PLATO'S *REPUBLIC*

PLATO'S
REPUBLIC
A Philosophical Commentary

R. C. CROSS
Regius Professor of Logic
University of Aberdeen

AND

A. D. WOOZLEY
Professor of Philosophy
University of Virginia

MACMILLAN

First published 1964 by
THE MACMILLAN PRESS LTD
Houndmills, Basingstoke, Hampshire RG21 2XS
and London
Companies and representatives
throughout the world

ISBN 0–333–19302–4

A catalogue record for this book is available
from the British Library.

First edition reprinted 1966, 1970, 1971
First paperback printing 1979
Reprinted 1980, 1986, 1989, 1991, 1994

Printed in China

PREFACE

Every year thousands of bewildered university students are introduced to philosophy, and many of them meet it first in Plato's *Republic*. Most of what Plato has written in the *Republic*, but not quite all, is, in our opinion, philosophically important; and views about what is important, and how important it is, vary from one philosophical generation to another. What we have tried to do is to produce a book that will serve as something of an introduction to philosophy via the *Republic*, rather than a specialised Platonic study. We have therefore chosen to concentrate on the main themes of the work, rather than produce notes on almost everything. And, because we do think that some parts of the *Republic*, whatever other interest they may have, have no philosophical interest, we have said nothing about them; for example, there is no discussion of Plato's views on school education.

Introductions to philosophy cannot be easy — they would be no use if they were — but, although we have not tried to make out the philosophical doctrines and arguments contained in the *Republic* to be easier than they are, and although consequently students at different levels of advance may find different parts of the book more useful, we have throughout aimed at presenting the arguments and our comments on them as clearly as we could.

The disadvantages of reading the *Republic* in an English translation, and of discussing it without constant reference to the Greek text, are considerable, partly because in certain respects the conceptual structure of thought in Western Europe of the twentieth century A.D. is very different from that of Athens of the fourth century B.C., with the consequence that it is impossible always to find words and phrases in English to match at all neatly the words and phrases in Greek; partly because a given word in one language often has a wider range

v

of meaning than its nearest single counterpart in the other, with the consequence that a reader dependent entirely on a translation may be seriously misled. This may be illustrated in a minor way by the title of the work, and, more importantly, by its subject-matter. The title '*Republic*' is quite inaccurate, if the word is used in its modern sense, to mean a constitution headed by an elected president, as contrasted with either a dictatorship or a hereditary monarchy. Plato's word πολιτεία (*politeia*) was far more general, meaning any form of political organisation at all which a community the size of a Greek city state was capable of assuming. 'Republic' therefore has to be understood, not in its specialised modern sense, but as the literal equivalent of 'respublica', which was the standard Latin translation of πολιτεία. Again, the subject-matter of the *Republic* is usually said to be Justice, simply because 'justice' is the most commonly used translation of the Greek word δικαιοσύνη (*dikaiosyne*). Now *dikaiosyne* is the main topic, or the main official topic, of the *Republic*, but 'justice' is a thoroughly unsuitable word to use as a translation of the Greek word. First, 'justice' has for us a strongly legal flavour: justice is what magistrates, juries and judges of appeal concern themselves with, i.e. the realm of civil and criminal law. But that is not in the least what Plato is talking about; nowhere in the whole work is there more than passing reference to the administration of justice or to provision for litigation. His *dikaiosyne* was something which a man could, or could fail to, exercise or express throughout his personal and social life. Again, while we do use the adjectives ('just' and 'unjust') and the adverbs ('justly' and 'unjustly') much more commonly than the noun ('justice') in a moral rather than a legal context, it is a very special moral context, viz., that in which one person is in a position of superiority, or power, or authority over another. A stepmother, a schoolmaster, a prefect may treat a small boy unjustly, but one small boy cannot treat another unjustly, if their positions are roughly equal. What he may do is to treat him wrongly or badly; and right or wrong, good or bad, conduct is what Plato is talking about. The *Republic* has for so long been said to be about Justice that there is now little hope of changing the usage, but 'justice' has to be understood in a fundamentally moral, not a legal, sense, and in an unrestricted moral context. That Plato's *dikaiosyne* turned out to be political is true, but this is because he thought the specification of the moral life for man in society was political. The word itself was a word of morals, as even more clearly were the adjectives δίκαιος and ἄδικος (*dikaios* and *adikos*) which could be applied to a man's character, meaning that it was good or bad, or to his conduct, meaning that it was right or wrong.

Two translations of the *Republic* are most widely in use at present: *The Republic of Plato*, by F. M. Cornford (Oxford: Clarendon Press, 1941), and *Plato: the Republic*, by H. D. P. Lee (London: Penguin Books, 1955). From time to time we have quarrelled with each; but, where we give translations from passages in the Greek, we often use one or other of these renderings, although we have also in many cases made our own translations.

We have tried to keep down to an unavoidable minimum the use of Greek words, and have instead employed their English transliterations which, although ugly, do serve to remind the Greekless reader that he is trying to grapple with an author who neither wrote nor thought in English.

Finally, we have two people to thank, a pair of very efficient secretaries, Miss V. Harvey and Miss D. Robertson, who by the speed and accuracy with which they typed out our manuscript disposed of the myth that each of us has almost entirely illegible handwriting.

R. C. C.
A. D. W.

CONTENTS

INTRODUCTION

PLATO's writings are unusual in their literary form in that they are prose dialogues in which the chief characters are historical personages, and in particular in most of them, including the *Republic*, the leading speaker is Socrates. Socrates lived at Athens from about 470 B.C. to 399 B.C., when he was put to death by the restored Athenian democracy on a charge of impiety. The date given for Plato's birth is usually 428–427 B.C., and for his death 347 B.C. He was a member of the group of friends with whom Socrates conducted his philosophical discussions, in Socrates's last years probably one of the innermost circle, and there is little doubt that when he began writing his dialogues he made Socrates the chief speaker with the intention, in part anyhow, of preserving his memory. It is not known precisely when Plato began writing, but the *Apology*, which is certainly one of the early dialogues, presupposes the trial of Socrates in 399 B.C., and it seems safe to assume that most, and indeed probably all, of Plato's writing belongs thus to the fourth century.

It can be seen then that, arising from the literary form in which it is cast, there are two dates relevant to the *Republic*. There is first what we may call the dramatic date, i.e. the date of the historical setting of the dialogue, and there is the date of composition; and for reasons which will emerge as we proceed it would be convenient to know these two dates. Since Socrates is the chief speaker, the dramatic date must be sometime before his death, i.e. sometime in the fifth century. A. E. Taylor (*Plato: The Man and his Work*, pp. 263-264) for various reasons suggested that the time around 422–421 B.C. fits best. The date of composition, both in the case of the *Republic* and of Plato's writings generally, is a much more tricky matter. There is no question here of a "date of publication" appearing on the manuscripts. Moreover, references in the dialogues to

easily dateable historical events are few; and further, there
are scarcely any references within the dialogues to other dialogues or to works of other contemporary writers. Thus even
the order of composition, let alone dates, presents a problem.
Attempts have been made to put the dialogues in an order
of composition by tracing through them the development of
various Platonic views, and by assigning an earlier or later
date according as a dialogue is taken to represent an early stage
of a certain doctrine or a later more developed stage. This
method, however, involves an element of subjectivity in assessing whether a doctrine is more or less mature, and has
produced widely differing conclusions about the order of composition. It was not until Lewis Campbell in 1867 initiated
the stylometric method that progress began to be made in
reaching a considerable measure of agreement about the order
in which the dialogues were written. It is generally accepted
that the *Laws* is the latest of Plato's works, and the stylometric
method consists in taking the style and language of the *Laws*
as a standard, and comparing the other dialogues with it in
detail — comparing for example the use of particles in the
Laws and elsewhere, grammatical peculiarities, choice of synonyms and so on. When this is done, though there are still
some doubts and uncertainties, a fairly definite picture emerges
of the order in which the dialogues were written. In particular,
for our purposes, many of the shorter dialogues, such as the
Apology, Ion, Charmides, Laches, and among the longer dialogues
the *Gorgias, Meno, Symposium* and *Phaedo* precede the *Republic.*
Thus any doctrines they contain that might be relevant to the
Republic would be already known, and we are justified in using
them to amplify and illustrate things said in the *Republic.*
Again, the *Parmenides, Theaetetus, Sophist, Politicus, Philebus* are
later in composition than the *Republic,* and if we use them in
connection with what is said in the *Republic,* this fact has to be
borne in mind. To have in this way obtained some idea at
least of the order of composition of the dialogues is obviously
a major step in handling any of them.

It would, however, also be useful if we could assign an
actual date for the writing of the *Republic.* This is a difficult
matter. A. E. Taylor, for instance, thought that the *Republic*

itself (as well as the other dialogues earlier than the *Republic*) was already written by 388. It seems more probable however on various grounds that its date of composition is later than this. G. C. Field has suggested 375 B.C., and there is a good deal to be said for this suggestion, though on the evidence available it cannot be more than a reasonable guess. The reason why an actual date for the *Republic* is of interest is that we can then compare the gap between the dramatic setting and the actual composition of the dialogue, and this in turn is of interest for the following reason. If there were a long gap between the two dates, we might begin to wonder whether we should understand the dialogue against the background of its dramatic setting, or whether we should understand it in the setting of its date of composition; and in certain cases this might be important. For example, to take an extreme case, suppose someone in the nineteenth century wrote a dialogue in which the speakers were historic characters of Queen Elizabeth's reign, in understanding the dialogue it would be important to decide whether the writer was trying to convey the ideas of the sixteenth century and the dialogue should be understood against a sixteenth-century background, or whether he was simply using these historical characters as a mouthpiece for ideas relevant to the nineteenth century. In the case of the *Republic* this is fortunately not an acute problem. It is true that, assuming there is anything in the suggestions of a dramatic date of 422–421 and a date of composition around 375, there is a gap of some forty-odd years — or let us say, to allow for errors in the suggested dating, at least a gap of some thirty years. Even the latter figure looks quite significant, especially when we think that within it fall the final defeat of Athens by the Spartans in 405 and the passing of what we regard as the great age of Athens. In fact, however, in relation to the problems in which Plato was primarily interested and which he discusses in the *Republic*, there is no abrupt change between the closing quarter of the fifth century in which he grew up and the fourth century when he was writing the *Republic*. The problems about moral standards and about government with which the *Republic* is concerned, which were brought prominently to attention by the fifth-century Sophists, and sharpened by the pressures of the Peloponnesian War, continued over into the fourth century, and indeed are perennial problems anyhow. There are particular parts of the *Republic* that are better read against a specifically fourth-century background, but for much of it the gap between its setting and its date of composition is much less significant than it looks. The reader will find an admirable discussion of this whole topic in G. C. Field's book *Plato and his Contemporaries*.

A last point may be made here about Plato himself. He was a member of a highly distinguished Athenian family with many political connections, and had intended himself, as we learn from the Seventh letter (324b), to enter politics. This same letter, written in his old age, describes (325d-326b) how he was deterred from a political career through despair of finding suitable men with whom to work, and records also his views on the great deterioration in law and morals. He adds, however, that he did not give up considering how these matters might be improved and indeed the whole constitution reformed, and the particular passage ends with the remark, of which the whole of the *Republic* is an elaboration, that he came to the view that there would be no escape from ills until philosophers became kings or kings philosophers. The *Republic* then grew out of what Plato regarded as pressing moral and political problems, and it sought to provide an answer to these problems in the way of a programme of reform. Now there are many philosophers who would say that it is important to distinguish between the moral or political reformer and the moral or political philosopher. They would say that it is not the job of the philosopher as a philosopher to make moral or political judgments, to say that this ought to be, or that ought to be. Rather they would say, if we describe the making of actual moral or political judgments as a first order activity, that the philosopher's task as a philosopher consists in the second order activity of analysing and examining such moral and political judgments, trying to see how they are arrived at, by what evidence and of what sort they are backed, and so on. If one wanted a modern way of putting this one might say that the philosopher as a philosopher is concerned not with the making of moral or political judgments, but with their logic. We have just seen, however, that the *Republic* grows out of an actual situation which it seeks to reform : the present state of morals and politics Plato judges to be bad, and he sets out what ought to take its place.   It might be thought then that however interesting the book may be as a programme of moral or political reform, it is not a good example of what the philosopher as a philosopher should be doing.   In fact, however, it succeeds in combining reforming zeal with philosophical analysis of the highest order.   The passion of the reformer is there with all the power that, for better or for worse, this gives to the book, and the reader has to be on the alert for it ; and at the same time there is philosophy in plenty, which makes the *Republic* one of the best introductions there are to the subject.

Chapter 1

THE ARGUMENT WITH POLEMARCHUS

PLATO's earlier dialogues have a more or less constant pattern, both of subject-matter and of method. Indeed, it is generally accepted that they reflect the actual philosophical interests and methods of argument of the historical Socrates, whose pupil Plato was. They are mainly concerned with ethical problems, they proceed by posing a large, abstract question of the form 'What is X?' (e.g. *Protagoras:* "What is virtue?" *Charmides:* "What is temperance?" *Laches:* "What is courage?"), and by Socrates, as the chief character in the dialogue, demolishing the successive attempts to answer the question made by the other members of the group; and they tend to conclude in a negative way, with the party agreeing that none of the suggested answers will do, and that the original question is more difficult than all but Socrates believed at the outset. The *Republic*, which belongs to Plato's middle period, starts out in the same way, its question being "What is *dikaiosyne*?", "What is right conduct?", and it proceeds throughout Book I along the negative lines of the Socratic dialectic. But in Book II a more positive approach is attempted, in the hope of finding out what justice or right conduct really is, instead of just clearing away misconceptions about it. The final answer (at the present level) comes in Book IV (443d); and the rest of the work is devoted to solving the philosophical, educational and political problems raised by an attempt to realise a community in which men lived, and were glad to live, in accordance with the principles evolved in the answer to the main question.

The question "What is right conduct?" is introduced very early in the dialogue, and introduced in a way that ensures that it will first receive conventional answers, the inadequacy

of which can be readily exposed. The old man Cephalus, who
indirectly suggests the first answer, and his son Polemarchus,
who directly propounds the second and makes various amend-
ments to it in an attempt to meet Socrates's objections, represent two quite common and quite respectable types of the
plain man : Cephalus the practical and successful man of
affairs, who has led a decent and honourable life, and who has
some ideas about right and wrong but shies away at an argument about principles and generalities ; Polemarchus, willing
to have a go and to commit himself, but very limited in his
capacity for clear thinking, and insufficiently trained intellectually either to have seen for himself the subtleties and distinctions
which Socrates's argument forces him to acknowledge, or to
detect any flaws or dishonesties in that argument itself.

The discussion opens much in the style of a modern television or radio interview, with Socrates asking Cephalus, as a
prosperous business-man, what he considers to be the main
benefit to be gained from the acquisition of wealth. When
Cephalus replies that it is the prospect of being able to face
death with equanimity, in the knowledge that one has not
deceived anybody and not left any debts unpaid, Socrates asks
(331c) whether that will provide a satisfactory definition of
justice, viz. to tell the truth and to repay what one has
borrowed. He suggests that this will not do, because it is
possible to think of a case where such action would be wrong.
For instance, if one borrowed a weapon from a man in his
right mind, and he then became insane so that he would not
be safe with a weapon in his possession, it would not be right
in those circumstances to return it to him ; nor would it be
right always to tell the truth to a man in that condition. Polemarchus intervenes to disagree with Socrates, and Cephalus
takes no further part in the conversation. What Socrates's
objection has shown is that the suggested definition will not do
as it stands, because there are cases which would satisfy the
proffered definition but would not fall under the term or concept to be defined. Either a new definition must be found, or
the suggested definition must be modified so as to exclude the
exceptions. That is, either we must not define justice in terms
of truth-telling and repaying debts at all, or we must modify

that definition so as to exclude truth-telling and repayment of debts in certain circumstances. Socrates has here made a general point about definition: that if you define X as being Y, i.e. say that X is the same as Y, then that definition can be shown to be wrong if you can find an instance of Y which is not an instance of X. That is enough to refute the alleged identity of X and Y. Although Socrates does not need here to say so, an equally effective refutation would be to produce an instance of X that was not an instance of Y. For example, if Cephalus had agreed, as he probably would have done, that it would be right for a wealthy man to help a poor man who was in distress, or that it was wrong to inflict gratuitous injury on another, this too would have been enough to show that justice could not consist simply in telling the truth and repaying debts; for it would have shown that the field of justice included some things not included in the fields of truth-telling and re-payment of debts. That is, justice (X) cannot be the same as telling the truth and repaying debts (Y), not only because, as Socrates's example of the madman shows, some Y's are not X, but also because, as the other examples show, some X's are not Y. That is the first and basic condition of any satisfactory definition that takes the form of an answer to the question "What is X?", that the instances covered by the defining concept must exactly coincide with the instances covered by the concept to be defined.

Polemarchus, taking over from his father, gives it as his opinion (331e) that the poet Simonides was correct in saying that it was just or right to give back to each man what was due to him; this he then specifies (332a-b) as doing good to one's friends and harm to one's enemies; this, in turn, under pressure from Socrates's objections, he modifies (335a) to doing good to one's friends provided they are good men and harm to one's enemies provided they are bad; finally, when Socrates objects (335d) that it cannot be the part of justice to do harm to anybody, Polemarchus caves in altogether, and he too, apart from an occasional remark, takes no further part in the conversation. His position is treated as being only very slightly superior philosophically to his father's, or what Socrates took to be his father's, and he is almost as easily disposed of. But

Polemarchus's position raises a number of interesting philo-sophical points ; and it is questionable whether he should have been disposed of as easily as he was. Socrates's counter-arguments contain a number of mistakes or even dishonesties, which a better philosopher than Polemarchus would have challenged.

Some commentators (e.g. H. W. B. Joseph, *Essays in Ancient and Modern Philosophy*, I) have objected that Polemarchus's whole procedure was wrong, because he attempted to answer the question "What is Justice?" by giving examples of justice or a list of duties. This raises three questions : whether Pole-marchus was attempting at all to answer the question "What is Justice?", i.e. whether he was offering a definition of jus-tice; whether, if he was, he was trying to do it by giving examples of it; and whether, if that was what he was doing, he was wrong to do it.

The first question, whether Polemarchus was attempting to define justice, to say what justice is, is not easy to answer, simply because he was not sufficiently trained as a philosopher to appreciate the distinction between giving a definition and saying something about justice that nevertheless would not count as a definition. When Socrates concludes the conversa-tion with Cephalus by saying (331d) that it has shown that truth-telling and repayment of debts do not define justice, Polemarchus intervenes to say that they do — if we are to believe the poet Simonides. But when he goes on to quote Simonides he does it, not in the form 'Justice is . . .' or 'Justice consists in . . .', but in the form 'It is just to . . .' And, on the strength of that, one might be inclined to say that he is not attempting to tell us what justice is, but that he is offering an example of justice, which might help us to see what justice is. Similarly, if bravery were the subject under discus-sion, and if a man were to say that it was brave to maintain a moral principle or a religious belief in the face of threats of persecution or torture for maintaining it, we should take this as an instance or an illustration of bravery, which might help us towards seeing what bravery is and how to define it. Alterna-tively, by using the form 'it is just to . . .' Polemarchus might be offering us one of the defining characteristics of justice, but not claiming that it was the whole story, or that there were no other characteristics to be mentioned. If the subject under discussion were democracy, and if a man were to say that it was democratic to allow freedom of speech, we might want to allow that this was the beginning of an answer to the question what democracy is, because freedom of speech is a necessary element of democracy; but not the whole answer, because a constitution would not be a democracy if it possessed that characteristic but did not possess certain others, e.g. direct self-government, or representative self-government where the representatives were freely elected by wide or universal suffrage. Consequently, from Polemarchus's first contribution one cannot conclude either that he is offering Simonides's statement as a definition, or that he is not; and, if he is, whether it is intended as a complete or only partial definition. However, as the discussion proceeds, Socrates takes it to be a complete account and Polemarchus does not protest at his taking it so. When on the next page (332d) Socrates asks "Do you say that justice consists in treating your friends well and your enemies badly?", Polemarchus replies "It seems so to me"; and two pages later, after some objections by Socrates, he repeats (334b) that it still seemed to him that justice consisted in helping friends and harming enemies. We must, therefore, conclude that, however Polemarchus started, he finished, or at this stage he had finished, by supposing himself to be producing a definition of justice.

Next, does Polemarchus try to answer the question what justice is by giving a list of duties, by citing examples of justice? The answer seems fairly clear, that he does not. If we take his first remark as an attempted definition, he is saying that justice consists in giving back to a man what is due to him, i.e. that what constitutes an action being just is that it is an action which gives back to a man what is due. That may or may not be a good statement of what it is for an action to be just, but it is certainly not in the form of giving a list of examples, whether complete or incomplete. It would have been a statement of that form, if Polemarchus had said that justice consisted of performing acts like x, y, z, etc.; but he did not say that. What he next does is further to specify the notion of giving back to a man what is his due by saying that it consists in helping one's friends and harming one's enemies, which he further qualifies by saying that it is helping one's friends if they are good and harming one's enemies if they are bad. One could object to this definition by pointing out that it appears to be a too narrow specification of justice. For it would be a consequence of accepting it that no question of just or right conduct could arise in the relationship between the two men if they were neither friends nor enemies, or if the second man were either a friend of the agent but a bad man or an enemy of the agent but a good man. That is, one could object to Polemarchus's elucidation of the notion of giving back to a man his due that it too much restricts justice, and would require us to say that we could not act justly to strangers or even casual acquaintances; for instance, that I would not be failing in right conduct if I jumped my place in a bus queue, or if I helped myself to an article from the counter of a chain-store and tried to get out of the shop without paying for it. But that is a different kind of objection from the objection that justice is here being defined in terms of a list of duties.

Thirdly, it may be asked what would be wrong with trying to define justice by means of a list of examples. Philosophers do not all agree what definition is. Some wish to say that all definition is of words or other verbal or symbolic expressions, and therefore that a correct definition is one which gives the meaning of the word or expression in question, that is, one which correctly states how the word is used. This might be called Verbal or Dictionary Definition, for that is the kind of information which a full dictionary like the Oxford English Dictionary purports to give.

The point to notice here is that the definition is of a word in a given language, such as English or French or Greek. The question "What is the definition of w?", where w is an English word, is the question "What is the meaning of w in English?", or "How is w used in English?"; and the answer is an answer about linguistic usage, and not about linguistic usage in general, but only about English usage in particular. Other philosophers have maintained that, in addition to that kind of definition, there is another kind which may be called Real Definition.

Here the question is not about a word in the context of the language to which it belongs, but about the concept conveyed by, or the thing referred to by, the word. The answer will consist in saying what the concept or the thing is, and the answer might be of the kind which an encyclopaedia, but not a dictionary, purports to give. The question whether this second kind of activity is or is not to be called a defining activity is here not of great importance. What is important is to recognise that it is a different activity from, although not unrelated to, the first. The Frenchman learning English, who asks for the definition or meaning of 'motor car', is not asking the same question or seeking the same information as the Eskimo who asks what a motor car is. The Frenchman knows or has some idea what a motor car is, because he is familiar with motor cars in his own country; he is asking a question, not about a concept which is new to him (for it is not) but about a word, an English word, which is new to him. The Eskimo, on the other hand, we may suppose never to have seen a motor car, or a picture of one, before, and being confronted with motor cars for the first time on his arrival in this country he is puzzled by the enormous variety in shape, size and other appearances of the objects which we call cars. He is asking, not primarily what 'motor car' means (although he will be asking that, in so far as he is trying to learn English, and 'motor car' is the only expression which he happens to have available), but what a motor car is. He will want to know, as the Frenchman does not, the difference between a motor car and a motor bicycle, between a motor car and a farm tractor, and so on. Whether the answer to his question is or is not to be called a definition, it is a different kind of answer to a different kind of question from what the Frenchman asked.

It is not in dispute that the questions which Socrates and Plato were asking were of the second kind, not the first. They were asking about highly abstract concepts like beauty, courage and justice, but they were not asking questions about actual Greek or Athenian linguistic usage. They thought that, however the word *dikaiosyne* was in fact used, there still remained the question what justice *really* is, because they thought that there was a real essence of justice which it was the task of philosophy to uncover. And when Socrates asks Polemarchus what justice is, and Polemarchus offers his answer, they take themselves to be looking for the second kind of definition, not the first.

But, although the two kinds are to be distinguished, they are, as mentioned before, not unrelated. The way people use a given word or verbal expression will be determined, to a large extent, by the beliefs which they hold about the concept conveyed by or the things referred to by the word in question. Thus word-meanings change as beliefs change or knowledge increases. 'Atom' does not mean now even what it meant in the nineteenth century. Sometimes the opposite happens : words and phrases continue to be used, although people no longer hold the beliefs for which they were the appropriate expressions. Thus, we continue to talk of the sun rising in the east and traversing the sky from east to west during the day, although we have long ago abandoned the geocentric view of the universe. But, in general, we do adapt our linguistic usages to our changes in beliefs, where that becomes necessary, and to our increase in knowledge. Consequently, although Socrates was seeking a real definition of justice, the question could be put as a question about meaning, as long as it is put in the right form. "What is justice?" for him would not be equivalent to "What does 'justice' mean?", if the latter is understood as "What *is* meant by 'justice' by people who use it?". But it would be equivalent to "What does 'justice' mean?" if that is understood as "What *is to be* meant by 'justice'?". The two kinds of definition, or rather the verbal formulations of them, tend to coincide for the reason already given, that people tend to make their linguistic usage conform to their beliefs. For people knowingly to use a word in a way which conflicts with their beliefs would be deceitful in a way which contradicts the purpose and value of having words or a language at all. Real definitions, therefore, while expressions of knowledge or belief about something which is not a word, may at the same time be regarded as *proposals* for the definition of a word.

It is not obvious, whichever kind of definition we are talking about, that it must be wrong to try to define by means of examples. That it has traditionally been thought to be wrong is due to a confusion in the traditional view of definition : the confusion between purpose and method of defining. The purpose of defining is to enable the person seeking the definition to understand something that he did not understand before, whether it is the meaning of a word, or the nature of some kind of object. A definition which, even if he understood the expression in which it was given, did not give him the information which he asked for would not be a good definition ; and one which did would be. Now, because his request for a definition is of the form "What does 'x' mean?" or of the form "What is x?" (depending on which kind he is after), it is natural to suppose that a satisfactory answer must take the form of providing an expression which means the same as 'x', or which states the essential nature of x. That is to say, it seems natural to suppose that a definition must take the form of an equation, and that, unless the expression on the one side of the equation is equivalent to the expression on the other side, the definition cannot be satisfactory. And it is true that many dictionary definitions are, or try to be, of this form, providing expressions equivalent in meaning to that defined. Similarly, a legitimate method of answering "What is x?" is, if it can be done, by answering in the form "x is . . .", where the blank is filled by a statement of the nature of x. But, although these are legitimate methods of defining, and although it may seem natural to suppose that they are the only legitimate ways, and although under the influence of the Aristotelian notion of real definition that was long supposed, yet it is wrong. If the purpose of definition is to gain or to provide some understanding, then any method which will provide it will be legitimate. Many words can only be explained in a clumsy, inadequate manner by the synonym-method, and can be much better dealt with by a statement which says something about the function of the word (e.g. that 'good' is the most general word of commendation), or which by example exhibits the word at work (e.g. that 'red' is the word for the colour of ripe tomatoes, G.P.O. vans, etc.). You would not directly *tell* a person what x was if you gave him a list of examples of

x, but you might thereby enable him to understand what x
was, or to come nearer to it. Consequently, even if Polemarchus had (as he did not) attempted to define justice by
citing some instances of it, or by giving a list of examples, he
would not have been guilty of any objectionable procedure. (It
would be difficult to give at all a clear account of what a game
is, if one were forbidden to mention any games in the account.)

What Polemarchus in fact does do is to follow a perfectly
legitimate procedure, by clearly defining the field of relationship of justice (it is conduct restricted to a man's relationship
with those who are his friends and are good, and those who
are his enemies and are bad), and then by specifying the kind
of conduct within that field which is just (helping the former,
and harming the latter). Unfortunately, he is persuaded by
Socrates's objections to make various admissions which he
need not have made, agreeing with Socrates that his account
of justice has unacceptable implications — implications which
in fact it does not have at all. Socrates leads him on by a
succession of *reductio ad absurdum* arguments to an admission
that the consequences of his view of justice are such as to make
it an impossible view to hold. They are not *reductio ad absurdum*
arguments in the strict sense of arguments leading to a conclusion which is logically absurd, or which is logically incompatible with one or more of its own premises. But they are
reductio ad absurdum arguments in the looser sense of arguments
leading to a conclusion which nobody in his right mind would
be prepared to accept. The conclusion which Socrates draws
from Polemarchus's statement of justice is threefold : (a) that
there is no field of activity for justice, which is therefore useless
(332-333) ; (b) that justice could be used equally for good or
ill purposes, so that some conduct which we would not accept as
being right, e.g. stealing, would on this view be so (333-334) ;
(c) that it would be the function of justice to make men worse,
rather than better (335). Polemarchus agrees (correctly) that
any view of justice which leads to such a conclusion is untenable, agrees (incorrectly) that his own view does lead to that
conclusion, and therefore agrees that his view is untenable.
Had he questioned or denied the assumptions which Socrates
was attributing to him, the demolition of his view would have

been far less impressive. Socrates in fact fathered on him assumptions which he neither made nor was committed to. But, while Polemarchus was thus treated unfairly, Plato was enabled, through the mouth of Socrates, to bring out several points, one of them most important.

Socrates develops his objection against the Polemarchus-Simonides account of justice, that it consists in rendering to each man his due, by proposing an analogy with certain skills or arts. It being agreed that the art of medicine is that which prescribes drugs and diet for the body, and that the art of cookery is that which provides flavour to cooked food, the question is what does the art of justice provide, and to whom does it provide it? When Polemarchus offers the guarded reply that, *if* the analogy is to be accepted, justice will be the art which provides benefit to one's friends and harm to one's enemies (332d), Socrates proceeds to draw out the implications of the analogy, without at any point examining the assumption that it is a sound analogy, and entirely ignoring Polemarchus's "if the analogy is to be accepted". Socrates's argument takes the form of showing first that each art has its limited sphere of operations, and secondly that there will be no sphere of operations for justice which is not already occupied by some other art. The doctor's skill is useful only in matters involving the maintenance or restoration of bodily health; the sea-captain's skill is useful only in navigation at sea and will have no place on land, etc. By gradual elimination he persuades Polemarchus to agree that there is no activity in which justice might be engaged which is not already pre-empted by some other skill, e.g. that of a business-man in money affairs, of a farmer when it comes to producing crops, of a builder when it comes to erecting a house, and so on. The negative conclusion is reached that when anything is to be done at all some other skill is useful, and that justice can therefore only be said to be useful where nothing is to be done, i.e. that justice is entirely useless. Polemarchus weakly accepts this conclusion, but he need not have done. First, he could have pointed out that, although skills have limited fields of operation, they are not necessarily exclusive but may overlap. For instance, the conduct of a military campaign is a matter, not just of skill in the tactical handling of troops, but also of the skills of maintenance of supplies and ammunition, of communications, of intelligence and of medical services. Therefore, the fact that a given activity falls within the field of one skill does not, as Socrates assumes and as his choice of examples suggests, preclude other skills; and consequently, as far as the argument has yet gone, the fact that one kind of activity, e.g. that of business, requires commercial expertise does not by itself show that there is no room there for justice — if justice is a skill at all. Secondly, he might have suggested that, while it may be true of each of the other arts that there will be some field of activity to which it does not apply, as the sea-captain's skill does not apply on land or the general's skill does not apply in politics, this might not be true of justice. Nothing has been said in the argument which would rule out the claim that justice has the whole field of human activity for its sphere of operations, and consequently, again if we assume justice to be a skill at all, that it will apply in every case as well as the particular skill or skills involved. To ask of a man in a given occupation whether in a particular case he has used his occupational skill does not preclude us from asking whether he has in that case acted justly, or whether his conduct was right. This indeed is the point which Socrates himself is trying to make, and which by his next argument he successfully does make — that it is always proper to ask whether a man has acted as he should, when we have already answered the question whether he has exercised his skill as a doctor or a lawyer, or whatever he may be. The point is that the question whether a man has acted rightly is a question of a different kind from the question whether in his action he has exercised his occupational skill. And Socrates is wanting to show, again quite rightly, that justice is not a skill at all. But his method of trying to show it by his first argument fails entirely. He has not succeeded in showing that the exercise of one skill excludes the exercise of another, and therefore that justice cannot be a skill, because there is no activity which does not call for another skill. So far as this first argument goes, justice might still be a skill overlapping each of the others, its field of activity embracing all of theirs.

Socrates's next argument (333-334) is much more powerful and shows why it is a mistake to regard justice as being a skill at all. If we consider other admitted skills, such as those of the fighter or the doctor, we see that the skill can equally well be used either to promote or to defeat the acknowledged end of the art in question. Thus, a skilful doctor is as well able to prescribe an unsuitable as a suitable medicine for his patient's disease. The doctor who wishes, from whatever sinister motive, to prolong the patient's illness or even to bring about his death, will be using his skill or technical know-how in deliberately giving him the wrong medicine or treatment as much as the doctor who prescribes what he thinks will be best for the patient. There is all the difference in the world between the incompetent doctor who through faulty diagnosis or ignorance of drugs or even through carelessness prescribes treatment that will not effect a cure, and the competent doctor who deliberately uses his skill to achieve the same end. Ignorance or incompetence may be culpable, depending on the circumstances, but they are evidence of lack of skill. And when they are culpable, they are so in a different way from a deliberate abuse of skill for a bad end. The dishonest solicitor who uses his knowledge of the law to exploit his clients' trust in him and to embezzle their funds is different from the inefficient solicitor who through ignorance gives them bad advice or invests their money badly. In general, any skill is what Aristotle subsequently called "a capacity for opposites": it can be used well or ill; and the practitioner who deliberately uses it ill is not deficient in the skill, he is not displaying lack of skill, as the incompetent or inefficient practitioner is.

The same thing will have to be true of justice, if it is a skill. If a man is just who treats others honestly and fairly, and if his treating them so is the exercise of his skill of justice, then we shall have to say that he is as much exercising it if he treats them unfairly and dishonestly. The rogue and scoundrel will be as much a just man as is the honest dealer, the difference between them being that the former uses his justice for bad ends, the latter for good. We shall have to say of the former that he is both a just man and a cheat or swindler, and that the more just he is the better he will be at swindling.

This is an absurd and unacceptable conclusion : to say of a man that he is just is incompatible with saying of him that he is a cheat or a swindler. But it is a necessary conclusion of admitting justice to be a skill. Therefore justice is not a skill.

Here Plato has brought out an important point about justice, or about moral qualities in general — although not, it should be repeated, a fair point against Polemarchus, who neither said nor implied that justice was a skill. What Plato is here doing (and possibly also in *Hippias Minor*, 375-376) is calling attention to the difference between what have been called a man's *capacities* on the one hand and on the other hand his *dispositions* or *character*. His capacities are what he *can* do (if he chooses), his dispositions are what he may be expected to (choose to) do. When a man applies for a job and the would-be employer asks another man, such as his teacher or his former employer, for a testimonial, the statements or opinions given in the testimonial will fall some into the one category, and some into the other; and if all the statements made fall into only one of the categories the potential employer would be unable to form a reasonable assessment of the candidate's suitability for the post. That the man can handle figures accurately, that he has a fluent command of Russian, that he has a good sales technique, that he has had previous experience in that kind of industry, that he has a mechanical flair, even that he is a good golfer, etc., will be relevant to the question whether he is a suitable candidate for the job ; so also will be any such unfavourable information about him, e.g. that his knowledge of mathematics is limited to what he learned at school, that his French, while once good, is by now rusty, that he knows nothing of the intricacies of company law, etc. From such information the employer will be able to tell what qualifications the man has, what he is good at, or not good at. But even if, on this side of the report, the candidate seems to have all the necessary qualifications, the employer still only knows half of what he needs to know. So far he knows about the man's abilities, what he is capable or incapable of doing. He *can* do this, that or the other thing, *if* he wants to, if he sets his mind to it. But that is not enough ; a man may be capable

of doing all sorts of things, but in fact not do them when required, because of laziness, weakness of will, lack of interest,
neurosis or even sheer cussedness. This is the other side of
the report which the employer requires, telling him not what
performance the man is capable of producing if . . . he can
be bothered, or is sufficiently interested, but what performance
the man may be expected to produce. The questions here to
be answered are those which would ordinarily be said to be
questions about his character. Is he honest? practical? Does
he measure up to responsibility? Does he get on well with
others? Does he keep his head in an emergency? Is he to be
trusted with secret information? Is he ambitious? Is he a
hard worker? Does he work with one eye on the clock? Is
he a heavy drinker? Is he superficial in his judgments? Does
he take trouble with the details of work that does not much
interest him? Is he careless in his research? Does he jump
to conclusions without careful enough attention to the evidence?
and so on. Again, information in this category is not by itself
enough: a man may be extremely conscientious and hard-
working, but quite unsuited to a particular appointment,
because he just does not possess the particular ability or qualifications required. The employer needs the two kinds of
information, both what the man is capable of doing, and what
sort of man he is, whether he may be relied on to use his
abilities at all (as opposed to failing to use them through idle-
ness or lack of interest), and whether he may be relied on to
use them in the required way (as opposed to using them on some
line of work other than that to which he is assigned, or using
them, through disloyalty, to the disadvantage of his firm and
the advantage of a rival).

What is to be said about a man, then, falls into one or
other of those two categories: what he is capable of doing —
leaving it open whether he is in fact to be relied on to use or
abuse his abilities; and what he may, with more or less con-
fidence, be depended on to do — leaving it open what is the
range of his abilities, and what their limitations are. Plato,
in this argument to show that justice is not a skill or an ability,
is making the important point that knowledge of a man's
ability is knowledge only of what he can do, not knowledge of

what he will do. For that, you need to know about his character, how he may be expected to conduct himself in a situation. Justice belongs not to the first category, but to the second. To say that a man is just is to say something about his character, telling you not how he can behave (if he wants to, or can be bothered), but how he may be relied on to behave. Whereas an ability by itself is non-committal or, in Aristotle's phrase, "a capacity for opposites", and knowledge of a man's ability tells you nothing of what you may expect from him, a disposition or character-trait is committal: knowledge of it tells you something of what sort a man is, and what sort of conduct you may expect from him. It is precisely because justice or honesty belong not to the category of skills, but to the category of dispositions or character, that we say of the fraudulent solicitor, not that he is a just or an honest man who has chosen to use his justice or honesty in that particular way, but that he is an unjust or a dishonest man. 'Just', 'unjust', 'honest', 'dishonest', are not capacity-words (like 'clever' and 'stupid') but character-words (like 'hard-working' and 'lazy', 'trustworthy' and 'unreliable'). In saying that a man is just we are not only saying something different about him from saying that he is clever, but we are saying something of a different kind. Therefore, although Plato's first argument that justice is not a skill (it has no field of operation not already occupied by another skill) fails, his second argument (distinguishing capacities from character) is entirely successful and illuminating.

At this stage in the discussion (334b) Polemarchus confesses that he is in such a muddle that he no longer knows what he was trying to say, but nevertheless he wishes to maintain his original position, that justice consists in doing good to one's friends and harm to one's enemies. Socrates finally silences him with a twofold objection: first, that a more careful and precise account is needed of what it is to be a friend (334c-335a); and secondly, that, even when the necessary qualifications have been made, this account of justice will not do, because it cannot be the part of justice to harm anyone, so that even if it were just to help one's friends it could not be just to harm one's enemies (335b-336a).

The first objection in itself is designed not so much to refute

Polemarchus's account as to show up its inadequacy without further specification; and Socrates does not lay as much weight on it as on the second objection. When Polemarchus says that a friend is a man who seems good, and an enemy one who seems bad, Socrates rightly insists on the possibility of making a mistake in one's judgment of friends, and on the need to distinguish between the man who seems good (whether or not he really is) and the man who is good (whether or not he seems so). If our duty is to help those who seem good and harm those who seem bad, we may in fact be helping bad men and harming good; can it be right to do that? Polemarchus therefore tightens up his account so as to make it now run that justice consists in helping a friend (i.e., a man who seems good) provided that he really is good, and in harming an enemy (i.e., a man who seems bad) provided that he really is bad. With this Socrates is satisfied, and moves straight on to his second, more fundamental, objection. Although no more is heard of this first difficulty, it does raise two points, neither of which probably occurred to Plato, but both of which are relevant to ethics.

First, in asking whether we should help the man who *seems* good or the man who *is* good, Plato is raising in a particular form a general moral question, whether a man is to be judged morally for acting (or failing to act) as he thinks the situation requires, or for acting (or failing to act) as the situation actually requires. This is the issue between what have been called the Subjective and Objective theories of duty. Is a man to be blamed for acting in a certain way in a given set of circumstances, provided that he sincerely (however mistakenly or misguidedly) believed that his action was the right one? He may have made a factual mistake : he may have been mistaken in his belief what the circumstances were, or in his belief what the consequences would be of acting as he did in those circumstances, or he may have been mistaken about both. Seeing a car being driven headlong through a busy street, I may think it is a criminal trying to get away from the scene of a hold-up — but I am mistaken, for it is a police driver rushing an urgently needed serum to a hospital: I have made a mistake as to the circumstances. Deciding to stop him, I may think I shall succeed by giving chase in my own car — but I am mistaken, for my car is not fast enough, or I am not a skilful enough driver, and, before I can catch him, am involved in an accident myself. Or again an agent, although making no factual mistakes, nor acting in factual ignorance, may make what might be called a moral mistake : he may think it would be right to do x, when it is clear to others (and perhaps afterwards to himself also) that it is wrong to do x, but right to do y instead. If he honestly (however incorrectly) thought that the circumstances were a, b and c, and honestly (however misguidedly) thought that it was right for him then to do x, is he morally reprehensible for having done x? We blame a man for doing wrong. Does this imply the Objective view, that the man is to be judged by the actual circumstances, regardless of what he himself thought about them? Or does a man successfully exculpate himself if he can truthfully say that, however ignorant he was or mistaken in his view of the situation, he did what he thought was right? Each view has its difficulties, which cannot be pursued here. But they are difficulties which have to be faced in ethics, and they are difficulties which are hinted at by Socrates's distinction between the man who seems good and the man who is good, and by his question which of the two is it the business of the just man to help. Our inclination may be, as Socrates's is, to take the Objective view and say that we should help the man who really is good, whatever he may seem ; but we cannot, on the other hand, ignore the fact that a decision to act (whether this way or that) is a personal matter : a man must take his own decision (otherwise it is not a decision at all), and, however hard he tries to find out what the facts of the case are (and often there is very little time in which to do it), he can never entirely escape from his belief as to what the facts are. We can say what we like about the moral mistakes of, for example, the Spanish inquisitors, or again the follies and shortsightedness of almost any political leader whom we care, with the benefit of hindsight, to criticise ; but we must, in fairness, not fail both to acknowledge and to question the assumptions which we are making in condemning or criticising them.

Secondly, we must recognise a difference which Plato fails to make, either through Socrates or through Polemarchus, in his brief statement of what it is to be or to have a friend. It is the difference between liking somebody (or having him as a friend) and approving of him (or thinking him good). It is true that Plato's position implies a distinction between the notions of "liking" and "thinking good", i.e. he is not supposing that 'to like' means the same as 'to think good'. If he were supposing that, his statement (334c) that "it is to be expected that a man will like those whom he thinks good" would be an empty tautology, saying that a man will like those whom he likes, or think good those whom he thinks good. What Polemarchus is maintaining is not a logical connection, but some kind of a causal connection, between A liking B and A thinking B to be good (the latter being then altered to B's being good); as a matter of fact, a man may be expected to like, and to do good to or to help, those who seem to him to be or who are good. As a generalisation about most of us most of the time, this may be true. But it is not a generalisation without exceptions. Our likes and dislikes are not entirely governed by our approvals and disapprovals. It is not uncommon to say of a man, "I don't think he is a good man (or I disapprove of him) but I can't help liking him all the same"; and to say this is not only not logically contradictory, it is not even odd — which it would be on the hypothesis which Polemarchus and Socrates share. Our likes and dislikes are feelings, or even attitudes, which in a sense one cannot help having; but they are quite different from *moral* attitudes. Maybe we would be better people if our likes and dislikes of others exactly coincided with our moral attitudes towards them, but it is no good pretending that they always do; otherwise we could not truthfully say, as we sometimes can, not only that we cannot help liking a particular man of whom we disapprove, but also, in reverse, that we wished we liked (which implies that we do not) a particular man whom we are bound to admit to be a good man. To suppose that our likes, or our choices of friends, are entirely or even mainly determined by our moral views as to their virtues is simply to ignore elementary facts of human psychology. In this passage Plato has tried to tie together the notions of liking and approving far more closely than in fact they are tied.

Finally, Socrates attacks the second half of Polemarchus's definition of justice, that it consists in harming one's enemies if they are bad men (335b-336a). He asks whether it is the part of a just man to harm anyone at all, and when Polemarchus replies that it is, viz. to harm those who are bad and his enemies, he proceeds to develop an analogy, the steps of which may be tabulated as follows :

(1) If you harm a thing (e.g. a horse or a dog) it becomes worse, and worse in respect of its particular kind of excellence (e.g. it becomes a worse horse or a worse dog).

Therefore (2) If you harm a man, he becomes worse, and worse in respect of his human excellence, i.e. he becomes a worse man.

(3) Justice is (the) human excellence.

Therefore (4) If you harm a man, that is the excellence in respect of which he becomes worse, i.e. he becomes less just or more unjust.

Therefore (5) On Polemarchus's account of justice, just treatment of a bad man will make him more unjust.

But (6) In the same way, as a musician cannot by the use of music make another man more unmusical than he was, so a just man cannot by justice make another man more unjust than he was.

Socrates's conclusion, therefore, which Polemarchus accepts, is that it cannot be the role of justice to harm anyone, because harming him would make him more unjust than he already was. Polemarchus, having accepted (2) (and (3)), is bound to accept this conclusion. But Polemarchus might have objected that, starting from (6), that just treatment cannot make a man more unjust, it cannot be true that justice, by harming a man, makes him worse. That is, although Polemarchus, by accepting (2) and (6), cannot avoid Socrates's conclusion, he could have avoided it by accepting (6) but not accepting (2) : he might have refused to admit, *either* that justice would harm a bad man, *or* that it would make him worse. (Strictly, on his own definition of justice, the first alternative would not be open to him, but the second still would be.)

The truth is that Socrates has exploited an ambiguity in the Greek word βλάπτειν, which has been translated 'to harm' ;

and it is by no means clear that the sense which he gives to it is the same as that with which Polemarchus originally used (or might have used) it. Unfortunately, as ordinarily used, the English word 'harm' is not as conspicuously ambiguous as the Greek word, but nevertheless even with it the ambiguity can be brought out. 'Harm' sometimes (indeed commonly) is used to mean (a) make worse. But it is also sometimes used to mean (b) hurt. We can hurt a man without necessarily making him worse. We may hurt a man by thwarting him, by interfering with his interests, by making life somehow more unpleasant for him (e.g. by fining him, sending him to gaol, depriving him of cigarettes, disqualifying him from driving a car), even by injuring him (e.g. by corporal punishment, by castration, by cutting off his hand); but we do not thereby necessarily make him a worse man. Punishment, in this sense of 'harm', might even, on a remedial view of punishment (for which Plato himself argues elsewhere), actually do the man some good. Those who argue in favour of corporal punishment, at least in some forms and in some situations, that it actually does good to the person punished, may be right or they may be wrong; but, even if wrong, their wrongness does not consist in contradicting themselves. The proposition that all physical hurt makes a man worse, or can do him no good, is not a necessary, or logical, truth.

That is, if you use 'harm' in sense (a) (where 'harm' has the notion of making worse built into its meaning), then the proposition that by harming a man you make him worse becomes a tautology; and, on this view, the question which Polemarchus should have asked is whether in fact the application of justice to a man does harm him, i.e. make him a worse or more unjust man. If, which is doubtful, Polemarchus had meant this by 'harm', he should have questioned his own claim that it is the role of justice to harm bad men. On the other hand, if you use 'harm' in sense (b) (and it seems more likely that this is what Polemarchus had in mind, for this is the sense which naturally contrasts with 'help'), then 'harm' does not have the notion of making worse built into it. And, in this sense, to harm a man does not necessarily make him worse. It might therefore still be true (as on some views of punishment it would be) that justice, by harming a bad man, instead of making him worse would make him better.

As an exercise in Socratic dialectic to silence Polemarchus the argument is effective, but as an argument designed to produce rational conviction it leaves much to be desired : it contains one serious ambiguity and too many unexamined assumptions to be acceptable. A surprising feature of Socrates's attack on Polemarchus's position is the absence from it of an argument that he might have been expected to develop, but did not use at all. His initial objection had been that Polemarchus's view of justice was too narrow, that it confined the exercise of justice to situations not already covered by other arts. But he might well (and more fairly) have developed this point against Polemarchus's view of justice as confined to one's treatment of friends and enemies. He might have asked whether the fact that a man is my friend or my enemy is the only fact relevant to the justice of my treatment of him. For it certainly is a consequence of Polemarchus's position that it will be impossible for me to treat justly (or unjustly) a man who happens neither to be my friend nor to be my enemy. Many of our dealings are with those who fall into neither category ; and, if we accepted Polemarchus's account, we should have to say that, however badly we treated them, however much we cheated or swindled casual acquaintances or total strangers, we could not fairly be accused of having treated them unjustly. By confining the range of justice and injustice to the comparatively narrow field of our friends and enemies, Polemarchus has precluded us from treating either justly or unjustly the vast majority of the human race ; and any account which precludes us from that may fairly be criticised as being seriously defective. This is the most damaging criticism that could be made of Polemarchus's position ; and it is at least surprising that Plato failed to make it.

Chapter 2

THE ARGUMENT WITH THRASYMACHUS

THE next stage in the conversation is taken over by Thrasymachus the Sophist, who bursts explosively into the dialogue (336b) with the familiar complaints made by Socrates's opponents — that he uses childish arguments, makes an absurd parade of politeness, plays to the gallery and, above all, indulges his usual practice of asking all the questions and getting his victims to provide the answers which he then demolishes without ever offering any positive contributions himself. This characterisation of the Socratic method is fair enough, although the implication that Socrates's purpose was negative is not; Socrates wanted to get at the truth, and he did it by eliminating accounts that were *prima facie* plausible but would not stand up to examination. By this means he was trying to show how much more difficult an innocent-looking philosophical question was than appeared at first sight, and what a serious business philosophical inquiry was. By his persistent questioning Socrates naturally irritated the Sophists, exposing the inadequacy and superficiality of the answers which they too readily put forward in their teachings. It was characteristic of the Sophists, itinerant teachers who tended to centre on Athens as the chief intellectual and cultural city of Greece, that, while professing to teach *arete* or virtue, they concentrated mainly on the arts which made for practical success and would be of value to men who wished, as politicians and public figures, to get to the top. Instruction in rhetoric and debating skills was their speciality. A disinterested pursuit of abstract truth, such as Socrates and Plato tried to engage in, aroused the scepticism of many of them as an attempt to attain knowledge on matters where it was unattainable. This is reflected in Thrasymachus's condescending, contemptuous manner towards

Socrates in this conversation, and his impatience with his questioning.

Thrasymachus demanded that, for a change, Socrates himself should offer an answer to the question "What is Justice?", and furthermore that it must not be an answer in terms of what should be done, or was beneficial, or was in some unspecified persons' interest; i.e. no answer along the general lines propounded by Polemarchus, and apparently taken seriously by Socrates himself, would be acceptable. To this Socrates not unreasonably suggests that it is unfair simultaneously to demand an account of justice and *a priori* to preclude certain types of answer in advance; for it might turn out that one of those types was correct. It is as if a man were to demand a definition of the number 12, and at the same time to say that no answer in terms of 6×2 or 4×3 would do. The only way to show that a given definition must be wrong is to show how and why it is wrong, not to assert dogmatically at the outset that it would not be counted as right, with no reasons given.

By further ironical sparring Socrates provokes the impatient Thrasymachus into doing just what he wants him to do, viz. to give *his* answer to the question, thus enabling Socrates to employ once more his familiar question-and-answer technique, retaining for himself the dialectical initiative. Thrasymachus gives his answer at 338c1, that "justice is nothing else but the interest of the stronger". This at once raises two related questions : (a) what *kind* of a statement is that intended to be? and (b) what does the statement mean? We shall find that the main difficulties over the argument with Thrasymachus are difficulties of interpretation. Many different interpretations have been put forward; and about none of them is it possible to be certain, beyond any dispute, that it is the right one; all that one can hope to do is to arrive at an interpretation which suggests itself as being more or less reasonable.

(Incidentally, it might appear inconsistent of Thrasymachus to have given an answer which looks to be of the kind, in terms of interest, which he had forbidden to Socrates; and Socrates indeed points this out (340a). But what Thrasymachus had prohibited was a general answer in terms of interest, without clear and accurate specification. This, as he shows in his answer to Socrates's objection, he claims himself to have provided by saying *whose* interest determines what is just, viz. the interest of the stronger man or party. It is clear therefore that his original remark was intended to rule out, not any account of justice in terms of interest, but only an account which was too vague and indeterminate.)

What *kind* of a statement is Thrasymachus purporting to make when he says that justice is nothing but the interest of the stronger? Is it intended as a definition of justice? or simply as some kind of remark or comment about justice, possibly somewhat derogatory? The word which Thrasymachus actually uses is ἀπόκρισις (337d1), which is a very general word meaning 'answer', with sometimes a legal flavour about it, which may or may not be present here, meaning a defendant's answer to a charge brought against him. Now, that Thrasymachus is offering an answer to Socrates's question about justice is quite compatible with its being intended as a definition of justice, but does not entail that it is one. It is therefore unfortunate that both of the most recent translators of the *Republic* (F. M. Cornford, *The Republic of Plato*, p. 16; H. D. P. Lee, *Plato: The Republic*, p. 64) render ἀπόκρισις as 'definition'. This is simply a mistranslation of the text, and begs the whole question. The translators may be correct in their interpretation (at least to the extent of supposing that Thrasymachus is offering a definition of some kind), but they are not justified in so translating the Greek as to make it appear that their interpretation must be correct. And, even if Thrasymachus is offering a definition, it might (so far as anything yet said in the discussion goes) be a verbal definition, giving the meaning of the Greek word *dikaiosyne*, or it might be intended as a real definition, purporting to state the essential properties of a thing, i.e. in this case saying what justice actually is. Throughout this section Cornford (although not Lee) aggravates his original mistake by persistently mistranslating the Greek in a way which would indicate to the Greekless reader that Thrasymachus is beyond any doubt producing a verbal definition of 'justice'. For example, in 338c he makes Thrasymachus say: "What I say is that 'just' or 'right' means nothing but what is to the interest of the stronger party"; 343c "'right' actually means what is good for someone else"; and in 344c, "'right' . . . means simply what serves the interest of the stronger party", etc. Unfortunately for Cornford, none of this is in the Greek at all. If Plato had wanted to make it clear that what Thrasymachus was doing was giving the meaning of a Greek word, the resources of the Greek language were sufficient to enable him to do it; but in fact he does not. In none of the above, and other, passages, does any Greek word or phrase occur which could possibly be correctly translated as 'means'. In all those passages Plato consistently has Thrasymachus saying, not that " 'justice' means . . .", but that "justice is . . .", so that if he is talking about the word 'justice' (or the Greek word) at all, he is only talking about it indirectly; what he is directly talking about is justice. What Cornford has done has been to provide a paraphrase of what Thrasymachus said (according to Cornford's own interpretation), but to pass it off as a translation of what Thrasymachus actually said, which it most certainly is not. It is a lamentable illustration of a philosopher's tendency to allow his interpretation to interfere with his scholarship.

Of Thrasymachus's apparently straightforward answer that justice is nothing but the interest of the stronger, many interpretations are possible; and it is even possible to confuse one interpretation with another. Unhappily, Cornford does this too. In his translation he takes one view of Thrasymachus. In his preliminary remarks in his introduction (pp. xiii-xiv) he takes quite another view, without apparently noticing the difference between them. One or other may be correct (although we shall argue that they are not), but they cannot possibly both be correct, for they are entirely different from each other.

According to the interpretation in Cornford's translation Thrasymachus in saying that justice is the interest of the stronger is giving a verbal definition, saying in effect that 'just' and 'promoting the interest of the stronger' are synonymous expressions, not merely in the weak sense that both expressions have the same reference (as 'the capital city of the United Kingdom' and 'the largest city in the United Kingdom' have the same reference, viz. London), but in the strong sense that both expressions mean the same thing. In this sense the two expressions about London are not synonymous, for to say that London is the capital city of the United Kingdom is not to say the same thing about London as to say that it is the largest city in the United Kingdom. Both statements happen to be true, but they do not mean the same as each other. On the other hand, to say of a Euclidean triangle that it is equilateral is the same as to say that its three sides are equal; they are not different statements about the triangle, both of which are true, but the same statement expressed in two different verbal ways. Similarly, to say of a man that he is ambidexterous is the same as to say that he is equally proficient with either hand; in the same sense 'silent' is synonymous with 'noiseless', '10.45' with 'a quarter to eleven', 'laziness' with 'disinclination to work', and so on. If Thrasymachus means that, in this way, 'just' is synonymous with 'promoting the interest of the stronger', he will be maintaining, not that the question whether a given act is just is to be answered by first answering the prior question whether it promotes the interest of the stronger, but that they are the same question. All statements of the form 'x is just' can be rephrased in the form 'x serves the interest of the stronger', without any alteration of meaning whatever.

That might be the correct view to take of Thrasymachus, but it is not the same as the view which Cornford adopts in his introduction. There he refers to an episode in the Peloponnesian War when Athens required the surrender of the island of Melos, whose inhabitants wished to remain neutral between Athens and Sparta. When the Melians protested that it was not just for a stronger power to treat a weaker in this way, the Athenian government replied that it was not interested in questions of justice, only in getting what it wanted and needed. The powerful do what they can, and the weak must acquiesce. When the Melians refused to give in, the Athenians besieged and eventually massacred them. This Cornford describes as "the philosophy of imperialism", and adds "it is also the philosophy of Thrasymachus in the first part of the *Republic*" (p. xiv). Now again, this might be the correct view to take of Thrasymachus; but, if it is, then the view taken by Cornford

in his translation must be incorrect, for it is an entirely different
one. According to the translation, questions about justice are
the same as questions about the interests of the stronger party.
According to the introduction, they are different questions, and
questions about justice are to be subordinated to questions
about the interests of the stronger party. The mere fact that
one question is to be subordinated to the other is enough to
show that they must be different questions, for it is logically
impossible to subordinate a question to itself. The view represented by the Athenians in the Melian dialogue *might* be the
nihilist view that there is no such thing as justice, that justice
is an illusion which you must see through if you are to be
successful; in that case the question of subordination would
not arise. Or it might be (and this is the more likely interpretation) the cynical view that, although there is such a thing as
justice, it is something to be ignored and disregarded if you
want to get on. You cannot afford to bother yourself with
questions of right and wrong if you want to be successful and
come out on top. The only practical question is which of two
conflicting parties is the stronger and going to win. This
implies, not that justice and questions of morality are illusions,
but that they are unimportant matters, which a man will dis-
regard if he is strong enough to be able to get away with it. As
a description of the shadier side of public life it fits in many
places : the corruption of ministers by contractors and others
anxious for government backing or connivance, systematic tax
evasion by those wealthy and powerful enough to be able to
arrange it, vote-rigging at political or trade-union elections,
etc. But to characterise it as " the philosophy of imperialism "
seems at least misleading. For few imperialist powers have
not pretended, or even sincerely claimed, some justification for
their activities. Whatever reason you give to warrant taking
over other people and their country, whether it is that it is for
their good, or that it is for your own, or simply that your being
the more powerful entitles you to do it, you are purporting to
justify your action. And that is quite different from the attitude of not bothering with justification at all, just concentrating
on getting what you want.

Now we turn to consider the different interpretations of

Thrasymachus's claim that justice is the interest of the stronger, and to determine, if we can, which is to be accepted. His remark is ambiguous in the same way as is the slogan "Might is right", which would indeed serve as a translation of it. So many different interpretations have at one time or another been put forward that it would be impracticable to consider them all. We therefore confine ourselves to four, which between them cover the whole range. For identification and classification, they may be tabulated as follows:

1. Naturalistic Definition
2. Nihilist View
3. Incidental Comment
4. Essential Analysis.

1. NATURALISTIC DEFINITION

This, as already pointed out, is the interpretation followed by Cornford in his translation. According to it, Thrasymachus is giving a definition of the Greek word *dikaiosyne* (or the phrase *to dikaion*), and is giving a definition of it in naturalistic terms. That is to say, he is purporting to give a verbal definition, as indicated by Cornford's translation: "'justice' means . . .". And it is a naturalistic definition, because what Thrasymachus will be saying is that an apparently moral or ethical term ('just' or 'right') really is not an ethical term at all, but has a wholly natural or factual meaning. To understand this claim, it is necessary to consider the distinction made between moral and non-moral terms, or more generally between value terms and factual terms. It is the case that sometimes we want to say that something is a fact, without also wanting to make any comment, favourable or unfavourable, on its being a fact; and in this case our statement can be said to be, in respect of value, neutral. If somebody asks me the time or today's date, and if I give him the answer by saying that it is 10.20 a.m., or that it is 18 September, I am simply informing him of what is (I believe) a fact. Similarly, if he asks who the present prime minister is, who headed the first-class batting averages last season, what are the colours of the flag of Ghana, how many men have so far been put into orbit round the earth, and if I content myself just with answering the questions put to me, my answers will be factual. They may or may not be correct answers — for I may be ignorant, forgetful, careless or even deceitful — but they all purport simply to state what is the case. Comparatively few of the statements which we actually make are of this purely factual, neutral kind. Commonly we also in our statements convey something of our attitude to the matter in question. Thus, in response to the question who is the present prime minister, the answer "Mr. X is" is neutral in a way in which neither "Unfortunately, Mr. X is" nor "Thank goodness, Mr. X is" is, although the fact reported in all three statements is exactly the same. The last two statements convey the speaker's attitude to the fact of Mr. X being prime minister, while the first does not, and they are therefore not neutral statements. One says that it is a bad thing, the other that it is a good thing, that he is prime minister; they attach a certain value, negative or positive, to his being prime minister. Now, commonly, moral judgments about a man's conduct, or about types of conduct, are held, in the broadest sense, to be value judgments, to be commenting with favour or disfavour on the conduct in question. Thus, to say "It was wrong of him to do that" is both to say that he did it and to ascribe a negative value to, or to convey disapproval of, what he did: it is both a factual and a value statement. Many moral judgments are about the future, and although they may differ from each other in various ways — they may report an intention ("It is a good thing that the government intends to raise old-age pensions next spring"), or make a prediction ("Old-age pensions will be going up next spring — and quite time too"), or say not how things will be but how, at least, we want them to be ("They certainly ought to raise old-age pensions"), or be designed to influence the future ("You ought to press for a rise in old-age pensions") — they are all alike in taking a value-stand towards what is or is not going to be done. And the primary, if not the sole, function of words like 'good' and 'bad' is to ascribe value, one way or the other, to what is under discussion, whether it is a man's character, or his conduct, or the state of affairs brought about by his conduct.

Now, if Thrasymachus is taking the line attributed to him on this interpretation, he will be denying that 'just' and 'right' are words used to ascribe value or make favourable comments. He will not necessarily be taking the extreme position that there are no value-words at all, but he will be saying that at least 'just' or 'right' are not among them. For he will be saying that 'x is just' means exactly the same as 'x serves the interest of the stronger'; and whether x does or does not serve the interest of the stronger is a purely factual question. That is, the apparently moral judgment 'x is just', containing the apparently moral word 'just', is not really a moral judgment at all, making a favourable comment on x, for 'just' is not really a moral term, but a neutral, factual term such that 'x is just' means exactly the same as 'x serves the interest of the stronger', the latter expression being substitutable for the former without any change of meaning, wherever the former occurs. If 'x serves the interest of the stronger' is a morally neutral state-ment, and if 'x is just' means the same thing, then it too must be a morally neutral statement; and we should simply be wrong to suppose that 'just' is a moral term. There would be no question of our approving of, or attaching value to, certain actions or policies which promoted the interest of the stronger, by our calling them just; we should merely be repeating our-selves, or saying the same thing another way. One or other expression could be dropped from the language altogether with-out preventing us from saying something that we wanted to say.

Now, Thrasymachus's initial statement certainly is capable of bearing this interpretation. Nevertheless, the rest of the discussion makes it clear that it is not the correct interpre-tation, for two reasons. First, a consequence would be that Thrasymachus could never say, nor allow Socrates to under-stand him as saying, that it is just to serve the interest of the stronger; for to say this would be to make the uninformative statement that it is just to be just, or that serving the interest of the stronger serves the interest of the stronger. Yet Thrasy-machus repeatedly does say this, and allows Socrates to under-stand him as saying it (e.g. 338c, 339a, 339d, 341a). From these passages it is clear that Thrasymachus is, whatever else he is maintaining, at least maintaining that an action which

promotes the interest of the stronger *also* is just : i.e. it is just
as well as serving their interest; and this it could not be if
'just' meant nothing more nor less than serving the interest of
the stronger. Secondly, although this cannot be conclusively
proved, it is difficult not to believe that Thrasymachus is using
dikaiosyne and *dikaion* as moral terms, implying that people
ought to serve the interest of the stronger, with the subsequent
addition that subjects ought to obey their rulers. Admittedly,
this is complicated by the fact that Thrasymachus undoubtedly
despises justice and recommends a life of injustice, if you can
prosecute it successfully. And it is probably true that Thrasymachus is more interested in recommending injustice as a way
of life than in discussing the nature of justice. But none of this
is incompatible with his treating 'just' and 'justice' as moral
terms, which on this first interpretation he could not be.
Certainly, if *he* was not using them as moral terms, Socrates
was; and certainly too, if Thrasymachus was not so using
them he would have objected to Socrates using them, and
would have protested that Socrates misunderstood him. Now,
while Thrasymachus is quick to protest at Socrates misunderstanding him on various points, he never protests on this point.
We can therefore reasonably conclude, not only that Thrasymachus is not using 'just' and 'serving the interest of the
stronger' as synonyms, but also that he is using 'just' in a way
which is not morally neutral. The first interpretation is therefore to be rejected. And Cornford's translation according to it
is to be regretted, not only because it is misleading by suggesting that there are no difficulties over understanding Thrasymachus's exact position, but also because it is inconsistent with
much else that appears in the text (and in Cornford's own
translation of it).

2. NIHILIST VIEW

The suggestion here is that Thrasymachus is saying that
there is no such thing as justice, and that the belief that there is
is an illusion from which Socrates and others suffer, and from
which he proposes to liberate them. The connection between
the illusion of justice and the interest of the stronger will on

this view presumably be that the stronger hoodwink the weaker, to induce them to do what will serve their own (the stronger party's) interest. The strong man exploits the weak man's mistaken belief in justice, by persuading him that certain actions or policies of action are what ought to be pursued, when in fact all that is true is that they will, if pursued, promote the strong man's interest. Now, that such a programme of deceitful exploitation of the weaker by the stronger, often of subjects by their rulers, has from time to time in the world's history been carried out can hardly be denied. If you are dealing with a man of conscience, and if you want him to per- form a certain action, an effective way of inducing him to do what you want will be to persuade him that that is what he ought, or it is his duty, to do; it is more likely to be effective than the more straightforward and honest way of admitting that you want him to do it because it is in your interest that he should. Undoubtedly, the fact that people have a sense of right and wrong (whether or not they are mistaken or foolish to have it) is a valuable weapon in the armoury of the unscru- pulous exploiter, who will prefer to take advantage of people's sincere, though mistaken, beliefs, rather than to enlighten them by showing the beliefs to be mistaken.

From a practical point of view it would make no difference to the powerful exploiter of the gullible weak whether *all* belief in justice and in a difference between right and wrong is an illusion, or whether a less extreme line is taken, that *sometimes* (or even often) people are mistaken, or can be misled, about justice and a difference between right and wrong. But philo- sophically the extreme and the less extreme positions must be distinguished from each other, for they are certainly different. The extreme position, the one attributed to Thrasymachus on the Nihilist interpretation, is that whenever a man believes an action to be just or one which he ought to perform he is mis- taken, for there is no such thing at all as justice or what ought to be done. The difficulty about maintaining such a position is to see how one could explain people's suffering from the illusion at all. If there is, and could be, no such thing as justice, how could we ever make the mistake of supposing that there was? Any *prima facie* plausibility which this extreme position has it

derives from the confusion of it with the less extreme position,
that people can sometimes (or often, or even usually) be persuaded to believe an action to be just when in fact it is not.
But this less extreme position implies at least the possibility of
being correct in believing a given action to be just, a possibility
which is denied by the extreme position. Making a mistake is,
as the word itself indicates, mis-taking, taking a thing or person
to have an identity or a characteristic which in fact it does not
have, but which logically it could have. To give a simple
illustration : if I take somebody else's umbrella from the rack
in mistake for my own, that is only possible because there is
another umbrella which is my own, or at least I honestly believe
that there is. If I neither own an umbrella, nor honestly
believe that I do, I cannot make the mistake of believing that
an umbrella which in fact belongs to somebody else belongs
to me. I may take his umbrella absentmindedly, or even
deliberately, knowing it is not mine, but if I neither have nor
believe that I have an umbrella I cannot take his by mistake.
More generally, there cannot be an incorrect answer to a
question unless there could be a correct answer to it, i.e. unless
it were known what it would be like for an answer to be correct.
For an incorrect answer is simply an answer which is not the
correct one ; and, if there could not be a correct answer, there
could not be an incorrect one either. On the less extreme
position mentioned above, the statement 'x is just' *could* be
correct : either it sometimes is correct, or at least a situation
is conceivable in which it would be. People could be mistaken
in some (or many) cases in believing that x was just only because in another case they could be correct. It is only because
it is possible to stick swords through a human body from all
angles that the stage-illusionist can entertain and puzzle us
by shutting his assistant up in a box and then apparently doing
just that. His creating the illusion of sticking swords through
the girl's body from all angles depends entirely on his making
his performance look as like the real thing as his skill permits ;
but, if there could be no real thing, there could be no illusion
either. The entertainment for the audience lies precisely in
its failure to detect what the difference is between what the
illusionist is doing in his trick and what he would be doing if

it were not a trick at all, but he really were sticking swords through his assistant's body.

Consequently, while it is easy to see that on particular occasions we can be hoodwinked into mistakenly believing an action to be just, it does not follow from this that we must always be hoodwinked and that our belief could never be correct. Indeed, the reverse follows, that on occasion, however seldom (if ever) in practice, our belief could be correct. And that the belief could be correct is what the extreme position, here attributed to Thrasymachus, denies. The less extreme position not only does not provide support for the more extreme position, but is actually incompatible with it. And, when this is acknowledged, any initial plausibility which the extreme position might appear to have disappears.

Even so, Thrasymachus might have held it. Two questions then arise. Did he hold it? And how, if at all, does it differ from the first interpretation, according to which justice also seems to be an illusion, 'justice' being simply another name for what serves the interest of the stronger? To take the second question first. On the Naturalistic Definition view, that there is something properly to be called justice, and that some actions are or may be just, is not denied. What is denied is that any distinction is to be drawn between an action's being just and its serving the interest of the stronger. That is, it is being maintained, not that justice is an illusion, but that any alleged distinction between justice and what serves the interest of the stronger is an illusion. According to the Nihilist view, on the other hand, justice is an illusion — nothing at all corresponds, or could correspond, to the word 'justice'; in no circumstances could a statement of the form 'x is just' be true. Summarily, it may be put like this. Given that in our language we have two words or expressions 'a' and 'b': the Naturalistic Definition view, while allowing that there is such a thing as a and that there is such a thing as b, denies a distinction between them, but grants that a statement of the form 'x is a' (which means exactly the same thing as 'x is b') might be true; the Nihilist view denies that there is such a thing as a at all, and consequently denies that the question could arise whether there is a distinction between a and b; a statement of the form 'x is *b*' might or might not be true, but a statement of the form 'x is *a*' could not be true, because nothing is or could be *a*. If there is no such thing as justice, the question whether or not it is to be distinguished from what serves the interest of the stronger cannot arise.

That this Nihilist view is not the correct interpretation of Thrasymachus's position can be shown by the same reason as the first of the two reasons operating against the Naturalistic Definition view. Whether or not we agree that Thrasymachus in making statements throughout the discussion of the form 'It is just to . . .' is purporting to make moral statements, we cannot deny that he does make statements of that form. He repeatedly asserts that it is just to serve the stronger, and to obey the ruler, that the just man behaves one way and the unjust another. If the Nihilist interpretation were correct, Thrasymachus could not say any of those things. If justice is an illusion, then it could never be the case that just actions are of a certain kind, or that the just man behaves in a certain way; for there could not be any just actions or just men. Now certainly, Thrasymachus believes that there are : he despises both, and thinks that men are fools to be just, unless they are compelled to be. But he could not think that they were fools to be just unless he thought that they really were just; and he could not think that they really were just if he thought that there was no such thing as justice. We may therefore unhesitatingly reject this interpretation; although it has been seriously advanced as what Thrasymachus meant, it cannot be what he did mean, for it cannot be squared with his reiterated assertions that actions which are just and that men who are just are of a certain kind.

3. INCIDENTAL COMMENT

On this interpretation Thrasymachus is not attempting to define justice, or to say what it really is, at all. Neither is he concerned to deny the existence of justice (as on the second view), nor to deny a distinction between it and serving the interests of the stronger (as on the first view). The present view assumes the fact of the existence of justice, or at least a belief in its existence, and contents itself with making a remark about justice, intended to bring it into disrepute. Thrasymachus's statement that justice is merely what serves the interest of the stronger might, in this respect, be compared with Marx's remark that religion is the opium of the people, or with the remark that horse-racing is the sport of kings. Neither of these remarks tells us what religion or horse-racing is, and they would be quite unintelligible to anybody who had no notion of them. A foreigner who had no idea what horse-racing was, and who asked what it was, would be in no way enlightened by being told that it was the sport of kings. He would need to know or to have a belief what it was, in order to understand or to appreciate the observation that it was the sport of kings. Similarly, Thrasymachus would not be claiming to explain what justice was, but would be pointing out what he claimed to be a fact about it, namely that it served the interest of the stronger.

This interpretation does fit much of what Thrasymachus has to say, particularly in the latter part of the conversation. He undoubtedly is concerned to show up justice in a poor light, to emphasise that the just man always comes off worst, and that only a fool will be just unless he is compelled to be. This thesis is again taken up by Glaucon and Adeimantus at the beginning of Book II. Thus, it is certainly true that Thrasymachus is far less interested in answering the question what justice is than he is in recommending a life of injustice if you can practise it successfully. But to say that his interest in defining justice is less than his interest in disparaging it is not the same as to say that he does not attempt to define it at all. Yet the latter is what we must say, if we accept the present interpretation. But, if we seek for evidence in the text that he does not begin by asserting what he thinks justice to be, we cannot find it. We must not confuse the undoubted fact that he takes a poor view of justice with the hypothesis, advanced by this interpretation, that he offers no view as to what it is for an action to be just. And against this hypothesis is to be set the fact that Thrasymachus repeatedly does say what it is for an act to be just, viz. that it serves the interest of the stronger. If no better argument for the present interpretation can be offered than that Thrasymachus's interest in defining justice is less than his concern to recommend injustice, we have no reason to accept the interpretation, and strong reason to reject it. An economist, writing an article about inflation, may hurry over his account of what inflation is in order to concentrate on his argument that controlled inflation is a sound economic policy for a country to pursue. But we are not entitled to conclude from that that he has or offers no view as to what inflation is. The same consideration applies to this interpretation of Thrasymachus.

4. ESSENTIAL ANALYSIS

We are therefore left with the view that Thrasymachus does say what he thinks justice is, and that, *after* making his statement he then goes on to what most interests him, viz. pointing out the disadvantages of justice and the advantages of injustice. He does not think that justice is an illusion, and he does not think that there is no distinction of meaning between 'x is just' and 'x serves the interest of the stronger'. In saying that justice is nothing but the interest of the stronger, he is maintaining that an action is just if and only if it serves the interest of the stronger, and that it is the fact of an act's serving the interest of the stronger that gives it the characteristic of being just. A just action is just *because* it serves the interest of the stronger : if asked for the reason or justification for claiming of a given action that it is just, you provide it by pointing out that the action serves the interest of the stronger.

While the terminology of duty and obligation is not altogether appropriate to Greek thought, Thrasymachus may be represented as maintaining, on this interpretation, that it is the duty of the weaker to help and serve the stronger. We may find this principle, advanced as a principle of morality, highly objectionable, but we must recognise that, if we do object to it, we are objecting because it conflicts with our own moral beliefs, e.g. the Christian belief that it is the duty of the stronger to help the weaker. Furthermore, we must acknowledge both that throughout human history a great deal of the world's affairs have in fact been organised as if the principle were true that it is the duty and function of the weaker to serve the stronger, and that from time to time it has been explicitly maintained as a principle. In the twentieth century, to go no further back, it can be found embedded in the philosophy of National Socialism in Germany, in the doctrine of the master race. Hitler believed, for instance, not only that it was foolish of the Poles to resist the German onslaught in 1939 (for they had no hope of resisting successfully), but also that it was wrong or wicked of them to resist; for, by doing so, they were trying to interfere with the destiny of the German master race. Thrasymachus therefore would be by no means alone in maintaining the doctrine that it is for the weak to serve the strong. Where he differs from Hitler is in his taking a cynical view of morality as a whole, and in recommending us not to behave in the way in which we ought to behave, provided that we can be *successful* in avoiding it. This interpretation does escape the difficulties which faced the other views. It is consistent with Thrasymachus continuing to talk about just men and just conduct, with his treating statements of the form 'x is just' as though they were or could be true, and with his using and allowing Socrates to use 'just' as a moral term. He will be maintaining the doctrine which is simple and straightforward, however perverse we may think it, that a man will be acting justly if and because he serves the interest of the stronger. Does this view, as an interpretation of what Thrasymachus said, run into any difficulties of its own? It must be admitted that it does: we must face them and see whether or not they can be surmounted.

If justice consists of promoting the interest of the strong man, what are we to say of the strong man himself? Are we to say that it is just for him to promote his own interest (because he is the stronger)? Or are we to say that Thrasymachus conceives of justice simply from the point of view of the weak man, and that therefore questions of what is just and unjust do not apply at all to the strong man's conduct? On the latter view the strong man simply does what he does, and no moral comments, at least in terms of justice and injustice, are appropriate to his conduct. It is certainly true that Thrasymachus, in putting forward serving the interest of the stronger as a rule of conduct, is thinking from the point of view of the weak man;

and therefore we might be inclined to suppose that he is maintaining that the strong man can be neither just nor unjust.
Unfortunately, he does more than once (e.g. 343e) speak of a
ruler being just or unjust (he tends in the argument to identify
the stronger with the ruler, and the weaker with the subject —
a point to which we shall have to return later). In favour of the
other view, that questions of what is just do apply to the
stronger, and that he will be acting justly in pursuing his own
interest, it can be argued that his original statement was not
that justice is the promotion *by the weaker* of the stronger's
interest, but simply that justice is the promotion of the stronger's
interest, the implication being that both the weaker and the
stronger will be acting justly in promoting the latter's interest.
The weak man will be acting justly in promoting *another man's*
interest, viz. the stronger's, and the strong man will be acting
justly in promoting *his own* interest. This would be a perfectly
consistent line for Thrasymachus to take, it would allow moral
terms like 'just' and 'unjust' to apply to any man's conduct,
whether he was weak or strong, and it would lay down the
same principle for them both, that they were to promote the
interest of the strong man.

But there is a serious difficulty in the way of thus interpreting
Thrasymachus, namely that he does explicitly say that justice
is *another's* good. This has led some commentators to conclude
that Thrasymachus is maintaining that while it is just for the
subject (the weaker) to promote the interest of the ruler (the
stronger), it will be just for the ruler to promote the interests
of his subjects. For, by promoting his own interests he will
not be promoting *another's* good, and therefore will not be
acting justly. We now have the previous position reversed,
in the case of the ruler himself. Instead of saying that for him
justice will consist of promoting his own interest, we have to
say that it will consist of promoting the interest of others, viz.
the subjects. Yet, if we accept his statement that justice is
another's good, with the consequence that justice for the ruler
consists of promoting, not his own, but his subject's interest,
what now becomes of his original claim that justice is simply
the interest of the stronger? It looks as though his two claims,
(a) that justice is the interest of the stronger, and (b) that

justice is another's good, not one's own, are flatly inconsistent
with each other, and that the inconsistency could only be
avoided by confining the applicability of justice to conduct by
the weaker subject. But that line is closed by Thrasymachus's
recognition that a ruler can be just or unjust; and the supposed
inconsistency cannot therefore be resolved.

In fact, however, Thrasymachus does not simply say that
justice is another's good, but immediately follows that statement with a specification of what another's good is, viz.
"what is to the interest of the stronger and the ruler" (343c4).
Clearly, by using 'another' to refer to the stronger, he is here
thinking of justice, not from anybody's point of view, but from
the point of view of the weaker. He makes the same point on
the next page (344c), where he says that "while justice is the
interest of the stronger, injustice is what is to one's own advantage and interest". The truth seems to be that Thrasymachus
has advanced two different criteria of justice :
  (a) that it is what serves the interest of the stronger
  (b) that it is another's good,
without appreciating that they do not necessarily coincide. In
the case of the weaker they do coincide, but in the case of the
stronger they do not. And because he advocates injustice and
the pursuit of his own interests, Thrasymachus tends, when he
does talk about rulers, to think in terms of (b), forgetting about
(a). He admires the ruler who, by his power, pursues his own
interest rather than that of his subjects, and he admires the
man who by injustice, the pursuit of his own interest, can
seize power and subject others to his rule (348d). The man
who, when he is in power, continues to act justly, in the sense
of promoting others' interest, is not a bad man, but simply a
fool to waste his opportunities (343e and 348c). Thus, Thrasymachus is not being perfectly consistent, but because he thinks
of justice primarily from the point of view of the weak subject,
and because he admires injustice as the pursuit of one's own
interest, when he does talk of the just and the unjust ruler he
thinks of them in terms of (b) rather than of (a).

We must now turn to a consideration of Socrates's objections to Thrasymachus's assertion that justice is nothing but

the interest of the stronger. He begins (339b) by agreeing,
that justice is to be analysed in terms of serving an interest,
with the consequence that the question to be considered is
whether that interest is to be specified as Thrasymachus has
specified it, as the interest of the *stronger*. (Incidentally, it will
be found that when an account of justice is finally reached
which Socrates is prepared to accept, in Book IV, it is not given
in terms of interest at all; perhaps this is some evidence
that Book I originally comprised a separate dialogue which
Plato subsequently used as a preface to the *Republic* proper.
It is true that he does think that justice, as finally analysed,
is to the interest of those concerned; but that it is so is
not part of the analysis. It may be that the fact that justice
is to the interest of those concerned would be his reason, or
part of it, for saying that men ought to be just; but that is
not the same thing as its being an element in the analysis of
justice.)

Socrates next suggests, and Thrasymachus agrees, that it is
just for subjects to obey their rulers (339b); and from now on
the stronger is identified with the ruler. Strictly speaking,
Thrasymachus should not have accepted this identification.
For, while it is characteristic of a stable government that the
government will be the stronger, i.e. will be able to enforce its
will and have its decisions carried out and laws obeyed, the
identification breaks down in the case of a successful revolution.
In that situation it is only because the revolutionaries during
the process of their insurrection are stronger than the government which they are engaged in overthrowing that their revolution can be successful. With their success, the stronger once
more becomes the ruler; but a revolution can only succeed
precisely because at the revolutionary stage the stronger and
the ruler are not identical. However, for the purposes of the
argument, the identification may be accepted, because none of
Socrates's objections or Thrasymachus's answers to them turn
on the error contained in it.

Having secured Thrasymachus's agreement to the proposition that it is just for subjects to obey their rulers, Socrates now
points out an inconsistency between it and the original proposition that justice is what promotes the ruler's (the stronger's)

THE ARGUMENT WITH THRASYMACHUS   43

interest.   What happens when the ruler passes a law or gives an
order which, if obeyed, will not be to his interest?   If the subject is to promote the ruler's interest, he must disobey the law;
if he is to obey the law, he must do something which will not
serve the ruler's interest.   For, as Socrates points out, and as
Thrasymachus agrees (339c), rulers in legislating are capable
of making mistakes as to what is in their interest.   The subject,
therefore, would be faced with an insoluble dilemma.   Whichever line he takes, he will be transgressing one of the rules of
conduct which Thrasymachus has laid down for him.   As long
as we admit the fallibility of rulers, the dilemma is neither
soluble nor escapable.

Cleitophon here makes a suggestion (340b) as to what
Thrasymachus really meant, with the implication that it is
only by misunderstanding and misinterpreting his meaning
that Socrates has been able to develop the charge of inconsistency.   It is not entirely clear what the suggestion is, partly
because the Greek is capable of either of two interpretations,
partly because Thrasymachus immediately brushes it aside,
and it gets no further discussion.   It turns on the two phrases
'the interest of the stronger' and 'what the stronger believes
to be his interest'.   Cleitophon may be saying:

(1) that Thrasymachus meant that the interest of the
     stronger is what the stronger believes to be his interest;

or (2) that by 'the interest of the stronger' Thrasymachus
     meant what the stronger believes to be his interest.

Whichever suggestion Cleitophon is making, we have to accept
it that it is not what Thrasymachus meant, not only because
he explicitly denies it, but also because what he goes on to
say would not fit Cleitophon's suggestion.   Nevertheless, it is
worth briefly examining Cleitophon's intervention, if only to
consider whether it represents what Thrasymachus *ought* to
have said.

(1) *Thrasymachus meant that the interest of the stronger is what
the stronger believes to be his interest.*   This cannot provide a possible way out of the dilemma posed by Socrates, for it contains
a logical fallacy of a kind that needs to be exposed, for it is
often enough committed.   It attributes to Thrasymachus an
assertion of the form 'x is the case if A thinks (believes) x is

the case', instantiated by statements like "If I think it is right to do that, then it is right to do that", or Hamlet's "There is nothing either good or bad, but thinking makes it so". The statement that if I think an action is right then it is right is not *logically* objectionable if all that the speaker means is that his thinking the action right is a sufficient criterion or guarantee of its being right, the implication being that the speaker does not make mistakes about what is right and wrong. He will be claiming an infallibility on matters of right and wrong, like the infallibility attributed by Roman Catholics to the Pope on certain religious matters; and although the claim may be objected to more readily than those responsible for the up-bringing of children, such as parents and schoolteachers, care to believe, it cannot be objected to on logical grounds. But if the statement that if I think an action is right then it is right is construed as meaning that my thinking that the action is right makes it right (which is what Hamlet is committing himself to in his "There is nothing either good or bad, but thinking makes it so"), then it does contain the same logical fallacy as Cleitophon's suggestion (on this interpretation of it). For what is being claimed is that x's being the case is determined by A's thinking that it is the case. The claim as a whole is asserting something the contradictory of which is implied by the latter part of the claim. It is part of the logic of verbs like 'believe' and 'think' (where it is used as a synonym of 'believe') that whether what is believed to be the case in fact is the case is *independent* of what the speaker believes. If I say that I believe that it is raining now, then quite apart from my im-plying that I do not know that it is raining and that I may be wrong, I also imply that whether or not it is raining is inde-pendent of what I think, is not determined by what I think. Either it is raining or it is not; and whichever it is doing is independent of what I think or believe it is doing, or whether I am attending at all to, or interested at all in, the state of the weather. That is, my assertion that I think that x is the case implies that whether or not x is the case is not determined by my thinking that it is. But Cleitophon's suggestion on this interpretation maintains that my thinking that x is the case does determine its being the case; according to Hamlet, my thinking something to be good makes it so. So, the claim as a whole maintains that something's being the case is determined by my thinking that it is the case; while the logical force of 'think that' in the latter part of the claim maintains the exact opposite — that something's being the case is *not* determined by my thinking that it is the case. Therefore anybody asserting a proposition of the form 'x is the case if A thinks that it is the case' ('A's thinking that x is the case makes x the case') is contradicting himself; he is making a claim which is contradicted by part of itself. And, if this is the suggestion which Cleitophon is putting forward on behalf of Thrasymachus, that whether an act is in the interest of the stronger is determined by the stronger thinking that it is in his interest, then Thrasymachus did well to reject it; for it would not rescue him from Socrates's dilemma. (The only way to rescue him along some such lines would be by replacing 'thinks that' or 'believes that' by some verb of a kind that has been called "performative", such as 'deem' or 'decide'. In a newspaper competition, where the editor's decision is final, the winner of the competition is the person whom the editor decides to be the winner, however incompetent, careless or corrupt the editor may be; the same thing applies to the decisions of umpires and referees in games. But Cleitophon does not use a performative verb; and there is not the slightest reason to suppose that the notion of performative verbs ever entered Plato's mind in writing this passage.)

(2) *By 'the interest of the stronger' Thrasymachus meant what the stronger believes to be his interest.* This, it must be said, is a simpler and more natural translation of the Greek than the former way; and this is what Socrates understands Cleitophon's suggestion to be, as his immediately following remark makes clear (340c), when he asks Thrasymachus whether he meant that justice was what seemed to the stronger to be his interest. What Cleitophon is suggesting, in fact, is that Thrasymachus in saying that justice is the interest of the stronger had expressed himself badly or carelessly, for what he actually *meant* was that justice is what the stronger *believes* to be his interest. In effect Cleitophon is saying that throughout the discussion so far we should for 'the interest of the stronger' read 'what the stronger

believes to be his interest'. This suggestion is not open to the
objection to which the other interpretation was, for Thrasymachus would not be saying that an act was to the interest of
the stronger if the stronger thought that it was to his interest.
He would be acknowledging that what he had *meant* by his
original statement, although those were not the actual words
he used, was that justice was what the stronger thought to be
his interest. Thrasymachus immediately denies that Cleitophon had conveyed his meaning correctly. But he might have
done better to have accepted the suggestion, either as a clearer
version of what he meant or as an emendation of it, for it would
have rescued him from the charge of inconsistency. There
would be no conflict between its being just to serve what the
stronger (ruler) believes to be his interest and its being just to
obey the ruler, for while a ruler may make a mistake as to
what actually *is* his interest he will hardly make a mistake as to
what he *believes* to be his interest; and if it is right for subjects
to do what the ruler believes to be in his interest, it will not
matter that the ruler is mistaken in believing so. This would
raise again the issue of subjectivity in moral judgment, which
came up in connection with Socrates's question to Polemarchus
whether a friend is a man who *seems* good or a man who *is*
good (cf. Chapter 1, p. 17).

Thrasymachus, declining Cleitophon's way out of the possible conflict between serving a ruler's interest and obeying
his laws, argues that the conflict cannot arise because, strictly
speaking, a ruler cannot make mistakes, with the consequence
that he cannot be in the position of legislating in a way which
he believes, but *wrongly* believes, to be in his own interest.
True, he agreed with Socrates earlier that a ruler can make
mistakes, but that was only a loose way of speaking. A ruler
is like any other expert, such as a doctor or a mathematician or
a craftsman, in that he operates from a fund of knowledge or
skill. When his knowledge fails him (as through forgetfulness
or carelessness), he makes mistakes, but at that time he is not
the expert, ruler, doctor, etc. It is true that we might still say,
for example, that the doctor had made a mistake, if his diagnosis
was wrong or his prescription unsuitable, but this would be a
loose, imprecise way of talking. Really, we would not want to

call him a doctor at the time at which he made the mistake. Similarly with the ruler: *qua* ruler he cannot make mistakes, for at any time at which he does make a mistake he is not being a ruler. Therefore the dilemma posed by Socrates cannot arise. There is no possibility of the ruler making mistakes about his own interest, and therefore no possibility of a subject, by obeying his ruler's laws, acting contrary to the ruler's interests.

This is simply a quibble by Thrasymachus, and no answer to Socrates's dilemma. Granted that his point is, not that men who are doctors (or rulers, or experts of any other kind) are infallible, but that *as* doctors they are infallible, and are therefore not properly to be called doctors when they make mistakes, there appears no reason why we should accept his point. In fact we say of a doctor in respect of a mistake that he has made, not that he is not then a doctor, but that he is a bad doctor (if his mistake is culpable), or that he is an unfortunate, or overtired or overworked doctor (if his mistake is not culpable). So far from saying that he is not a doctor when he makes mistakes, we may deplore the fact that he is a doctor. Furthermore, even if Thrasymachus were allowed his point that a supposed ruler only *is* a ruler when his legislation really is in his own interest, this would only be a verbal patching over of his difficulty. If a subject believes that obedience to a particular law would not serve the ruler's interest, he may be correct in believing so; he will still have to choose between the two courses. And, if Thrasymachus means that a subject should not obey a law which does not serve the ruler's interest, on the ground that at the time of making that law the supposed ruler was not really a ruler (for, if he had been, he could not have made the mistake about his interest), then he is saying that it is for the *subject* to decide whether a law ought to be obeyed. The fact that the man who is the supposed ruler claims not to have made a mistake, and therefore to be the ruler, establishes nothing, for that claim itself may be mistaken. A situation in which the right to decide whether or not the laws are to be obeyed belongs to the subjects is hardly what Thrasymachus, with his general view of government, contemplated; if the subjects are the ones who have to decide whether the supposed ruler is in any piece of legislation *really* the ruler, it is they, not he, who are in control.

Fortunately for Thrasymachus, Socrates does not pursue him in this direction, but takes him up on three propositions which seem to be implied by his general praise of injustice and denigration of justice as a way of life. They are:

(1) A ruler governs in his own interest, not in that of his subjects.
(2) Injustice is more profitable than justice.
(3) The unjust man has a better life than the just man.

(1) *A ruler governs in his own interest* (340d-347d). Socrates's argument against this proposition follows the three-stage pattern of analogy which he frequently uses. He suggests (341c), and Thrasymachus agrees, that a man is a doctor, not because he makes money out of his occupation, but because he cures the sick; the art of medicine looks not to its own interest, but to that of the patient's body (342c). That is the first stage, in which he cites examples of men (he gives others besides doctors) who practise their occupation not in their own interest, but in the interest of those on whom they practise. At the second stage (342c4-5) he generalises by induction to the proposition that "no other art looks to its own interest — for it has no need to — but it looks to the interest of that of which it is the art". An art stands to the subject-matter on which it works as ruler and stronger to the weaker and ruled, and it works for the interest of that over which it rules. Therefore (third stage reached deductively from the second) the political ruler, who exercises rule over his subjects, as the doctor does over his patients and the sea-captain over his crew, practises the art of government not in his own interest, but in theirs.

As it is from particular instances which favour his thesis that Socrates has reached his generalisation that no art (or practitioner of it) pursues its own interests, Thrasymachus not unnaturally retorts with a counter-instance, in which he falls back on what actually happens. Is Socrates really prepared to maintain that sheep-breeders look after and fatten up their animals for the animals' sake, and not for their own (343b)? And in fact governments do the same thing; they are looking after themselves, not their subjects.   One has only to keep one's eyes open to see that injustice pays, but justice does not. Clearly, if Socrates's pattern of argument is legitimate, so is Thrasymachus's — for it is exactly the same.   From particular instances Socrates argues to a given generalisation, and from particular counter-instances Thrasymachus argues to a generalisation which appears to be a contrary of Socrates's.   The matter is further complicated by the fact that they are arguing at cross-purposes, so that their two propositions are not in fact in contradiction.   Socrates is talking about the way it is right for things to be, Thrasymachus about the way he thinks they actually are.   The claim that the true doctor, the man who really deserves the title of doctor, is the one whose prime interest is in his patient's health, and not in his own fees, is quite compatible with the claim that, as a matter of fact, doctors think far more about their fees than about their patients.   Both Socrates and Thrasymachus could be right, for neither is denying exactly what the other is asserting ; but this goes unnoticed. Indeed, Socrates accuses Thrasymachus of inconsistency (345c), for having agreed on the one hand that a doctor looks to his patients' interests, while insisting on the other that a sheep-breeder looks to his own rather than that of his sheep — which is to regard him as a profit-maker rather than a sheep-breeder. A distinction must be made between doing one's job and making money out of it (346a-b), which Socrates somewhat artificially treats as another art or craft which a man pursues side by side with his pursuit of his particular art of medicine, seamanship, government, etc. ;   the various arts differ from each other in performance of their particular functions, and are alike in that they have in common that their pursuit earns a livelihood.   By the practice of his art a man benefits that on which he works (e.g. patients, subjects), not himself;   it is by the money which he earns by, or receives for, his services that he himself is benefited.   A ruler must be paid to do his job, just because his job consists of working not for himself but for his subjects.

The truth about this discussion seems clearly to be that both Socrates and Thrasymachus are wrong in their claims. Socrates's claim that an art (by which he means an activity grounded on expert knowledge or skill) works for the good of that of which it is the art is the claim that it is altruistic, and is at its most plausible when the art in question is one which has people for its subject-matter or the material on which it works, and is one which is readily accepted as beneficial. The art of medicine which he selects as his prime example is the best he could have chosen, and he could have added many others. But it is difficult to take seriously his claim that *every* skilled activity is altruistic, even if we think only of arts which have people for their subject-matter. The activities of criminals may be skilled, but it is idle to pretend that they are altruistic. And Socrates's case looks even sillier if we consider arts which do not have people as the material on which they work; we shall have to say that the sculptor works for the good of the stone, the painter for the good of the canvas, the architect for the good of the building and so on. On the other hand, Thrasymachus is equally wrong in maintaining that *no* activities are altruistic, for it is perfectly clear that many are. Both disputants have made the mistake of over-generalising from their instances. Socrates, starting from some clearly altruistic arts, concludes that all are altruistic; Thrasymachus, starting from some equally clearly self-regarding arts, concludes that none is altruistic; and both are wrong in their conclusions.

If we ask what is the proper aim of any man exercising his expert skill, the answer is not to be given in terms of interests to be served, whether his own or others'. It is rather that the exercise of his skill should be disinterested, i.e. that he should be concerned solely with exercising his skill to the best of his ability, whether he be doctor, barrister, musician or anything else. Simply as an expert, the man's job is to exercise his skill to the maximum, and for him as an expert or artist the question whether he is really working for his own advantage or somebody else's does not arise. It may arise for him as a *man* as a question about his profession, but it does not arise for him within his profession. A man who is a barrister may well wonder whether he ought to be spending his life trying to secure acquittals for shady characters, i.e. he may wonder as a man whether he ought to be a barrister, or a criminal barrister, at all. But in court he should not be thinking like that. In court he is a barrister, and his job is to make out the best case he can for the defence (or for the prosecution, as the case may be) without any consideration at all whether it will be to his own or to somebody else's advantage. Socrates could have made out a good case for maintaining that rulers ought to promote the interests of those whom they govern, but he quite fails to make it out by the method which he actually follows. For he deduces it as a conclusion from the general proposition that all arts work for the interests of those on whom (or that on which) they work, a general proposition which Thrasymachus has no difficulty in showing to be false.

(2) *Injustice is more profitable than justice* (347e-352b). Strictly speaking, the question whether injustice or justice pays better (if this means that it leads to honours, wealth, etc.) is not a philosophical question at all. It is an empirical question, to which there is no single answer covering all situations. As advice to the impressionable young, the warning that injustice or crime does not pay may be salutary, and as a broad generalisation it may be true. But to what extent it is true will depend on the efficiency and incorruptibility of the law, i.e. of police and judiciary; and that is something which notoriously varies from one political community to another. Even in a community such as our own, where the rule of law is probably regarded as highly as anywhere, it would be idle to pretend that injustice never pays; and the question whether or not it does is not a question which the philosopher has any special claim to answer.

Nevertheless, Socrates does produce certain arguments in support of his denial that injustice is the more profitable, which must be considered. The first, which again makes use of the notion of the expert, and depends on an analogy with activities such as those of the doctor and the musician, is the longer (348c-351c). Its gist is as follows. If we look at experts in a field such as music, we see that the expert does not try to outdo everybody in that field, but only to outdo the less expert. A player will not try to tune his instrument better than another player who is as good as himself, but only better than the man who is not as skilled as himself. The non-expert, on the other hand, because he does not know all that he needs to know in that particular field, will try to outdo everybody — expert and non-expert alike — and will show his ignorance and foolishness. Similarly in the case of justice. The just man will try to outdo, not other just men, but only unjust men. The unjust man, on the other hand, like the non-expert musician, will try to outdo everybody, just and unjust alike — and, again like the non-expert musician, will show his ignorance and foolishness in doing it. Therefore it is not true that injustice is more profitable than justice.

It is difficult to believe that Plato intended this argument seriously, for it is almost embarrassingly bad, and calls for at least two main criticisms. First, he has exploited the ambiguity of the Greek word πλεονεκτεῖν, which we have rendered by 'outdo' as being the most nearly corresponding ambiguous word in English. In the case of music, what Plato means is that the expert will try *to do better than* the non-expert, will try to make a better job of whatever it is that he is doing; and the non-expert will make the mistake of trying to do better than anybody else. In the case of justice, on the other hand, Plato means not that the unjust man will try to do better than everybody else, but that he will try *to get the better of* everybody else. The unjust man is not trying to do the same thing as the just, and trying to do it better. He is, in fact, trying to do the very opposite of what the just man is doing. The outdoing in which Plato supposes the unjust man to indulge is a different kind of outdoing from that in which he supposes the non-expert musician to indulge.

Secondly, Plato's argument assumes, without any kind of justification offered for it, that the unjust man will display his foolishness because he will be less good at pursuing his job of crime than the just man will be at leading his honest life. But there is no reason at all for thinking of the unjust man as a second-rate or third-rate version of a just man, as the bad musician is of the good musician. The unjust man is not pursuing the same object as the just man, but not doing it as well — he is pursuing a quite different object, and may do it just as well. The suggestion is that an unjust man, simply because he is unjust, will overreach himself, and that that will be his downfall. No doubt, plenty of bad men do overreach themselves in this way, but it would be wildly optimistic and ingenuous to suppose that all do. Why, because a man is wicked or a criminal, he should also be more stupid or less skilful than the honest man, Plato makes no attempt to explain.

Finally, the question must be asked whether in drawing this analogy between the just man and the expert musician Plato is not being inconsistent with what he said earlier, in the argument with Polemarchus (cf. Chapter 1, pp. 13-14).

There he had argued that justice could not be a skill (*techne*) by showing the absurdities to which one is forced on the assumption that it is a skill; there (332c7) he had used the example of the doctor as a man who exercises a skill, and here again he mentions the same example (349e8). Consequently, it appears that in this argument designed to establish that injustice is not more profitable than justice by showing that the unjust man will make errors of judgment which the just man will avoid, even as the inexpert musician will make errors of judgment which the expert will avoid, Socrates is himself making the very assumption which he has claimed earlier to have refuted, viz. that justice is a skill. If this is so, we must wonder whether Plato is being intellectually dishonest, or whether he is unaware of his inconsistency, or whether this is a case of his not uncommon practice of making Socrates use in one discussion a line of argument inconsistent with an argument used in another discussion, just to see whether his interlocutors are capable of detecting the inconsistency.

However, it is not entirely clear that he is being inconsistent. The keyword, *techne*, of the earlier discussion with Polemarchus nowhere occurs in the present discussion with Thrasymachus; and the most we could say would be that Socrates's argument here *implies* that justice is a skill or *techne*. But another word does occur here, which did not occur at all in the previous discussion, viz. *episteme* (350a6); and the difference may be significant. Later in the *Republic*, *episteme* comes to bear a technical and highly specific meaning, but at this stage and in some of its subsequent occurrences it means, in a quite general sense, 'knowledge'. That is to say, Plato is not yet restricting the sphere of knowledge in the way in which he goes on to restrict it in Books V-VII; and he is here allowing to the expert practitioner of an art such as medicine or music a knowledge of his art in a way which he would not later allow unless further conditions were met. And it is one of Plato's main doctrines that virtue is knowledge, that a man does not voluntarily do what is wrong, that he only does wrong through ignorance.

How then are we to reconcile the view, which emerges here, that the just man, like the expert musician, has a knowledge lacking to the unjust man or inexpert musician with his previous argument against Polemarchus that justice is not a matter of expertise? The two views can be reconciled, if we appreciate that against Polemarchus he is maintaining that justice is not a skill *tout court*, i.e. that being just is not simply the same as possessing a certain skill or know-how. We might want to say of somebody that he knows what he ought to do in a certain situation, but that he is not to be relied on to do it. There does not seem to be any obvious contradiction between saying of somebody that on the one hand he knows how to conduct himself in certain circumstances — i.e. he knows what he ought to do, what conduct is expected of him — and saying that, on the other hand, the trouble with him is that he is not to be depended on to behave that way. He knows that it is wrong to get drunk at the Christmas office party and then to insist on driving his car himself afterwards, but he is not to be trusted to refrain from one or the other. We are not going to call him good or virtuous merely because he knows what he ought and ought not to do, or because he is *capable* of refraining from drinking before driving (as shown by the fact that sometimes he does refrain). Possessing this knowledge is not enough to make him virtuous, for while knowing that it is wrong to drink before driving he may choose to ignore it, say, out of bravado or a desire to show off, or he may forget it under the influence of the party. He must actually behave, and be dependable on to behave, in the right way if we are to call him virtuous.

That is as far as Plato goes with Polemarchus, that justice in particular (or virtue in general) is not *simply* a matter of knowing how: it is a matter, not of capacity for behaving in the right way, but of a settled disposition or reliability to behave in the right way. Justice may require a skill, but it is not simply reducible to a skill.   On the other hand, in this passage with Thrasymachus he is saying something more in line with his positive view that virtue is knowledge.   Not merely does virtue require knowledge (as does expertise in the arts, such as those of medicine or music), but also, if a man really knows what is good, that is how he will try to behave. Conversely, if a man does not try to do what is good, it shows that he does not really know what is good.   In the true sense the man getting drunk at the office party does not really know that it is wrong to drink before driving; if he did, he either would not drink or would not insist on driving afterwards. Just as the real musician could not bring himself to try to do something musically wrong, which would be something, not indeed beyond his skill, but contrary to his art, so the virtuous man, possessing real knowledge of what is good, could not act in a way contrary to that knowledge.   Plato's thesis that virtue is knowledge is open to dispute, and was immediately after-wards disputed by Aristotle (*Nicomachean Ethics*, VII. 2-3), on the ground that succumbing to temptation was the result of weak-ness of will, and that weakness of will or of character was to be distinguished from ignorance : a man can, from a variety of causes, fail to apply knowledge which he has.   But at least it can be maintained that Plato's thesis does explain away the apparent inconsistency between the passage in which he argues against Polemarchus that justice is not a skill and the passage in the argument against Thrasymachus in which *prima facie* he seems to be presupposing that it is.

Plato has a second argument (350d-352b), much more effective than the first, to show that injustice is not more profit-able than justice.   It is that injustice cannot in itself be a source of strength : it is not a unifying force, but exactly the opposite, a divisive force.   The practice of it in a community does not bring men together : it sets them against each other.   Here Plato might be said to be making the point of the need for honour among thieves.   If a group of men conspire together for some wrong purpose, then within the group they must behave justly; they must be able to rely on each other, and to be relied on; if they cannot rely on each other, the group flies apart, and they will not be able to fulfil whatever purpose they came together for. Here Plato's point is a good one, although not quite as good as he thinks or wants. What is true is that in a gang of criminals unity must be preserved, and in that sense they must be able to depend on each other. But to say that is to say much less than what is meant by 'honour among thieves'. The latter means that although thieves will not respect the rights of others, will not regard themselves as having duties to others, yet among themselves, within the gang, they will respect rights and regard themselves as having duties to each other. But if this in turn means, and if Plato wants to suggest, that a gang of criminals cannot be kept together unless they recognise duties to each other, it seems patently untrue. A gang can be kept together by mutual fear, or by fear of the boss if he is a strong enough personality; or it can be kept together just by the continuing success of its exploits. In either case, a member has much to gain by staying in, and much to lose by trying to get out; and, as long as that is so, the gang will cohere. When mutual fear, or fear of the boss, ceases to operate, or when successes decline or turn to failures, then the unity of the gang begins to disintegrate. The history of gangsters, whether Chicago racketeers or Nazi war-lords, illustrates that well enough. Still, Plato's main point is fair — that injustice as such is not a unifying but a dividing factor. He later applies it to the individual man, saying that a man who is unjust is at war with himself — the different elements in his soul are fighting against each other.

(3) *The unjust man has a better life than the just man* (352d-354c). One of Thrasymachus's main points of recommendation of injustice was that it gave you a better life, a life for which you might reasonably be envied by others less fortunate. This is not the same thing as saying that the unjust man was happier than the just, although no doubt Thrasymachus would have maintained that too. The Greek word in question, εὐδαιμονία, is frequently translated as 'happiness', but misleadingly so. For us, for a man to be happy is for him to be in a certain general condition of enjoying his life, of having a certain outlook on the world, of being free from worry and so on; essentially, to say of a man that he is happy (even more obviously in the case of saying that he is unhappy) is to say something

about his mental or spiritual or psychological condition. It is to say something personal about him, not something about the circumstances of his life. On the other hand, for the Greeks *eudaimonia* meant something different, and consequently Thrasymachus, in maintaining that the unjust man is *eudaimon*, is talking rather about the circumstances of his life than about the man's psychological state in those circumstances. He is maintaining that the unjust man's life is enjoyable, that he is in the best position to be happy. It is like our saying of a man who has won several thousand pounds on the football pools that he is a very lucky (or very unlucky) man ; we do not think it necessary before saying that he is lucky to find out what he himself thinks or feels about suddenly having so much wealth.

That is the position — that the unjust man's life is more enjoyable than the just man's — which Socrates now tries to destroy. His argument depends on the two notions of the function of a thing, and of the excellence (or good quality) of the thing which enables it to perform its function ; for instance, the function of a knife is to cut, and the peculiar excellence of a knife is the sharpness of the blade which enables it to carry out its function or job of cutting. The function of a thing, says Socrates, is (a) that job which it alone can perform, (b) that job which it can perform better than anything else can, (c) that job which has been assigned to it. For example, (a) seeing is the function of the eyes, for they are the only organs which can see, (b) pruning is the function of a pruning knife, for, although you can make some kind of a job of pruning with a carving knife or with a sculptor's chisel, you will not do it as well with them, (c) again, pruning is the function of a pruning knife, for that is what it is made for. Next, if a thing's excellence is destroyed or weakened, its performance of its function will be impaired, as in the case of blindness in the eyes or bluntness in a knife. Now, this is applied to the human soul (353c) : the function of the soul is to live (i.e. to direct the man's life) ; therefore the soul must have an excellence, and if deprived of that excellence cannot perform well its function of living ; but we have already agreed (350d4-5) that justice is the excellence of the soul ; therefore the just soul is the one which lives well ; and the man who lives well is *eudaimon*, the man who does not

live well is not; therefore it is the just man who has a better
life, not the unjust man.

Socrates's argument, which concludes Book I, calls for
various comments. First, he is rather free and easy in his
mention of three criteria of the function of a thing, as though
it made no difference which was used. Certainly, it is true
that where (a) applies (b) applies also, although in such a case
it would be pointless to say so. If (a) there is a job which only
one thing can do, then necessarily (b) that thing must be
able to do the job better than anything else can, since *ex hypo-
thesi* nothing else can do the job at all. But (b) might apply
where (a) does not, as in the case of the pruning knife and the
carving knife used for pruning. And (a) might apply where (c)
does not, (b) where (c) does not, or (c) where (a) does not or
(b) does not. Consequently, the question arises which of the
three different criteria of the function of a thing we are to suppose used in Socrates's assertions about the function of the soul.
If, as 353d indicates, he is using criterion (a) and saying that
living is the function of the soul, for it alone can perform that
function, then it needs to be pointed out that the function has
only been mentioned so far in a generic way, and that just as
the soul alone can live well, so the soul alone can live badly.
Socrates has in fact moved from saying

(1) that living is the function of the soul (which is compatible with living either well or badly) to supposing

(2) that, if the soul is performing its function well, it will be
living well.

But this is a fallacious argument. For, if the soul were
carrying out its function by living in a bad way (which by
criterion (a) it might), then it would be performing its function
well by living badly. That is to say, Thrasymachus could, if
he had wished to remain consistent with his general position,
have used against Socrates an argument of Socrates's own form,
by maintaining (i) that the soul alone can lead a bad life; (ii)
that the excellence of the soul which enables it to perform that
function is injustice; therefore (iii) it is the unjust soul which
best performs its function and (iv) it is the unjust man who has
the enjoyable life. Thrasymachus's mistake was to have agreed
with Socrates that justice is the excellence of the soul; such

an admission was inconsistent with, and fatal to, his own general thesis.

If Socrates was making any use at all of criterion (c) of a function, it needs to be pointed out that it has teleological and theological implications. If a thing has a function assigned to it, or has been designed for the performance of a function, the assigning or designing has been done by someone. If living, by this criterion, is said to be the function of the soul, this presupposes the existence of a God who assigned that function to the soul, or designed the soul to perform that function. You cannot, merely by examining a thing and finding out what it can do or what you can do with it, establish that that is its function according to criterion (c). For you cannot, by that method, establish that it *was* designed to perform a function at all. This kind of argument from design cannot therefore be used as an argument for the existence of God (although attempts have often been made to use it so). An argument which, when applied to the function of the human soul, has the existence of God as a presupposition cannot also have the existence of God as a conclusion. To know that the soul has a certain function assigned to it we should need to know independently that God had assigned that function.

What Socrates has not brought out is that the notion of function presupposes purpose — the purpose for which we use a thing which we find, or the purpose for which we have the thing designed. We can talk of seeing as being the function of the eyes only because that is the purpose for which we can and do use them (and for which we have nothing else as a possible substitute). Where a thing has been designed to perform a certain function, like a knife or a watch or any artefact, the notion of purpose comes in twice, the purpose for which the designer designed the thing, and the purpose for which the user uses it. If the thing is well designed, these purposes are likely to coincide, for the designer's purpose is to enable the user to meet *his* purpose. But they need not coincide : the user might find that the object better served some other purpose which he had than its designed purpose, or that it served some other purpose which he had more need to satisfy ; an ornament used as a doorstop, or a book used to prop up one leg of an uneven table would be an instance of one or other of these cases.

Clearly, the argument from function in general, and from living being the function of the soul in particular, does not establish that the just man has a better life than the unjust, nor does Plato himself regard it as satisfactory. For he points out in the final paragraph of Book I that it is preposterous to try to settle whether injustice rather than justice is a virtue, whether injustice is the more profitable, and whether the unjust man has the better life, without first having settled what justice and injustice are. Until they know exactly what it is that they are talking about, claims made about it one way or the other cannot be seriously discussed. He therefore ends this first book on an inconclusive note, and only returns in Book IX (576b) to the question whether the just or the unjust man has the better life, after he has answered the question what justice is.

Chapter 3

A NEW APPROACH TO THE PROBLEM
OF JUSTICE

THE preliminary discussion of justice in Book I had served two purposes. First, by finding fault with the two accounts of justice advanced by Polemarchus and by Thrasymachus respectively, Plato had revealed the inadequacies and the superficialities of conventional approaches to the subject, and the difficulty of giving a satisfactory analysis of an abstract concept, however familiar the concept, or the everyday use of it, might be. Secondly, Thrasymachus's thesis had raised the question whether justice was any kind of a good at all, Thrasymachus having maintained that it was none, and Socrates claiming that it was a good, but having done little more to show that it was than attempting to demolish Thrasymachus's arguments that it was not. The rest of the *Republic* is devoted to these two main questions: What is Justice? And what kind of a good (if any) is it?

Book II begins with a preliminary formulation of the latter problem, the speakers being, apart from Socrates himself, Plato's two brothers Glaucon and Adeimantus. It is significant for the thesis that Book I was once a separate dialogue, both that Glaucon and Adeimantus, who had been present throughout the conversation of that book, took no part in it, and that, apart from interjections, none of the characters who had taken part speaks again anywhere in the course of the remaining books. From now on the only three talkers are Socrates, Glaucon and Adeimantus, the last playing such a minor part that the conversation becomes virtually a dialogue between Socrates and Glaucon. There are two further points to note about the abruptness of the transition to Book II, the second being of some philosophical importance. First, it is striking, in contrast to the Socratic method of Book I, that now it is Glaucon who asks the questions, and that it is Socrates who offers answers to them, a sign that the character "Socrates" is now becoming more of a spokesman for the views of Plato himself. Glaucon outlines the different kinds of good (357), asks Socrates to which kind justice belongs, and receives an unhesitating answer (358a), which is adhered to without modification throughout the rest of the *Republic*. Secondly, Socrates, having concluded Book I by saying that until they have settled what justice *is* they cannot profitably consider questions about it, immediately does accept such a question and proposes an answer to it. This raises two problems: whether Socrates's practice at the beginning of Book II is inconsistent with his profession at the end of Book I; and whether, apart from the issue of consistency, it is illegitimate to consider questions *about* a concept before considering the central question of the definition or analysis to be given of the concept itself.

The charge of inconsistency can hardly be maintained, for all that Socrates does at this stage is to state his answer without arguing for it. There is nothing objectionable about a philosopher stating at the outset of a discussion what his conclusion is going to be, provided that he then proceeds to develop the argument which leads to that conclusion. As a matter of procedure, it is often clearer to make the order of exposition the reverse of the order of proof, a practice with which we are all familiar from our learning the theorems of Euclidean geometry: there, the theorem to be proved is first stated, then follows the proof, with at the end the formula *quod erat demonstrandum*. This is exactly the procedure which Socrates professes to pursue. He asserts that justice is something which is *both* good in itself *and* good in its consequences. In Book X at 612b he claims that they have now proved that justice is good in itself, and that they may now go on to establish that justice is good in its consequences, the argument for which immediately follows. Had Socrates at the beginning of Book II tried to argue for his conclusion about the goodness of justice, in advance of giving his account of justice itself, he could fairly have been accused of inconsistency with his statement at the end of

Book I; but as he follows exactly the opposite procedure, the charge of inconsistency fails.

Inconsistency apart, would it have been illegitimate for them to discuss what kind of good justice belonged to, in advance of having settled what justice was? Socrates had just said (354c) that if you do not know *what* justice is, to ask other questions about justice is a waste of time. But, in fact, the procedure is not illegitimate, and may even help towards settling what justice is. Certainly, there is some *prima facie* plausibility about saying that, if you do not know what the thing is that you are talking about, you cannot usefully say anything about it. But there are two ways of knowing what a thing is, or two senses of 'knowing what a thing is', which need to be distinguished from each other. In the first sense, we know what an x is if we can recognise an x, can distinguish it from non-x's, and can linguistically apply the word 'x' correctly to x's. In this sense, most of us, even children and some domestic animals, know what motor cars, apples, meat and so on are: we recognise a car, an apple, or a lump of meat when we see one, we have no difficulty in distinguishing them from other things such as a bicycle, a turnip, or a lump of clay, and we (not animals, nor all children) have the linguistic ability to use the right word for the right thing. While knowing what an x is, in this sense, consists mainly in our ability to recognise x's, this is not incompatible with failure to recognise an x if it is disguised, or with inability to decide whether something is an x if it is a borderline case between being an x and being, say, a y. A man would not be said not to know what an aircraft is if, faced with the request to point out all the aircraft within his view, and then to point out all the seacraft within his view, he were unable to decide to which class to assign the hovercraft which happened to be present. He knows what an aircraft is, as long as he can recognise standard or not unusually deviant cases of aircraft. But knowing what an x is, in that sense, does not necessarily, and seldom does in fact, carry with it knowing what an x is, in the other sense of being able to say what an x is, to give the defining properties of x, or explain what constitutes being an x. That very few people have any knowledge of this kind about almost anything at all is due, not so much to inarticulateness or stupidity, as to their having little occasion to try to acquire the knowledge. For most people, and for most of their practical purposes, ability to discriminate between an x and a y is enough: they neither need the other kind of knowledge, nor have the curiosity to pursue it. Most people in this country could now tell the difference between an AM or an FM radio, either by the look or by the sound of the sets, but very few could give at all a coherent or accurate account of what the difference is: for their practical purposes of buying or of operating a set of one kind rather than the other they do not require the knowledge which would be expressed in their saying what the difference is.

The same is true of abstract concepts. Plain, unreflective men like Cephalus and Polemarchus know what some (at least of the most straightforward) of these are, in the sense that they recognise, say, a standard case of justice or injustice when they meet it. In that sense they know what justice is, but in the other sense they do not — they cannot *say*, accurately and coherently, what it is. Again, for the practical business of living, they do not need to, except for either extremely complicated or borderline cases; and such cases, fortunately, seldom occur in the life of the private citizen. Knowing what justice is, in the sense of being able to recognise actual cases, or what would be cases of it, might well enable a man to answer some questions about justice, even although he could not yet answer the direct central question — what justice is. Indeed, the whole process of determining the answer to the central question and answers to more peripheral questions (such as to what kind of good justice belongs) works on a principle of conceptual feedback. A man must be able to recognise some (at least standard) instances of x, and to achieve some discrimination between what are and what are not x's, before he can begin to answer the question what an x is: if he had not that recognition-knowledge, he would have no material for his answer, no reason for giving one answer rather than any other. On the other hand, the answer he gives to the central question, i.e. the successive improvements he makes on his first answer, will determine his future discrimination between x's and non-x's; and so the two kinds of 'knowing what' activity are complementary. For instance, a legal definition of 'aircraft' clearly must cover what are obviously cases of aircraft and must exclude what are obviously not cases of aircraft, but it may not matter for some time that some people (possibly even some legal authorities) treat a hovercraft as an aircraft and that others do not. But with an increase in the number of hovercraft, it may come to matter, e.g. for traffic control and for deciding responsibility for accidents. And then the definition of 'aircraft' will be tightened up, either in legislation or by judicial decision, in a way that will either definitely include hovercraft in, or definitely exclude them from, the class of aircraft.

Therefore it would not have been wrong for Socrates and the others to have discussed what kind of good justice belonged to, before discussing what justice was. It needs to be realised that both types of question are reciprocal, and that neither can be finally answered without finally answering the other. However, as already stated, they do in fact not discuss the question: the question is asked, an answer is given, and the justification for the answer is provided by the remainder of the dialogue.

At 357 Glaucon classifies the three kinds of good, and asks to which justice belongs. They are:

(1) those which we welcome for their own sake, and not for the sake of their consequences, e.g. happiness, and harmless pleasures that do not have any unpleasant after-effects. That is to say, these are goods which we choose in themselves, neither because of nor in spite of their consequences.

(2) those which we welcome both for their own sake, and for the sake of their consequences, e.g. good sense, judgment, eyesight and health.

(3) those which we do not welcome for their own sake, but which we would say bring consequential benefits, and which we would therefore choose to have for the sake of the rewards and other advantages to be gained from them, e.g. physical training, medical treatment and earning a living. Things of this class we do not merely not regard as intrinsically good, but we actually regard

as irksome or disagreeable. That is to say, they are things which we choose, in spite of what they are in themselves, solely because their consequences are good.

Socrates unhesitatingly assigns justice to the second kind, and claims in Book X (612) to have by that stage shown that it is good in itself, having as a final task that of showing that it is good in its consequences. So, at the outset Socrates declares a scheme, and at the end claims to have followed it. But does he follow it ? This is not an easy question to settle, chiefly because what Plato writes implies a distinction which he does not seem to have noticed himself. It concerns his notion of consequences, in respect of which a thing may or may not be good, contrasted with its being good in itself. In Glaucon's classification of goods which, being accepted by Socrates, we may reasonably take to be Plato's own, consequences are characterised in a consistent manner : the consequences of x are these things which (a) happen, (b) happen after x and (c) happen because of x. This is a familiar notion of consequences, and raises no difficulties which are relevant here. And the instances of consequences which Plato gives under the third class, and which he elaborates in Book X, viz. the honours and rewards which come to a man who has led a life of justice, exactly fit his specification of a consequence. Honours and rewards are the consequences of justice, in the sense that it is a matter of fact, a contingent fact, that they do come to the just man ; they are what he may reasonably expect to receive sooner or later from having led a just life. But they are what might be called incidental consequences ; it is not in any way a necessary fact about justice that it does have such welcome consequences. Justice would still be justice even if it went unacknowledged, unrecognised and unrewarded : that is why Plato says that justice is good both in itself and in its consequences ; justice would not cease to be justice, nor cease to be good, even if it did not meet with the rewards which it deserves.

So far Plato's notion of consequences raises no problems. But if we look at his examples of the third kind of good, things that are good in their consequences, the problems begin. For there a quite different notion is involved, the notion of result, of an activity's outcome successfully achieved or not. While in ordinary, everyday English the distinction between 'result' and 'consequence' is by no means always observed, it frequently is, and rightly so. We ask what the result was of a football match, wanting to know which side (if either) won, and what the score was. We ask the researcher to report on the results of his researches, or whether he has achieved any results yet. If we asked what were the consequences of the football match or the man's research, we should be seeking entirely different information. It might be among the consequences of the match that one of the players was out of the game through injury for the rest of the season, that some of the supporters of the losing side, drowning their sorrows in drink, were later that evening arrested by the police, and so on. It might be among the consequences of the man's research that a major advertising campaign was planned to launch his discovery on the market, that other firms tried to lure him away from his employer, and so on. Where we distinguish result and consequence, we mean by 'consequence' exactly what Plato says he means in this passage, and we mean by 'result' something much more narrowly restricted. It is restricted to things that we do (as opposed to what happens to us), and to things that we do with a certain end or aim; and the result of the activity is its outcome in respect of success or failure in achieving the end aimed at. That is why the result (not consequence) of the match was a win (lose, or draw), and the consequence (not result) of the match was, among other things, that the ground was unfit for play for a week.

Plato was therefore quite right to think of the honours and rewards which a just man receives as consequences. But the examples he gave of things belonging to the third class of goods, as being good not in themselves but in their consequences, are in fact things which are judged in terms of their results. Physical training, medical treatment and earning a living are all activities performed with a certain aim, and they are judged good for their success in achieving their aim. Improved health or improved athletic performance is not an incidental consequence, or a by-product of physical training, as honours and rewards are the incidental consequences of Plato's justice. This improvement of health or performance is the aim of physical training, is precisely what makes it to be physical training at all; and therefore the training is to be judged good or bad in respect of its results, of the degree of success with which it performs that function which constitutes its being physical training. And the same applies to Plato's two other examples, and to innumerable others that could be added.

This failure to distinguish between result and consequence is slurred over by his use of the word *ophelein* meaning 'benefit'. For a benefit can be something aimed at, and therefore characterised as a result (as in the examples of physical training, etc.), or it can be something, not aimed at, but incidentally received or accruing (as in the examples of honours and rewards). This is relevant to what Plato himself has to say about justice. Here he claims that it is good both in itself and in its consequences. But it is fairly clear from many passages throughout the *Republic* that what Plato really means, by saying that justice is good in itself, is that it is good because of what it *does* to the man who is just. A quite explicit statement of this (admittedly made by Adeimantus, but not objected to by Socrates) comes a little later in the present book, 367b: mentioning justice and injustice, Adeimantus requests Socrates to show "what each does to the man who has it that makes the one bad in itself and the other good in itself". In the course of the same speech, Adeimantus twice repeats the same thing (367d and e); and there are many other such passages in speeches by Socrates himself (e.g. 392c, 457b, 505a), which show that Plato thought that the good which justice *is* must be characterised in terms of the good which it does. It is because of this that he has been hailed by some philosophers and decried by others as the first utilitarian. The answer to the question might have been clearer if Plato himself had recognised the distinction between consequences and results involved in his examples of the third kind of goods, and if he had in turn, with reference to justice, considered what distinction (if any) he should make between saying of something that it is good in itself and saying of something that it is good because of its results.

In order to obtain from Socrates a clear exposition and defence of his thesis, or rather of the first part of it, that justice is good in itself, Glaucon proposes to put forward the case against it as forcibly as he can (358b). This involves him in a statement of what he believes to be a widely held view of justice, which is a renovated and toughened version of Thrasymachus's view, and which he expounds polemically, not because he believes it to be true, but because he wishes Socrates to show that it is false. The popular view can be given under three headings (358c):

(1) The origin of justice
(2) Justice practised as a necessity, not a good
(3) Such practice quite reasonable.

(1) *The origin of justice* (358e-359b). In themselves, doing wrong is a good thing and being wronged an evil thing. The evil of being wronged outweighs the good of doing wrong, so that men, having had a taste of both, and finding themselves unable to escape the former and secure the latter, make agreements with each other neither to inflict nor to suffer wrong. Starting from this point they begin to make laws and mutual undertakings, and "to call that which is ordained by the law lawful and just; and this is both the origin and the essence of justice, being between the best state, which is to inflict wrong and not pay a penalty for it, and the worst state, which is to suffer wrong but not be able to obtain redress" (359a).

(2) *Justice practised as a necessity, not a good* (359b-360d). Justice, produced as a compromise between the naturally best and the naturally worst condition for man, is regarded and practised as an unavoidable necessity. Men look at it, not as something good in itself, but as the best terms which they can hope to get; and nobody would continue to practise it if he thought he could do better for himself by injustice. Even the most virtuous man would abandon a life of justice if he were suddenly given full power to do whatever he pleased with no risk of being caught and punished.

(3) *Such practice quite reasonable* (360c-362c). We can see that this attitude to justice is reasonable if we imagine the extreme cases: on the one side, the supremely unjust and villainous man who nevertheless, by the skill with which he operates and conceals his operations, retains an untarnished reputation for honesty and justice; and on the other side the

supremely just man, who nevertheless is misjudged and has a reputation for injustice. There is no doubt at all which of the two will have the better and more successful life. This shows both that men are quite right to treat justice of conduct as a necessity to be practised only where they cannot be successfully unjust (i.e. that justice is not good in itself), and that what is worth having is not justice, but the reputation of justice, because of the advantages it brings. The ideal is to combine the advantages of being unjust with the advantages of being thought to be just.

Adeimantus intervenes (362d), to reinforce Glaucon's thesis by making two points: first, that parents in praising justice to their children, and in impressing on them that they must be just, in fact do so not on the ground that justice in itself is good, but because of what it brings in the form of honour and prestige — once more it is not justice but a reputation for justice that counts; secondly, that it is a recurrent theme of religion and piety that doing wrong does not matter, if by the appropriate rituals you obtain remission for your offences. The challenge which Socrates must meet is that of showing that justice in itself is good even in the most unfavourable case, i.e. in the case where the man is not known or believed to be just and is deprived of the advantages which such a reputation would bring.

Glaucon's thesis about the origin of justice reduces to two propositions: (1) *Factual* — the allegedly historical proposition that it is only through individual weakness that men have come to form social communities and to make agreements not to exploit each other. (2) *Ethical* — that justice, the obligation to abide by rules of conduct, has its origin in the agreements and the laws which men have made. Here Glaucon is guilty of a minor inconsistency, for if justice has the origin which he assigns to it, then so must injustice — there could be no injustice prior to the agreement. And yet, as he has described it, men only come together and agree to co-operate precisely because they find the evil of unfettered suffering of injustice outweighs the good of unfettered practice of it; and the agreement is said to be an agreement "with each other neither to practise nor to suffer injustice". If justice and injustice are only created by the agreement, it cannot be an agreement to compromise between the advantages and disadvantages of injustice. To the condition of man prior to the agreement the concepts of justice and injustice are equally inapplicable : in such a condition a man does what he does, and he either gets away with it or he does not. Moral criticism would be as inapplicable to his conduct as it is to that of a fox raiding a poultry run. But the inconsistency can be removed, and Glaucon's thesis left essentially intact, if we amend his opening sentences : if for 'practise injustice' we read 'exploit', and for 'suffer injustice' we read 'be exploited', we remove from the natural condition of men the moral concepts which on Glaucon's account are introduced only with the mutual agreement to end unfettered exploitation.

Glaucon's thesis that the natural condition of man is one of purely self-regarding exploitation of others, and that it is only ended by men finding that, through their individual weakness, they suffer more than they gain under it, has more than once been asserted to be one of the earliest statements, or even the first statement, of what was later known as the Social Contract theory (cf. Cornford, p. 40; Lee, p. 90). And admittedly, there is a certain *prima facie* similarity, particularly to the version of the theory advanced by Thomas Hobbes, who conceived of the state of nature very much as Glaucon described it, as one in which every man was out for himself, and the weakest went under; neither Locke nor Rousseau, the other two leading contractualists, took the same unflattering view of man in the state of nature. But, even taking Hobbes as the model contractualist with whom Glaucon is to be compared, it seems misleading to assert that the latter is advancing a theory of Social Contract. It is true that a Social Contract theory does advance two propositions like (and in the case of Hobbes, very like) the two advanced by Glaucon, but the emphasis is entirely different in the two cases. It is, or used to be, a standard objection to the Social Contract theory that it has no historical basis, and that the state of nature is a historical fiction. The theory is a theory of political obligation, that men have an obligation to obey the government and the law, because they, or their remote ancestors, bound themselves by an agreement with each other and thus emerged from their previous state of nature. And it has been held against the theory that, quite apart from any other objections to which it is liable, it relies on the factually weak presupposition, for which no historical evidence is, or now can be, produced, that men did in fact once live in a state of nature, and that they did in fact come to form communities by making covenants with each other. Not only is there no historical evidence for the state of nature and for emergence by covenant, but the theory rests on a wildly implausible assumption, viz. that man is by nature a solitary, rather than a gregarious and social animal.

Now this, although a familiar objection to the Social Contract theory, is a thoroughly bad one, for it entirely misses the point of the theory. The essence of the theory is contained in the second, or ethical, proposition that men's obligation to obey derives from the agreement which they have made, i.e. that the fundamental obligation is that of a promise, to behave in a certain way because they have entered into an undertaking to do so. The first, or allegedly factual, proposition, that prior to the agreement men lived in a state of nature, is strictly irrelevant to the theory; and therefore the fact that this proposition is almost certainly false is no objection to the theory. As Locke saw more clearly than Hobbes, the factual proposition, even if it were true, would provide no support for the theory, because, even if our remote ancestors had entered into a mutual agreement, this would provide no explanation or justification of our present obligation to obey government and law. If we now have such an obligation, it rests on a quite different factual proposition, namely that *we ourselves* have given such an undertaking. Locke's attempt to show that by living in a community, and enjoying the advantages and services which it provides, we have given an implicit, if not an explicit, undertaking may or may not be successful. What matters is that that is the factual basis of the theory, not a proposition of extreme historical dubiety. That is, the emphasis in the Social Contract theory is on the ethical proposition, that men have an obligation of obedience in so far as they have undertaken it, with the consequence, alleged by Rousseau, that in actual states men have far fewer obligations than is generally supposed. It is an important consequence of the Social Contract theory that a man's obligations are self-imposed. By my explicit undertakings, and by those of my actions which can be construed as undertakings, I incur obligations or impose them on myself; they cannot be imposed on me by the actions of others.

The Social Contract theory, then, purports to explain the existence of obligation, specifically to state the conditions under which a man has the political obligation of obedience to government and law. But is this what Glaucon is professing to explain? In his account the emphasis is entirely on the factual, or would-be historical, proposition, supposedly giving an account of what induced men to emerge from a state of nature into the organisation of a social community; even within his community the emphasis is still on the allegedly factual side, that men only accept the compromise because it pays, and that no man would continue to tolerate it if he thought he could successfully violate it. If this were all that Glaucon had to say, we should have to conclude that it was simply false to maintain that he was advancing an early version of the Social Contract theory. In fact, he does have a little to say about the ethical proposition, but so little that it is at best misleading to label him a contractualist; misleading, not only because his emphasis is wholly on the other, factual proposition, but also because what little he does say leaves it quite unclear where he stands on the question of obligation. His actual words (359a), which have been already quoted, are: "they begin to make laws and mutual agreements and *to call that which is ordained by the law lawful and just*" (our italics). If by the italicised phrase Glaucon means that an act which is just or which a man has an obligation to perform is so because it is ordained by the law, there is nothing contractual about that. He would be providing a purely legal basis for obligation, that it was the fact that the law required a man to behave in a certain way which imposed on him an obligation to behave that way — with nothing said about the moral basis for the law itself. It would only be if Glaucon had meant that a man had an obligation to behave in a certain way because the law required him to do so, *and because the law itself derived from the agreement into which he had entered*, that Glaucon could be plausibly called a contractualist.

But it is far from clear that the latter is what Glaucon did mean. What he has to say about the basis of obligation is so sketchy, and is about a question in which he was, for the purposes for which he was talking, so little interested anyway, that it is to read far too much into him to maintain that he was advancing a theory of Social Contract. Modern labels are seldom, without adaptation, applicable to Greek thought of the fourth century B.C.; and the present case is a particularly glaring case of their inapplicability. Glaucon was not in the least interested in establishing the basis of political obligation, and well might not have understood what the question there was. What he did want from Socrates was an argument to show that justice was a good of the kind that Socrates had claimed, something that was worth practising quite apart from its incidental consequences, which in any case were the consequences, not of being just, but of that very different thing, of having acquired a reputation of being just.

Glaucon may indeed have misconceived Socrates's remark that justice was good in itself, and may have been wrongly inviting Socrates to show how justice was to the interest of, or profitable for, the man who was just. That is, he may have been confusing the question whether justice is good with the question whether it pays to be just (cf. "Honesty is the best policy"). Socrates was prepared to show that justice was good because of what it was or because of what it did. But there appears no reason to suppose that he was thinking solely in Glaucon's terms of what advantages it brought to the agent. Showing a man that just conduct does also serve self-interest may be, and often is, an effective way of inducing him to behave in the required manner, but it must be distinguished from showing him that justice is good, or what kind of a good it is.

Chapter 4

FORMATION OF THE FIRST CITY

HAVING declared what kind of a good he intends to show justice to be, Plato immediately reverts to his original question "What is Justice?", and proposes a new procedure for answering it (368d). We ascribe justice, not only to an individual man, but also to a whole community, such as a Greek city; that is, it makes sense to characterise Athens as being just, as much as it does so to characterise Socrates. And because a city is larger than an individual, they might find it easier to make out in it what they are looking for, and thereafter identify the corresponding property in the individual. He therefore proposes that they should begin by examining a city coming into being and find justice (and injustice) coming into being with it. Having located and identified justice in it, they can perform the corresponding operation for the individual with more hope of success than if they followed the method of Book I.

Before turning to Plato's account of his city's origin, we must understand what is involved in his proposed procedure. First, it presupposes that there is some degree of similarity between the nature of an individual and the nature of a city, indeed sufficient similarity for findings about a city to be illuminating, or even relevant, for questions about a man. *Prima facie*, we might be inclined to say, the unlikeness between a city (or a nation, or any politically organised community) and an individual man is so great that we could hardly expect to argue by analogy from one to the other. At least we should have to establish that they had a certain number of properties in common, in order to give any degree of reasonability at all to the supposition that what could be said of a city in respect of justice could also be said of a man. And the mere fact that in some cases the same *word* can be used of both would not establish that it was being used in the same way of each. For instance, in "Torquay is a healthy town" and "Jones is a healthy man" the same word 'healthy' is used both of town and man, but it is used to say a quite different thing of each. Similarly the mere fact (if it be one) that we can say both that Athens is a just city and that Socrates is a just man would not entitle us to conclude that justice in each was the same. In fact, Socrates does not argue by analogy from some known features of identity between city and man to an as yet unknown feature; and he does not argue from the fact that we may use the same word 'just' of both. His procedure is far bolder and less self-critical. As his example of the large and small letters shows (368d), he takes it as unquestioned that justice in a city is the same as justice in a man, and therefore there is nothing doubtful about examining the large-scale model straightaway. At 435b he explicitly asserts that in respect of justice a just man will not differ at all from a just city. But this is not an argument: it is a bare assertion which is accepted without question. He does not propose to establish the presupposition of identity of justice in city and man either by argument from analogy or by considering whether the same word might or might not have the same meaning in the two cases. As a procedure this may strike us as odd, indeed as unwarrantably dogmatic, but it becomes less surprising as the *Republic* proceeds, and as we find how close a parallel Plato draws between the nature of a state and the nature of a man. His initial procedure here, while questionable if regarded on its own, provides the key to his whole political philosophy, which is going to turn out to be that the state is itself an individual, and therefore that many statements which can be made about an individual man's character or psychology can be made literally, and not just metaphorically, about the state as well. This is the theory of the state which has been called the Organic Theory (cf. T. D. Weldon, *States and Morals*, Chapter 2), which sees the state not as a piece of political machinery, but as a political person with a life and a character of its own. Emotionally this view may answer a need, and politically, because of its emotional force, it is of enormous value to a state's government, but its intellectual claims are hardly comparable. Still, there is no doubt that in the *Republic* Plato was putting it forward, and in some detail. Consequently, while we may query the presupposition of his proposal to find justice in the large-scale model (the city) instead of looking for it at once in the small-scale model (the individual man), viz. the presupposition that justice will be the same in both, we cannot complain that this was a presupposition of which Plato was unaware, or which he perhaps hoped that his readers would not notice. Nothing could be further from the truth. He was well aware both of the presupposition, and of the need to argue for it. Furthermore, he does later argue for it (435e), when he maintains that the individual man must have the same characteristics as the city, for otherwise the city itself could not possess them : a city cannot derive its characteristics from any source other than the men who are its citizens. And having given his account of justice in the city, he insists (434d) that it must be regarded only as a provisional account until confirmed by the account to be given of justice in the individual man; if any discrepancies appear, the former, rather than the latter, will have to be revised. Therefore, although the assumption made at the beginning of Book II may seem, when taken by itself, an erroneous and implausible assumption, we must recognise that it is seriously meant, and that Plato is going to argue in support of it later. His argument at 435e may or may not be a good argument, but it is there.

Next, we should appreciate that Plato's declared reason for embarking on political philosophy at all is a moral reason, or at least that it is a reason about the individual. He is interested in the search for justice in the city only because it will enable him to make out justice in the individual. The individual is what he cares about, and the examination of a city is a device for solving a problem about him. But, in fact, as the argument proceeds, Plato's interest changes and his emphasis shifts from the individual to the city; not only is the happiness of the city as a whole more important than the happiness of any of the individuals, or any of the classes in it (421b), but also the individual comes more and more to be regarded as an element in the state, described in terms of the function which he performs and the contribution which he makes to the state's welfare. This indeed is a natural consequence of the organic view of the state which Plato embraces; and to that extent his first introduction of the city, to help solve a problem about the individual, is misleading. It has misled some readers into regarding Plato as the great Liberal, whereas it would be nearer the truth to regard him as the great Totalitarian. On the other hand, it must be acknowledged that Plato is not entirely consistent in his view of the individual as subordinated to the state. The only individuals about whom Plato talks in any detail are those comprising the small *élite* class who are to govern the state, the philosopher-rulers, and towards them he adopts an ambivalent attitude: on the one hand, their education and training is determined by their political function, and is designed solely to qualify them for their responsibilities in government. On the other hand, being men of philosophical temperament and wisdom, they will have no political ambitions whatever: they take it in turns to rule, and they do so willingly, if not enthusiastically, partly because as good men they recognise how dangerous and pernicious it is to allow government to fall into the hands of inferior men (347c), partly because they accept the requirement to govern as the price which they must pay for the privilege of spending the rest of their time in the way in which they want to spend it, in the pursuit of philosophy itself. For, as Plato insists, the most worth-while life, if you are capable of living it, is that of contemplation and research; the practical life is, compared with the theoretical life, only a second-best. So we find in Plato's thought this tug-of-war between the two opposing tendencies: when he is writing as a political philosopher, to regard as the ideal for man service to the state in whatever capacity his aptitudes assign him to; and when he is not writing as a political philosopher, to regard as the ideal for man the life devoted to the pursuit of knowledge, with service to the state as a necessary but irksome chore which he must perform as the condition of being allowed to spend the rest of the time on what really matters (520d-e; cf. 582).

Plato's account of the formation and character of his first city is quite short (369-372) and very clear. And the fundamental fact about it, as he indicates in the opening words of his description, is that it is an economic community. "A city comes into being, in my opinion, when each of us happens not to be self-sufficient, but lacks many things" (369b). That is to say, he imagines men coming together, not because they have any need of each other in social terms, for friendship or company, but because they have needs of economic goods such as food, housing and clothes which each man is unable to provide adequately or efficiently by himself. The minimum community will be one catering for these needs, with each man specialising in one trade, bringing the products of his work surplus to his own needs to a common stock, where they are exchanged for other producers' goods of which he has need. Thus the principle of division and specialisation of labour is brought in right from the start, for, as Socrates says, it is obviously more efficient for each of the four or five basic tradesmen to produce four or five times as much of his own commodity as he requires himself and to exchange with others, than for each one to try to be his own farmer, house-builder, clothes-maker, shoe-maker, etc. (369e). Not merely is this more efficient in terms of expenditure of time and energy, but it takes into account that different men have different aptitudes. This smallest imaginable community must expand immediately, and on the same principle as before : the primary producers will need tool-makers, cattlemen, shepherds, then importers and exporters (which in turn calls for a greater surplus of production, so that exports may pay for imports), merchants, sailors, shopkeepers and labourers. Although the resulting community will be enormously larger than the first group of four or five producers, it has, for Plato, altered only in size, not at all in character. It still consists of a number of individuals, each doing his own specialised job, selling his products and services and in turn buying those of others. It is still thought of wholly in material terms as a community devoted solely to production and consumption ; and although Socrates says that such a life as it provides will be pleasant enough in a simple, bucolic kind of way, he does not object to the suggestion that what he has described is a "city of swine" (372d).

It should be realised not only that Plato supposes men induced to co-operate by their *economic* needs, but also that he maintains that they do so entirely selfishly. The first city is no high-minded community, fired by ideals of brotherly love. It is a group of men, each still out for his own interest as much as if he were living in a state of nature, but now realising that enlightened self-interest is better served by a degree of co-operation. Socrates makes this quite clear at the start, where, immediately after saying that the city owes its origins to man's economic needs, he goes on, "One man gives a share of his produce to another, if he does, or accepts a share of the other's produce, *thinking it is better for himself to do so*". As the phrase which we have italicised indicates, there is no question here of either of the communist doctrines "to each according to his labour" or "to each according to his needs". It is straightforward capitalism : "to each what by economic exchange he can get". The attitude which Socrates ascribes to each of his imaginary citizens is that of putting into the common stock, or on to the market, whatever he must in order to get out of it what he wants. That another man might have need of what you produce would not be regarded by you as a reason for your supplying it, unless you yourself had need of what he produces. No doubt, prudence and enlightened self-interest might dictate the wisdom of supplying a man of whose products you had no need — in case later your positions were reversed. But it would be a question of prudence, not of love nor of morality.

So far the understanding of the first city presents no problems : it is clearly a purely economic community, and it is clearly one of which the members are moved by considerations of self-interest ; in fact Plato is offering a basic account of what has since been called Economic Man — an account, incidentally, which in certain respects, e.g. its division of labour, anticipates that given in the eighteenth century by Adam Smith. But, granted that the picture which he paints is clear enough, what kind of a picture is it intended to be — imaginary, historical or something else ? It can hardly be imaginary, in the sense of not being intended in any way to correspond to reality, for in that case it would be pointless and not help at all in the search for justice.

If in his description of the formation of the first city Plato is attempting an historical account of how some social organisation, or how all social organisations, in fact came into being, he will be open to the same objection as that commonly levelled at Social Contract theories, of writing *a priori* history, of arguing that this is how things happened, and the order in which they happened, not because he produces positive factual evidence that in a particular case or cases they did happen in this way, but because this is how things must have happened; it will be an argument not from historical evidence, but from an examination of the essential nature of man or of social organisation or of both. But this seems an unlikely interpretation of Plato. First, even if his first city depends on contract, it is not a Social Contract in the accepted sènse: the striking feature of the first city is precisely the absence from it of the very thing which the Social Contract purports to explain, the existence of government and the obligation of subjects to obey it. If in Plato's first city there is any question of obligation at all, there is certainly none of political obligation; this makes no appearance until the evolution of the third and ideal city. Secondly, and more important, there is nothing in the text to suggest that Plato was claiming to write history: there is no description of man first living in an individualistic state of nature, and then coming to find that unsatisfactory, such as Glaucon had attempted; furthermore Socrates's proposal had been to inquire "what justice is in cities" (369a), which suggests a quite different approach. If he states it in terms of picturing a city coming into being, this is a graphic, and not dangerously misleading, way of introducing a description of a city pared down to its minimum essentials. In fact, he seems to be asking what are the minimum conditions which must be met if a city is to exist at all, and he replies that they are economic conditions, the provision of necessities of human life, the provision of freedom from want. This, he could argue, was even more basic than the need of security, freedom from fear, because fear of insecurity presupposes the possibility of aggression, and this in turn presupposes that the economic necessities of the possible victim of aggression are, at least to some extent, met: if a man does not possess the means of biological survival, neither will he survive, nor will he be a desirable object of aggression by other men. If a community cannot meet its barest economic needs, it cannot exist or survive as a community at all. Another way of getting at Plato's point would be to take any actual community and ask whether there is any one feature of it such that, if that feature were removed, the community would disintegrate : Plato's answer would be that it is the economic feature. If, for any reason, the producers of goods (and one could add, in any but the most primitive communities, the providers of services too) were to cease to supply them, the community could not survive. We see the beginnings of this in the stoppage of labour in a producing industry, whether a strike or a lock-out, such as a closing of coal mines, or in a distributive industry, such as a complete cessation of transport, or in a services industry, such as a cutting off of electricity supplies. And the further a strike in one industry spreads to strikes in others, culminating in a total and complete general strike, the more disastrous and thoroughgoing the breakdown becomes. Every time we are faced with a strike of sufficient proportions or duration, we are given a reminder of Plato's point, that the meeting of economic needs comes first, and that without that no other needs can be met at all. It is a simple point, but an inescapable one, which Plato does well to lay down as the basis of his city. Furthermore he is stressing, not only that the basic principle of a community's life is economic, but also that the basic fact about economic life is that it is self-interested, the provision of one's own needs. If this leads to agreements and contracts, to the exchange of goods and services, it is only a more sophisticated and enlightened self-interest, dictated by the wish for improved efficiency and by the recognition of the prudence of taking a long-term view of one's interests. The man who prefers to spend a few pounds each month on insurance premiums against the unlikely risk of his house and furniture being destroyed by fire may be more prudent than his neighbour who spends the same amount monthly on hire-purchase payments for a television set, but he is no less pursuing self-interest; and the insurance company, in accepting his proposal, is being as self-interested as he.

But Plato is not saying that the only motives which determine men's conduct are those of economic self-interest, or even are economic at all; and any attempt to father on him the economic interpretation of history, or to regard him as a Marxist before his time, is surely mistaken. In Books VIII-IX Plato does offer a limited interpretation of history, but it is not solely, or even primarily, an economic one. According to the economic interpretation of history the course of events is wholly or mainly (depending on the form of the theory adopted) determined by the factors of economic need and ambition; and any other interpretation which admits into historical explanation political or religious factors, or the influence of dominant men, is either wilfully or mistakenly wrong. But there is none of that in what Plato is saying here. What he is saying is that economic needs come first, and that if they are not met a community simply will not have a history at all; on the other hand he would allow that, if they are met, the community's history will be shaped by many other factors as well. There is all the difference in the world between saying that economic factors determine history, in the sense of saying that if they had been different history would have been different, and saying that they determine history, in the sense of saying that nothing else does. Plato supports the first view, but there is not a shred of evidence for supposing that he supports the second.

As the declared object of constructing this minimal city was to identify justice in it, after the preliminary description of the city is complete, the question is put by Socrates where justice is (371e). It receives from Adeimantus the somewhat lame and imprecise answer that he does not know unless perhaps "it is somewhere in men's dealings with each other". To which Socrates replies that perhaps he is right, but they must examine the suggestion and not shirk the problem. But in fact they do not then examine it at all: Socrates next gives a short account of the sort of life that men lead in such a community, and then proceeds immediately to sketch the city's evolution into something more elaborate. The question of justice is dropped, and not taken up again until Book IV, beginning at 427e. The answer at which they eventually arrive could, as Socrates points out (432d), have been given

at this stage, but as it could not at this stage have been de-
fended, or shown to be the correct answer, perhaps he was
well-advised to defer it until they were better able to appreciate
its significance. Furthermore, Socrates here defends the post-
ponement of the direct search for justice on the ground that
they should be better able to identify it (and injustice too) in
a rather more elaborate and sophisticated community than in
the one so far sketched (372e).

Nevertheless we may ask, independently of Plato's own procedure, whether there is a place in the primitive city as so far
described for questions of right and wrong. And it is worth
asking, for what answer we give affects our interpretation of
his city. The problem whether there is a place in the city for
questions of right and wrong is in fact not one problem, but
breaks down into two, related but distinct : (a) *Are the notions
of right and wrong applicable by us, as observers or commentators, to
the first city ?* (b) *Do members of the first city themselves recognise the
applicability of the notions ?*

(a) *Are the notions of right and wrong applicable by us ?* That
is to say, if we imagine such a community as described, composed of economic men, is it significant (let alone true or false)
to characterise some conduct as right and other as wrong ?
For example, could we properly say that a man's conduct was
wrong if he did not stick to his own job, or if he did not produce
goods surplus to his own needs and make them available to
others, or if he tried to obtain for himself something of another's
products without making any contribution of his own ? More
generally still, we might ask what the difference is between the
situation to which we think moral notions are applicable and
that to which we think they are not. What is the difference
between a woman shoplifting and a dog grabbing a piece of
meat from a butcher's shop and making off with it ? Or between a thief breaking into a shop and stealing some of its contents and a fox raiding a poultry run ? Clearly in each pair of
examples we should regard moral comment as applicable to
the first member of the pair but not to the second ; indeed
words like 'shoplifting' and 'stealing' are not purely descriptive :
they are morally loaded words, while the words used to report
the dog's or fox's behaviour are not. The question is whether

moral words or morally loaded words are properly applicable to the activities of purely economic man.

The answer seems to be that they are, provided that one condition is fulfilled, viz. that in this city of economic men their activities of production and exchange of goods arise from agreement, and of the special kind of agreement that could be called contract or bargain. What is here meant is practical agreement, agreement to do something as contrasted with agreement in opinion. In the latter sense, two men may be said to agree with each other if they hold the same views on some matter (and to disagree if they hold different views), but they could not be said to have made an agreement or to have entered into an agreement with each other. They, or their views, are in agreement, but the agreement is something that they have found themselves in, not something in which they have engaged themselves. Even this contrast between practical agreement and theoretical agreement or agreement in opinion is not here sufficient, for two men might be said to be in practical agreement with each other and yet not to have entered into an agreement with each other. An example of the latter would be Hume's instance of two men rowing a boat together: they are co-operating with a common purpose, for the efficient achievement of which they will need to make their style of rowing and rate of striking conform with each other; each may have somewhat to modify the method of rowing which he would use if he were on his own. The fact that they have a common purpose or that their individual purposes coincide makes it prudent, simply in terms of efficiency, that each should try to fit in with the other, or adapt his rowing to the other's, as well as he can; but this does not require that they should have entered into an agreement with each other. In the latter stages of the last war Britain and the U.S.A. on the one hand and the U.S.S.R. on the other were allies in the minimum sense that each had a common enemy, and that each had at least the same minimum objective, to inflict military defeat on Germany. It is true that they did enter into some agreements with each other, but even if they had not it would still have been sensible, so far as it would have been possible, for each to have taken note of what the other was able to do, and was trying to do, and to adapt its own strategy and tactics accordingly. But it is only if men have a practical agreement into which they have entered with each other, that moral concepts are applicable to their consequent conduct. That is, it is only if they have entered into a bargain, an agreement of the "I will, if you will" kind, that we can comment favourably or unfavourably on their sticking to or breaking their bargain. There *can* be one-sided undertakings, where A unconditionally undertakes to B to perform some action. For example, a father promising to give his son a gold watch on his twenty-first birthday would be giving such an undertaking, to be contrasted with the father promising the son a gold watch on his twenty-first birthday if he does not smoke before then. But in a unilateral undertaking such as the first, while A has agreed to do something, or to do something under certain conditions, B has not; the condition of reaching the age of twenty-one is not a condition which B accepts, as the condition of reaching the age of twenty-one without smoking would be. Consequently, in a one-sided case, while A's conduct in respect of it can receive moral comment, B's cannot, because there is nothing that he has agreed to do. For moral comment to be applicable to each, both must have entered into the agreement, both must be parties to it. If two men do enter into an agreement, e.g. for the exchange of goods or for the sale and purchase of goods, each has let himself in for carrying out his side of the bargain. One party may release the other from the bargain, i.e. remove from him the obligation to complete it, but one party cannot release himself. Provided that I enter into a bargain, and am not released from it by the other party (either his letting me off or his failing to keep his side), I can only either discharge my obligation by fulfilling the bargain, or fail to discharge my obligation by failing to fulfil the bargain: in the first case my conduct is morally acceptable, in the second it is morally objectionable. What exactly constitutes an undertaking, let alone a mutual undertaking, it is not easy to say, for not all undertakings are characterised by the formalities of signed and witnessed documents. In most cases saying "I will" is enough, morally although not legally. But there will be plenty of cases that do not even approach to that. For instance, suppose that B has taken to grazing his horses in A's field without asking A's permission, that A does nothing about it either by way of giving permission or by way of ordering the removal of the horses, and then that after a long interval, say the passage of several years, A suddenly insists on the immediate removal of the horses, has B legitimate ground for complaint? Can he say that A, by allowing the practice to continue for so long, has entitled him to expect to be free from sudden eviction, that A has in effect consented to the practice, and therefore is under an obligation not to terminate it abruptly? Granted that B had no right to put the horses in A's field in the first place, has A, by not hitherto objecting or ordering them out, conferred a right? Probably we should say in this case that B has no legitimate ground for complaint, although we might want to say that A's sudden action was inconsiderate. But there will be cases about which we should be more doubtful what to say. Putting it generally, we may say that moral comments are applicable to the extent that an agreement has been entered into, without attempting here to specify exactly the conditions under which an agreement exists. There will be clear cases where it does, clear cases where it does not, and borderline cases about which there would be doubt and dispute; the latter are cases which would have to be settled by discussion, possibly even by litigation, and about which as lawyers and as philosophers we should find it interesting to argue, so as to clear up or to reduce the area of uncertainty.

The question whether the economic activities of men in the first city do arise from such agreements or contracts does not admit of a ready answer, for Socrates nowhere actually says that they do (or that they do not) nor makes any explicit mention of agreements. That is, we can neither firmly assert nor firmly deny that his meaning is that the first city depends on agreements between individuals. In this respect his account may be contrasted with Glaucon's earlier statement, which did envisage men making mutual agreements with each other (359a). Socrates's silence on this matter has led some to interpret his first city as a natural unity, not only in a moderate sense, but in an extreme sense as well. It is undoubtedly a natural unity in the moderate sense in that it has no leaders, no government, no laws and consequently no system of punishment for what would, if there had been government and law, have been disobedience or offences. It is a unity to the extent that the individual interests of the members do mesh harmoniously; and it is natural in that there are no legal or quasi-legal contrivances for preserving the unity, or for preventing or repairing discord arising from a clash of interests. If all goes well, the community is in a healthy condition, but if all does not go well, as through the personal ambition or uncooperativeness of individuals, there is no authority for restoring it to a healthy condition; it is simply a fact of existence in such a community either that all goes well or that it does not. But it has also been held to be a natural unity in the sense in which a beehive or an ant-colony or even the human body might be held to be one, an organisation which has resulted not from any organising, but from a natural process of growth and evolution. Different ants in a colony perform different specialised jobs, as workers, warriors, etc. and their jobs in fact complement each other in a way which maintains the life of the colony, just as the different organs of the human body perform different and complementary functions in such a way that, if each organ performs its own function adequately, the body as a whole continues in a healthy condition. The corresponding interpretation of the first city would have the different workers simply performing different jobs, with the different jobs being in fact sufficiently diversified that their performance did have the effect of maintaining the community's economic existence. What characterises the city, in this view, would be the absence of purpose. Just as we cannot say that the human heart or the human liver has a purpose in doing what it does, i.e. we cannot say that its performance of its function is purposive, so we could not say of the members of the city that their activities were purposive. And this seems to be the weakness of the interpretation, for although the individuals may not be acting for the purpose of maintaining the life of the city as a whole (indeed, Socrates clearly implies that they do not when he stresses that each man pursues his own interest), yet it is hard to conceive of human activities as being activities and yet not being purposive at all; and to say that each man pursues his own interest, that he engages in economic exchange "thinking that it will be better for himself" if he does, is to attribute some purpose to him.

Whether the "beehive" interpretation will do for beehives and ant-colonies or not, it will not do for human society, even of the most primitive kind, because it ignores the facts that human beings as agents are both purposive and self-conscious. Usually, a man knows what he is doing, and if asked what he is doing can give the answer — which makes him a self-conscious agent. And usually a man knows what he is trying to achieve, and if asked why he is doing what he is will give the answer in terms of what he is trying to achieve — which makes him a purposive agent. Neither of these statements is universally true, for a man can be doing something without being aware what it is that he is doing, or even that he is doing anything, and he *can* be doing something without any purpose at all. But these are the exceptional, not the normal, cases and do not invalidate the proposition that human agency is characterised by the two features of purposiveness and self-consciousness. It may not be clear whether we can attribute these features to bees or ants, but it is clear that, while we cannot attribute them to the function of bodily organs such as heart and liver, we must attribute them to men as agents. And therefore we must suppose that the men in Socrates's city, each producing his surplus of goods and exchanging it with others' surplus, know what they are doing and are doing it with a purpose. If men knowingly and purposively engage in the exchange of goods, are they entering into agreements or contracts? Again, it is just possible that they are not, that they are simply adapting their conduct to the conduct of others so as to achieve their own ends with the maximum of efficiency which that makes possible. But it is an implausible suggestion, particularly when we remember that man is also a speaking animal. Bees may or may not communicate with each other, heart and liver certainly do not, men certainly do. The notion of men as self-conscious, purposive agents, and able to communicate with each other by speech, entering into economic exchange, without entering into agreements for the conduct of that exchange, appears too unlikely to be acceptable. How, on such a supposition, could bargaining be possible? How could any but immediate exchange be possible? A baker or a butcher might be able, in this simple way of exchange, to meet their respective needs for the day, but how could either get the builder to erect a house for him? And how could a money system, with coins or anything else accepted as tokens of exchange value, be introduced? Yet Socrates mentions the introduction of such a system (371b). It therefore seems reasonable to suppose that even in such a primitive economic community as Socrates is envisaging men do knowingly and purposively enter into agreements, and consequently to conclude that the condition of the applicability of moral concepts is satisfied. We can use words like 'right' and 'wrong' of their conduct, at least of that conduct which consists of the production and exchange of goods. The positive evidence provided by the text that this condition is fulfilled is something more than slight. First, Socrates does say (369e) that each man "must deposit the produce of his work into a pool for all"; how there could be a common pool or stock without an agreement for making deposits or withdrawals it is difficult to understand. And secondly, as already mentioned, he does refer to a currency and to the notions of buying and selling, which is a more sophisticated system than that of simple barter; and that itself is more sophisticated than merely producing a surplus of goods, leaving it to others to help themselves, and in turn helping oneself to their surplus. Therefore, although Socrates nowhere explicitly asserts that the members of his city enter into agreements, it seems wildly implausible to interpret him as supposing that they do not.

(b) *Do members of the first city recognise right and wrong?* The answer to this is not entirely determined by our answer to the first question. We do not think that moral comments on a man's conduct are debarred by the fact (if it be one) that he himself has no sense of right and wrong. Such comments, made to him, may have no practical effect on his conduct and he himself may be quite unable to see what we are getting at, but it does not follow from his inability to see what we are getting at that we are getting at nothing. A situation then could exist in which moral comments are applicable to a man's

conduct, while at the same time he does not recognise their
applicability. His position would be, not of disagreeing with
us when we said of an action of his that it was wrong (for disagreeing would presuppose his admitting that moral comment
as such was applicable), but of his maintaining either that he
could attach no meaning at all to our use of words like 'right'
and 'wrong', or that the action was not of a kind that could be
either right or wrong, that with regard to it questions of right
and wrong simply did not arise. That is, members of the first
city, even if they recognised the applicability, or the possibility
of application, of right and wrong to some areas of conduct,
might not recognise their applicability to the economic conduct
of product and exchange. The question is whether they would
admit that they were doing wrong in failing to keep a bargain,
whether again, if the other party failed to keep a bargain,
their own annoyance would be simply annoyance at being
deprived of what they wanted or hoped for or expected, or
whether it would be moral indignation. Could they say that
the other party had acted unfairly, or had cheated or swindled
them? or would they be restricted to saying that the other
party had been too clever for them? Is it like being cheated
at bridge by your opponent breaking a rule or a convention of
the game, such as deliberately revoking? Or is it like being
outmanœuvred at bridge by your opponent's skill at bidding
or play? The difficulty of getting a clear answer from Plato
to this question arises, not, as in the case of the previous question, from what he does not say, but from what he does say,
for in different parts of his account he says different things; it
is doubtful whether what he says at 369b-c can be squared with
what he says three pages later at 372a-d. If we take the former
passage by itself, we can hardly suppose that men in the city
do recognise right and wrong, at least not in their economic
conduct which is the only part of their conduct which Plato
specifies. For there he insists that their conduct is entirely
self-regarding; and this implies that a man regards all other
men, in their capacity as consumers and producers, as means
only to his own end, that is to the end of his own advantage.
He treats them as people to be used for his own benefit, whom
there is no question of his supplying or helping if he has no need

of their supplies or help. There is no reason why such a community, composed entirely of thoroughly selfish men, not admitting that they owed anything to others, should not operate efficiently, provided that the members were sufficiently enlightened and long-sighted in their selfishness. We might not think of it as an agreeable or an admirable community, but that would be no reason for denying its feasibility. As long as men, in their dealings with others, show sufficient self-restraint for social life to be practicable, it does not matter from the point of view of practicability that we should not find them likeable or admirable people. And the self-restraint could be dictated by wholly selfish motives. As Bishop Butler maintained, the common failing is not that of caring too much for self-interest, but that of being insufficiently enlightened and provident in the pursuit of it.

If men do simply regard each other as means to their own ends, they will not recognise that conduct can be right or wrong. It can be skilful, silly, ingenious, infuriating, and plenty else, but it will not be regarded in moral terms. Such a man *might* apply moral terms to others' treatment of him, i.e. while he regarded himself as owing nothing to others, whom he treated as he did just because he thought it served his own interest, yet he regarded others as owing something to him. That is, he might not only object to others treating him for their own ends, but morally object. It would be a queer, perverse, egotistical kind of moral attitude, and it is typically the attitude of the thwarted and frustrated individualist, but it is a kind of moral attitude. However, whatever may be such a man's attitude towards the relation of others to himself, his attitude towards the relation of himself to others is clear : they are to be used for his own advantage, and their interests are to be served simply to the extent that serving them serves his own. To his conduct in relation to them he does not recognise the possibility of applying right or wrong : success or failure are the only issues.

It is only if a man regards other men as ends, and not only as means towards his own ends, that he will recognise that his conduct towards them may be right or wrong. For then he acknowledges both that other men have their own interests

which are as important to them as his are to himself, and that
there is no reason why they should be expected or required to
prefer his to their own — not merely that they will not prefer
his, but that he has no more reason for expecting that they
should than they have for expecting that he should prefer theirs
to his own. To have this much respect for other people, to
regard them as being as entitled to expect certain conduct of
you as you are of them is to recognise the applicability of moral
notions to your conduct. Of this there is no sign in the passage
where Socrates emphasises that every man's motive for joining
in economic exchange is purely selfish. But a few pages later,
the picture, or at least the emphasis, changes. He still does
not explicitly say that men recognise others as having rights,
but he does, in describing the contented, bucolic life which his
men will lead, make a point of its being a peaceful, healthy
life, and of the members of the city "living amicably with each
other" (372c). This, it is true, is not absolutely incompatible
with the view of the earlier passage, but it hardly fits it well.
It fits much better a view of men as having some respect for
each other as persons, rather than as beings to be helped and
supplied only to the extent that it pays oneself to do so. A
community of men producing enough to keep themselves well
above subsistence level, enjoying a certain degree of social life,
and joining together in celebrations such as harvest festivals,
may be a fairly rough and primitive community, but hardly
one to which the notions of honesty and fair dealing would be
entirely foreign. Consequently, the answer we give to the
question whether the members of such a society as Plato describes recognise right and wrong must be that we cannot give
a single answer. If we take our evidence from the first part of
Socrates's account, we must answer No. If we take our evidence
from the latter part, it is reasonable to answer Yes. And if it
is unsatisfactory not to be able to give a single answer, that is
no reason for distorting what Plato wrote; we have to acknowledge that the question is one which Plato gives no sign here of
having considered at all.

Chapter 5

EVOLUTION OF THE IDEAL CITY

WITH the sketch of the basic city complete, Glaucon protests (372d) that the life which it provides will be excessively austere, making it "a city of pigs", and that the inhabitants will demand some provision of comfort, such as household furniture and variety in food. Socrates, while still regarding the original as being the true, healthy city, is prepared to consider its growth into a "luxurious" and "swollen" community, for that way they might more easily discern how justice and injustice find their way into society (372e). From the description, first of this development of sophistication, and then of the measures required to restore and maintain civic health, evolves the final and ideal form of city, in which the nature of justice may be identified and characterised.

The innovations needed to raise the standard of living above the subsistence level of the first city carry with them two related consequences. First, an increase in the number and diversity of jobs to be done: producers of new goods such as tables, chairs, utensils and ingredients for cooking, clothing, household and personal ornaments, etc.; and the providers of new services, such as actors, artists, domestic servants, and doctors. Secondly, an increase in the size of the city and its supporting territory: the population will have to be larger not only to accommodate the increase in the number and variety of producers, but also to provide enough surplus commodities to support the non-productive activities of those engaged in service occupations. So, the growth in the city's complexity necessarily brings with it an increase in its size, which in turn will lead to competition between the city and its neighbours for further territory; and such expansion will, sooner or later, have to be fought for in war (373d-e) which, whether we regard it as bad or good, we must acknowledge as an inevitable consequence of a city's growth. To provide for this, one further occupation must be introduced, that of the soldier; and, following the principle of specialisation of labour, the army must be a full-time professional army, not a citizen army or militia manned by part-time or reserve soldiers, temporarily diverted from their normal civilian occupations: efficiency demands that a man should devote himself wholly to a single job, as much (if not more so) in the case of a soldier as in the case of any other trade, such as builder or farmer (374b-c).

With the introduction of the army we reach the beginning of the transition to the third and final city, a transition which, although Plato claims that it is simply an evolution of the original city in accordance with the single, original principle of the specialisation and division of labour, in fact introduces an entirely new principle, which Plato nowhere explicitly acknowledges, and which, as we shall see, affects his eventual account of justice.

In 374d Plato for the first time introduces the word φύλακες (Guardians) as a name for his army, which in itself is not significant, for the function of the army is to guard and protect the lives and property of the citizens. But the concept of the *phylax* rapidly develops, entirely changing the character of the city. Even at the outset we must recognise a fundamental difference between the soldier's occupation and that of any of the producers whom he is protecting, which shows Plato's claim that it is simply the addition of one more job to be misleading. It is one more job, but one of a quite different kind from any of the others, and not on a par with them. It is a job which presupposes the others, and is, in a sense, parasitic on them; for the soldier's job is to protect the performance of the other jobs. It is his business to preserve the situation in which other men may pursue their jobs in peace and undisturbed; and if there were no other jobs to be protected, the soldier himself would have no job. Thus a state could exist (although it might not last for long) in which the productive occupations were pursued, but in which there was no army; but a state could not exist possessing an army, but no productive occupations. In this way, the producer's job is primary, the soldier's secondary; not that it is less important, but that it has to be defined in relation to the producer's job, as that of protecting it and preserving the conditions of its continuance.

After a brief section (375a-376b) on the character and temperament required of the Guardians, and a long section (376c-412b) on their school education, Plato proceeds to the more detailed organisation of his city, in the course of which it undergoes significant changes in form from anything to be found in either of the earlier cities. (In passing, it should be noticed that at this stage Plato introduces two points, which, although they are here just mentioned, anticipate important elements in his later elaboration. Comparing a good Guardian to a good watch-dog he says first that he must be *spirited* (375a) so that he will be a good fighter; and secondly, so that he may be fierce only to his enemies and gentle to his friends, he must be *philosophical* in nature (375e), which Plato elucidates, so far as he does, in terms of a contrast between *knowledge* and *ignorance* (376b): the good watch-dog discriminates between friends and foes as being those whom he does and does not know respectively. These distinctions, between being spirited and being philosophical, and again between knowledge and ignorance, while here being made in an entirely general and non-technical way, foreshadow the two main themes of Plato's general argument throughout the rest of the *Republic*.)

With his account of school education complete, Plato returns to the Guardians, and makes a distinction between the older and wiser men who are to rule and the more energetic younger men who are to be ruled (412c), by which he means that the latter in obedience to the former are to carry out their instructions for the preservation and maintenance of the city. And at 414b he introduces a new term to designate these younger men, ἐπίκουροι (usually translated as 'Auxiliaries'); and from this point on, the two terms φύλακες and ἐπίκουροι are used in a technical and contrasted sense. Those who have hitherto been referred to in general as *phylakes* or Guardians are now subdivided into two grades, the *phylakes* or Guardians proper and the *epikouroi* or Auxiliaries who have the job of carrying out the rulers' will and are to be regarded as performing the functions of the military, the police, and the executive of the Civil

Service. Correspondingly, from now on, whenever we use the term 'Guardians', we shall, unless we indicate the contrary, be referring only to the top grade, i.e. to the rulers.

The bare outline structure of the city is now complete; and it is time for us to consider what changes have been introduced with it. The chief differences to be noted are three. First, there is an important change of attitude. In the primitive city (and in the second which differed from it only in being somewhat less austere) every man pursued his own interest, and promoted that of others only to the extent that, as he thought, it served his own. In the final city, on the other hand, we have the notion of working for the interests of the city as a whole; and when Adeimantus objects (419a) that the Auxiliaries and Guardians, under the severe burden of service imposed by Socrates, will not have a happy life, he receives the reply that the aim is to provide the conditions of happiness, not for one class (ἔθνος) but for the city as a whole. Whether or not this entails the concept of a city as an entity over and above the individuals who comprise it (and the analogy of the statue in 420c-d perhaps suggests that it does not), at least it entails the idea of mutual co-operation, of a man being expected to be prepared to subordinate his own interests to those of others. Secondly, the city no longer consists of a number of individuals each pursuing his own job, the different jobs fitting in with each other in a way which makes life economically supportable. Now we have the total population divided into three classes, with movement from one class to another prohibited except under stringent controls. At the top there are the Guardians or rulers, who, whether they are administrators only or administrators-cum-legislators, are in complete control of the city and the lives of its members. Below them are the Auxiliaries, their executive assistants. And below them again comes everybody else. For this third class Plato does not in fact provide a single and official name, possibly an indication of his comparative lack of interest in them. It is a striking change of emphasis that, having originally conceived the notion of constructing a city at all, in order to solve a problem about justice which had throughout Book I been thought of as a moral problem, concerning the relationship between individuals as men, Plato becomes more and more engrossed in political philosophy. The city, from being a large-scale model for helping us to solve a problem about the smaller-scale man, is becoming the thing which matters; the individual man is now primarily regarded in respect of the performance of his function of contributing to the life and unity of the city. The third class, consisting of everybody not engaged administratively or executively in the tasks of government, might be called Subjects, which is what they are. But a better name would be the Economic Class. (Plato himself usually refers to them in this kind of way, as money-makers or men in business, e.g. 434a, 434c, 581d.) For it is the function of everybody in it to pursue his particular job of providing goods, distribution or services in a way which will ensure the city's economic survival and such limited degree of prosperity as is desirable; excessive prosperity, indeed, is as much to be avoided as excessive poverty, for either is equally corrupting (421d). When it comes to a war a comparatively poor and small but united city is a match for one which is wealthier and larger but internally divided (423a-b).

The third and most far-reaching difference between the final city and either of its predecessors is marked by the basis of its class-division. Merely to divide a community into classes, whether grounded on differences in social status or on differences in earning and purchasing power, would not by itself represent any major change of principle from a more primitive single-class community. But this is not how in fact Plato does it. What he does is to introduce the entirely new principle of *political* classification. The basis of the first two cities had been entirely economic. Every man pursued his own trade, the results of which by mutual interchange of goods and services kept life going. And the consequent unity of the city might be called a *natural* unity, in that life was made tolerable or even enjoyable by the mutual give-and-take of the individuals concerned. But there was no provision whatever for ensuring and maintaining its unity, for warding off threats and dangers to it, or for repairing and restoring it if damaged by the selfishness of individuals. Nobody was in charge of anybody else; there were no punishments or provisions for the infringement of laws, for there were no laws. There were agreements for the exchange of, and payment for, goods, but there was no system for the enforcement of agreements, and no sanctions for their violation. As a result, such a community either would work well economically or it would not, its unity either would be preserved or it would not. Success would depend entirely on the mutual good sense and forbearance or on the enlightened self-interest of the individuals concerned. At best, they would be one happy family, at worst a collection of self-seekers whose activities either did or did not go the length of wrecking economic life. Whether such a community could actually exist, or could for long survive, does not here matter. What does matter is that that is how Plato envisaged it, as a community held together, so long as it was, by the natural economic forces of supply and demand, possibly also by some degree of respect and love for one's fellowmen. The fundamental fact about the first cities then is the total absence from them of any system of control of one man, or group of men, by another.

The third and final city is entirely different, in that it is based on a political principle, making it no longer a *natural* but an *artificial* community. Plato introduces the army as simply one more trade in addition to those already being performed. But when he develops the notion of an army into that of rulers and subdivides that more specifically into administrators and their executive assistants, he brings in a quite new and political principle, viz. that of government. True, these new functionaries, first soldiers, then Guardians and Auxiliaries, are pursuing each his own particular job; and to that extent Plato could claim to be sticking to his original (economic) principle of division and specialisation of labour (even if the tasks assigned to the Auxiliaries were more various than might ordinarily be thought to fall within the scope of a single job). But the new jobs to be done by the new functionaries are different, not only in kind, but also in status, from those performed by everybody else. The new jobs are precisely those of ruling, that is of controlling all the other jobs. The city now consists, not of economic equals, but of subjects pursuing their economic functions, the rulers seeing to it that they do, and that they do it in a way which maintains the life and unity of the city as a whole. The unity of the new city is artificial because in government we have a group of men whose function it is deliberately, and as a result of a decision, to maintain its unity; successful survival of the community is a matter no longer of good fortune, but of conscious political contrivance. With the introduction of government, of laws (415e), of some men in authority over others, issuing orders and prohibitions to them, we now have an entirely new conception of a city as a self-conscious organisation, constructed to achieve a certain communal purpose, and to do it by entrusting to one group of men the task of governing the rest. Consequently the class-structure of Plato's final city is neither economic nor social, but political, first dividing the population into the two classes of rulers and subjects, and then dividing the rulers again into Guardians or rulers proper and into the Auxiliaries or the executive branch of government. The trades of the first two cities which had been divided among their total population now belong to one class only, the Economic Class, who are the bottom class of the state. From now on Plato has indeed very little to say about them, chiefly perhaps because there is very little of interest to be said about them. His chief concern now being with political philosophy, he rightly sees that success will depend almost entirely on finding men of the right kind to be rulers, and on providing for them education and training of the right kind to qualify them for the responsibilities of government. Within the political framework the Economic Class have only one function to perform, viz. that of doing what they are told to do; consequently they scarcely interest Plato at all or receive much more than an occasional mention hereafter. While it might be going too far to attribute to Plato the wish that they should be like the conditioned proles of George Orwell's *1984*, such an idea would not be as foreign or as abhorrent to Greek thought of his time as it might be to us. The existence of a slave class or of a helot class to support the leisure of free citizens was a familiar feature of Greek, in particular of Athenian, city life; and slaves could have a tolerable, even enjoyable, existence, while still being kept in their place as a submerged class. The claim that all men are equal, whatever that imprecise claim might mean, was certainly not then acceptable. And although, as we shall see, Plato did allow his Economic Class a degree of political freedom, it was only a limited and indeed counterfeit freedom, one which they were to be allowed only as long as they exercised it in the way which he desired, and of which he would not have hesitated to deprive them if their attempt to use it as real freedom threatened the constitution of his city.

One question about the status of the Guardians is nowhere unequivocally answered by Plato — whether they are to be administrators only or whether they are to be legislators also. In general Plato draws a contrast between the Founders of the city (Socrates and those assisting him in the discussion) and the Guardians who keep it going, once founded. In 458c and again in 497d he addresses Glaucon as "you, the lawgiver". And as it is a political Utopia, a perfect city, which they are trying to envisage, the city once founded should not undergo any fundamental changes, for any change is bound to be for the worse. Thus it is to be a static organisation, the Guardians having the responsibility of maintaining the equilibrium which Socrates has established. When the question is raised whether such a city is possible (471c), the answer given shows that Plato was no starry-eyed idealist with little regard for practical problems. The great danger to any political organisation, as Plato shows himself aware in the discussion of Books VIII-IX, is the corruption to which those in power are liable. And he insures against this by the ingenious device of insisting that only philosophers are to be rulers, because as philosophers they possess two essential qualifications : first, they possess knowledge and understanding in a way in which no other men do; and secondly, because as philosophers they are dedicated to, and consumed with a passion for, the pursuit of truth, they will have no political ambitions whatever. They will take their share of ruling, not because they want to, but because they recognise that other men, lacking the knowledge, would do the job worse than themselves, and because they acknowledge it as a duty which they must perform as the price of their privilege of being allowed to spend the rest of their time doing what they really want to do, viz. engage in philosophical research. By entrusting government to men who have no personal interest in governing, but who conscientiously accept it as their responsibility, Plato endeavours to insure against the risk of political degeneration. He was well aware that the inherent defect of the politician is that he enjoys politics.

Given that the city is established in a perfect condition, and that it is then ruled by men who, understanding that condition, make it their business to maintain it, it is natural that Plato should think of his Guardians as high-grade administrators rather than as legislators and as policy-makers ; the legislating and policy-making have already been done by the founders. Plato does refer to the Guardians as legislators in one passage (425e), but he is clearly speaking of detailed regulations governing commercial conduct, and he insists that they should be as few as possible. In a bad city a host of regulations are useless, in a good city they are either unnecessary or obvious. In the one passage (502b) where he does identify ruler with legislator, he is not talking about his particular city, but about government in general, and making a point not about governors but about subjects, that as a rule they are prepared to obey the laws.

It seems reasonable, therefore, to infer that Plato regarded the Guardians as administrators rather than legislators. But it is reasonable also to suppose that this was because legislation would not be required of them, not because they were incompetent to engage in it. At the present stage of the argument the Guardians are treated as being the older and wiser men who possess knowledge of political requirements, whereas even their assistant Auxiliaries possess only correct belief; but the precise distinction between knowledge and correct belief has not yet been worked out, so that these terms are not yet being used in the technical sense which in the course of Books V–VII they come to acquire. But when, as a result of the argument in these books, the contrast between knowledge and belief is made clear, providing the justification for insisting that only a philosopher is qualified to be a Guardian, the situation thereafter is different. The Guardians are then to be selected not merely on the general ground that they are the wisest members of the community, but on the specific ground that, possessing the philosopher's knowledge, they will know what form is to be imposed on the city, i.e. what form *has* been imposed on it by the founders, and which it is their own business to preserve. As philosophers, therefore, they would be competent to legislate and lay down policy for the city, were it necessary, i.e. if the latter had not already been performed by the founders (484d). And if the city were to send out men to form a colony elsewhere, the Guardians of the mother city could act as founder-legislators of that.

But it needs to be emphasised that that belongs to a later stage in the *Republic*. Proof that at the stage so far reached the knowledge which the Guardians possess is not at all what Plato later means by *episteme* is provided by the extraordinary insertion of the foundation myth (414c-415d), about which he explicitly says both that it is false, and that it is desirable that everybody, especially the Guardians, should be taken in by it. This is not a case of supposedly enlightened or well-informed rulers guiding their ignorant subjects by misinformation, as when in time of war military defeat and enforced retreat becomes a tactical withdrawal to prepared positions. Here it is a case of the rulers themselves being persuaded of something by being deceived. It is inconceivable that Plato would have proposed such treatment of his rulers, if the "knowledge" which at this stage they possess (cf. 428d) were at all what it becomes in Book VII. It is, in any case, difficult to understand why he supposed that the most intelligent members of the community were more likely to be able to grasp, and to be prepared to believe, the proposition that men are unequal in ability if, instead of being presented with that proposition and with the evidence for it, they were offered an allegory so simple-minded that Plato admitted his own embarrassment in producing it, to the effect that some men have gold in their souls, others silver, and others iron and bronze. As a figurative way of putting across a literal, possibly unpalatable, truth to the intellectually undeveloped or to the emotionally immature it might be effective. As a way of convincing those who have been picked out to rule because they are men of outstanding wisdom and good judgment, that they *are* men of outstanding wisdom and good judgment, it seems little less than insulting.

With the city now founded, Socrates proposes that they

return to their original task of finding "where justice is in it and where injustice, how they differ from each other, and which of the two must be possessed by the man who is to have a happy life, whether or not his having it escapes the attention of everybody else, gods and men alike" (427d). As the city is perfectly good, it will possess the four virtues of wisdom, courage, self-restraint and justice. If we can locate and identify the first three, we shall be able to identify justice as what is left. This is the procedure which Plato in fact adopts, identifying in turn wisdom, courage and self-restraint, and thence by elimination arriving at justice. As a procedure it leaves so much to be desired that it would be difficult to suppose that Plato intended it to be taken seriously, were it not for the fact that he appears to take it seriously himself. An argument by elimination depends on a set of presuppositions such that if any one of them can be challenged, the conclusion, even if correct, cannot be accepted as validly established. The presuppositions here are: (a) that the city possesses a known number of virtues (in this case four); (b) that the four virtues are exactly the four named by Socrates; (c) that the four virtues exactly fill out the structure of the city. A good example of such an argument by elimination would be provided by a jig-saw puzzle. If we were told that a box contained all the pieces of a puzzle but one, and were asked to locate and identify the shape and size of the missing piece, we should have no great difficulty in solving the problem, viz. by assembling all the pieces which we have and then seeing where and what the final gap was. But this is only possible because of the composition of such a puzzle; it consists of a known number of pieces which interlock in such a way that when all are used up they complete a picture of a known shape and size. If a puzzle consists of 300 pieces, and if, when we have fitted 299 of them into place, we have the picture complete except for one small gap, we can conclude that the missing piece is of precisely the size and shape to fill the gap. Plato's argument for the location and identification of justice is exactly analogous, but unfortunately he offers no reason why we should accept any, let alone all, of his three presuppositions. He started by saying that it was obvious that the city would possess the four virtues which he named (427e). We might accept that, for it would not be reasonable to suppose that a perfect city would not possess them. But his argument by elimination requires us to accept that the city would possess these, *and only these*, four virtues. Unless we accept that, the argument by elimination cannot begin; but Plato offers no reason why we should accept it. Again, he makes no attempt to argue for the assumption that the four virtues named, when identified and located in relation to each other, exactly fill out the city's structure in the way in which the 300 separate pieces of the jig-saw puzzle, when fitted into place, exactly complete the total dimensions of the puzzle. We must comment that, as a method of argument, Plato's procedure here is worthless, while being prepared to allow that his conclusion as to the nature of justice, although invalidly reached, might still be correct.

The city is wise through the good counsel and knowledge of its Guardians (428c). While it will have in it many kinds of knowledge and skill, e.g. those of its carpenters and other craftsmen, we should not call it wise in virtue of their kind of knowledge, which is concerned with a particular craft or trade. Its wisdom must come from that knowledge which is concerned, not with the interests of any particular person or group, but with the welfare of the city as a whole and in its relations with other cities (428d). This is the only kind of knowledge that can be called wisdom, and it is to be found only in one class, and the smallest class of all, viz. the Guardians (429a).

Where courage lies, in virtue of which the city as a whole is to be called courageous, is not difficult to decide (429a): it must lie in the military class, whose business it is to fight for and defend the city, and who have now developed into the Auxiliaries. And courage is not simply fearlessness or bravery in the face of danger, but educated bravery, the bravery of men who have learned, through the education outlined in Book III, what is and what is not to be feared. It is the courage of men who are loyal to the principles which have been inculcated into them during their upbringing. The Auxiliaries will be men of conviction, and the principal aim of their school education is to turn them out as young men who both hold the right convictions, and have sufficient strength of character to stand for and stand up for their convictions against all adversity and temptation. Their business is not to have inquiring minds, but to believe what they have been taught to believe about their city. Lacking the full knowledge and understanding possessed by the Guardians, they hold their beliefs and principles as a matter of faith, not fully appreciating why these are the correct beliefs and principles, but convinced that they are, and to be relied on to act in accordance with them.

These first two virtues in the city derive each from a corresponding characteristic in a particular class, its wisdom from the Guardians being wise, its courage from the Auxiliaries being courageous. In this respect they differ from the other two virtues which do not derive from the characteristics of a particular class. Both self-restraint and justice in the city are going to depend, not on features of one class in it, but on a relationship between classes. Furthermore the scheme is cumulative; the Guardians are wise, and they alone are wise; the Auxiliaries are courageous, but not they alone are courageous, for the Guardians are courageous too. Men who are Guardians have in their youth been Auxiliaries, and have, if they succeed in surviving the higher education to be described in Book VII, graduated to the Guardian class. By becoming Guardians, they do not lose the courage which they had as Auxiliaries, although strictly their courage will have been transmuted into something rather different. Plato does not mention this, but he is committed to accepting it. For as he has originally defined courage as loyalty to "correct belief" (430b), and as in the case of the Guardian correct belief is replaced by knowledge, the courage of the Guardian will not be exactly the same as that of the Auxiliary; it will stand to it in much the relation that Kant's concept of the holy will stands to that of good will. But although the Guardians will have courage, it is the courage of the Auxiliaries that makes the city courageous (432a). If courage were not to be found in them, the city could not possess the virtue of courage; and in this sense we may say that courage is characteristic of their class, as wisdom is characteristic of the Guardian class.

Self-restraint, Plato says, does not, unlike the first two

virtues, reside in a single class, but is more like a kind of
"concord or harmony" (430e); and later he asserts that it
actually is a "unanimity and concord" (432a). Just as an
individual man is self-restrained, if he is master of himself, i.e.
if the better side of him is in control of the worse side (431a),
so the city will possess self-restraint if the better part of it is in
control of the worse (431b). But while control of the worse by
the better part is necessary to self-restraint, it is not yet sufficient,
for it does not yet constitute the harmony and concord of
which Plato speaks. One party might be better than another,
and able to keep it in control, simply by having greater power
and being able to exercise severe discipline, keeping the worse
party in its place by sheer regimentation, with no element of
concord present at all; for example, a prison or a police state
might be kept in order in such a way. For concord to exist,
there must be some measure of agreement between those in
power and those under them that this is the way things should
be done. Self-restraint therefore requires not only that the
better should control the worse, but also that they should
agree that the better should be in control (431e). It consists
in fact, in the case of the city, in rulers and subjects agreeing
who are to do the ruling. This factor is important to an understanding of Plato's political philosophy, for it seems to imply
the attribution to the subjects (i.e. the Economic Class) both
of some degree of rationality and understanding of how the
city should be run (of which Plato nowhere else makes any
mention at all), and of some degree of freedom in accepting
their place as subjects. Were it not for the elements of rationality and freedom in self-restraint, the distinction between the
virtues of self-restraint and justice would turn out to be somewhat tenuous. (Plato also insists that the same account is to
be given of an individual man: his self-restraint will consist of
the control of his worse side by his better side, *with the consent of
his worse side* (432a). It is open to question whether this claim
makes sense at all in terms of individual psychology, as he
describes it later in Book IV; but the fact that he makes the
claim, here and again at 442c-d, cannot be denied.)

   To what extent rationality and freedom in the Economic
Class will reach Plato does not make explicit. Is he saying

that members of that class, while not intelligent enough to be
rulers themselves, are intelligent enough to recognise which
men are intelligent enough to rule? This would be something
like, although not going as far as, the principle underlying
representative democracy, in which the electorate are assumed
to be sufficiently intelligent and well-informed to choose between the rival candidates, parties and programmes being
offered to them. Or is he simply supposing that members of
the Economic Class are content to leave ruling to the
Guardians? For, as long as they are content, the concord or
unanimity of which Plato speaks would be there. Again, in
the case of freedom, does he suppose that they consent to rule
by the Guardians? Consent entails real freedom, for it makes
the Guardians' authority to rule depend on the Economic
Class's agreement that they should. To say that something is
done with my consent implies that it could not be done if my
consent were withheld. Or is he merely saying that members
of the Economic Class acquiesce in their status as subjects, and
that of the Guardians as rulers? Acquiescence does not necessarily carry real freedom with it, for I acquiesce in a state of
affairs as long as I do not object to it or do nothing to try to
prevent it, even although, if I did try to object or to prevent it,
my attempt might have no hope of success. If I had no hope
of preventing it, the state of affairs could not be said to exist
with my consent, but I could even so, if I raised no objection
to it and made no vain effort to prevent it, be said to acquiesce
in it. It would, on the whole, be more in keeping with Plato's
view of political philosophy in the *Republic* to suppose that he
thought of self-restraint in the city as implying acquiescence
rather than consent on the part of the Economic Class. It is
fairly clear that he regarded it as their business to stay in their
place and get on with their jobs, leaving the job of government
to better and wiser men. There is no suggestion that the
Guardians rule because the Economic Class allow them to
rule. It is not over-cynical to conclude that Plato thought it
was more important that the most competent men should rule
than that less competent men should have any say in deciding
who should rule; and that the freedom accorded to the
Economic Class was an exceedingly limited or even spurious

freedom, the freedom which they would be allowed only for so long as they used it in the way which Plato wanted. There is very little doubt what would become of their freedom, if they showed any signs of getting out of line. Consequently, to attribute to Plato the view that the city's unity derives from a community of purpose among *all* its citizens, if this is to mean that all alike, despite their differing degrees of rationality, are inspired by the notion of a single form to be imposed on it, would be to read into Plato far more than can be extracted from the text (cf. 500d-e, 590c-d).

With the three virtues of wisdom, courage and self-restraint in the city now identified, it remains to find the fourth and last, justice. And the discovery of this turns out to be, as Socrates says, something of an anti-climax, for they have had it under their noses all the time (432d) in the principle insisted on from the formation of the first city, that each man should perform one and only one job, that to which he is by nature best suited. "This principle, as it seems to me, or some form of it, is justice" (433a). Again, "this principle of sticking to one's own job appears, when it takes a certain form, to be justice" (433b). And the reason immediately given is that it is the adherence to this principle that makes it possible for the other three virtues to be present and play their parts. Wha are we to make of the fact that in the two passages just quoted Plato does not unequivocally say that the principle of one-man-one-job *is* justice, but rather that it *or some form of it* is justice? Is he here showing some recognition of the difference between the original economic principle of the first city and the new political principle of the final city? Or is he, by his somewhat indeterminate statement what justice is, here slurring over the difference? Certainly, in the next two pages, he abandons the purely economic principle, when he makes a point that appears to run wholly counter to it, viz. that it does not greatly matter and will do no great harm to the city if a member of the Economic Class changes his job or even *undertakes two jobs at once* (434a). To allow this is to admit that the original principle of one-man-one-job is not all that important, and is to weaken the claim that they have had justice staring them in the face from the very beginning. What is now important

is that a man should not presume to undertake the functions of
a class higher than that to which he belongs. In other words,
instead of the requirement that each man should stick to his
own job, we now have the requirement that he should stick to
his own class. Justice is now specified not in terms of each
individual *man* performing his proper job, but of each of the
three *classes* performing its proper job (434c). Whether or not
Plato did clearly recognise the difference between the economic
prirtciple of division and specialisation of labour and the
political principle of division of classes, it is certainly the latter
with which he has ended up. Justice in the city consists in
each of the classes performing its own function and not usurping
that of either of the others. This will correspond to what he is
shortly going to say about the virtue of justice in the soul, that
it is (or is produced by) the harmony of the three elements in
the soul when each discharges its proper function. Plato's not
wishing to abandon entirely the proposition that justice consists (in some sense) in each man doing his job might be a
reflection of something else which he says when talking of
justice in the individual. There he contrasts a man's acting
justly with his being a just man or possessing the virtue of
justice: the former, consisting of outward conduct or the
externals of justice is only an "image" of the latter, which is
the real justice, the state of his soul or character (443c-d). So
here he might say that men will be acting justly if they stick
to their jobs, but that this is only an image of the real virtue of
justice in the city, which consists in the classes remaining in
their proper relationship to each other. This can only be conjecture, for Plato makes no definite statement on the matter,
but it is reasonable conjecture in view of the close parallel
which at all points Plato wishes to draw between city and
individual. The whole operation of trying to identify justice
in the individual by first identifying it in the city would have
been quite pointless unless Plato genuinely believed in the
closeness of the parallel. Furthermore he explicitly says that
"a just man will not differ at all from a just city in respect of
the essence of justice, but be like it" (435b). And he maintains,
as his final point on this topic of justice in the city, that the
account now given of it must be regarded as provisional until

confirmed by the account, still to be given, of justice in the individual. We may have to be prepared to modify the former in the light of what we discover about the latter, but there is no question of the modification being the other way round (434d-e) : clear proof that, despite the fact that the order of exposition is first city and then individual, Plato's order of argument is the other way round, from individual to city. The city is to be regarded as a large-scale individual and what can be said of it is to be determined by what can be said of the individual (cf. 544d) ; and what can be said of the individual provides Plato's next topic (435e-444e). We must therefore not make the mistake of comparing the account of justice so far given with the accounts discussed and rejected in Book I. They were attempts to characterise justice in the individual as being based on the conduct of an individual man in his relationship to certain other individuals (Polemarchus) or on the conduct of an individual subject in his relationship to his rulers (Thrasymachus). On their accounts, a man's conduct was right, or morally acceptable, if it was of one kind, wrong if it was of another kind ; justice was a moral concept grounded in the relationship between a man and other men. But the justice of which Plato has at this stage in Book IV given his account is a political concept. His answer is not to the question under what conditions can a man be said to be a just man, but to the question under what conditions can a city be said to be a just city. Plato might now be prepared to say of an individual man that he acts rightly as a citizen if he performs only his own job, or if he performs only the functions proper to his own class, but he cannot be taken as saying that this is what right conduct for a man consists in, or that this is what justice in the individual is. For his statement of that we have to wait until 443, when he has concluded his account of the nature of the human soul.

Chapter 6

JUSTICE IN THE SOUL

RIGHT at the outset of his discussion of the soul Socrates raises a doubt about the procedure on which they are embarking. The question they are to answer is whether in a human soul there are to be found the three elements which would correspond to the three classes in the city. The conclusion is going to be that there are, viz. the Appetitive, Spirited and Rational elements, corresponding to the Economic, Auxiliary and Guardian Classes, and that the same four virtues can be found in the individual soul as in the city. But what is his doubt — that the method or argument is not exact enough, or not complete enough, or that the results are not precise enough, or that they are too tentative?

What he actually says is: "It is my opinion that we shall never reach an accurate answer to *this* question by *such methods as we are now using in our discussion* — for the road which leads to it is another one, longer and more difficult — but perhaps we can do it in a way which comes up to the standard of our arguments and inquiries so far" (435d, our italics). The problems are four: what is this question? what are the present unsatisfactory methods? what is the longer and more rigorous method? and what is it that is unsatisfactory about the first method but not unsatisfactory about the longer method? If we had only this passage to go on, the first two questions would be difficult to answer, and the third and fourth impossible, for Plato here says nothing further about them at all. It would be natural to suppose that "this question" is the one which has been mentioned immediately before (435c), and an answer to which is propounded in the following pages, viz. whether in the human soul there are to be found the three elements corresponding to the three classes of the city. But what then are the "present methods" about which doubt is being expressed? Is it the form of argument suggested in 435e, that the human soul must have the same characteristics as the city, for otherwise there could be no explanation of the city having them? Certainly this would be an invalid argument, in view of the fact that they have agreed on the previous page that their conclusions about the city must be regarded as tentative until confirmed (or otherwise) by what they discover about the human soul. To arrive at the conclusion that the soul must be threefold, in order to account for the city's being so, would not be legitimate or at any rate would not itself be more than tentative when the proposition from which the argument by analogy starts, that the city is threefold, is itself only tentative. But, in fact, Plato argues to the threefold division of the soul, not from a necessary analogy with the threefold division of the city, but from a quite different principle (436b), not previously mentioned and concerned with human psychology; although it is true that, when he comes on to assigning the four virtues to the human soul, he does so in very summary fashion and offers no more reason than that they will be the same as those in the city — which suggests that he does not in fact treat their conclusion about the city as being quite as tentative as he had claimed at the outset. Perhaps then he is doubtful about the validity of the psychological principle from which he does argue? But he shows no signs of being so; and, if he were, his whole argument for the threefold division of the soul would be quite illegitimate, which again he shows no sign whatever of suggesting. Again it could be that he doubts whether, using the method of argument which he does, the conclusion of the threefold division of the soul is exhaustive. Might not further argument show the presence in the soul of more than three elements? To this interpretation it can be objected that Plato does not claim that his account is exhaustive, and that in at least one place (443d7) he allows for the possibility of further division.

Fortunately, much later on Plato reverts to this topic at 504, where he refers back to our present passage, and where what he says helps to resolve our problems. "We said that for it to be possible to see *them* at their clearest there was another longer way round" (504b, our italics). It is reasonably clear from the context that the "them" here mentioned are not, as might be supposed from 435d, the three elements of the soul but the four virtues. The "this question" of the earlier passage is not then, as it appeared to be when that passage was considered in isolation, whether the three elements are to be found in the soul, but whether it has the four virtues; or rather it was "this whole question" about the soul, not only about the elements but about the virtues as well. And the difference between the "short" and the "long" methods is immediately afterwards stated. It could not have been stated in the earlier passage, for an understanding of it depends on the thesis which forms the major part of the intervening discussion in Books V and VI. We, in our turn, can only indicate the difference here, leaving it to be made clear when we reach that part of the *Republic* (v. Chapter 9, p. 200). Plato's point is that there is something even above justice itself, which is greater than justice, which is the object of the highest form of knowledge, and by relation to which justice itself derives its value, viz. what he calls the Form of the Good (505a) : and later, comprehension of this Form is claimed to be the culmination of a philosopher's training (517b and 534c). The two methods then which Plato is contrasting are those of psychological inquiry and of philosophical inquiry. The former, which he adopts in Book IV, is an empirical exercise in what might be called moral psychology, examining the nature of the soul and its virtues by means of the introspection which is available to any of us. But the conclusions of such an inquiry are necessarily incomplete and inadequate, as long as they lack the basis of a philosophical knowledge of the concepts involved and of their interrelation. Corresponding to the contrast between the two methods is the condition of the Guardians in Books IV and VI respectively. In Book IV they are marked out from other men simply by being wiser, but the discussion of Books V-VI, in which Plato develops his thesis that to be Guardians they must be philosophers, reveals that being wiser is not simply a matter of being more intelligent or of sounder judgment than other men; it is a virtue which arises from the possession of *knowledge* of the truth, as contrasted with the *beliefs* (even the *correct* beliefs) which other men may have. The psychological method followed in Book IV is to be regarded as good enough for working purposes, and indeed is the only method available until the nature of philosophical knowledge and inquiry has been elucidated. But the answers arrived at by it are only second-best, and a matter of belief, until they are shown to be grounded in knowledge, which only the methods of philosophy can attain.

Starting from the facts of observation that men engage in different kinds of activity, such as the appetitive (the pursuit of bodily desires, for food, drink and sex), the spirited (the pursuit of ambition and self-assertion), and the rational (the pursuit of learning), Plato asks whether we engage in these different pursuits all with the same element in us, or each of these with a different element. "Do we learn with one element in us, do we show anger with a different one and do we with a third desire the pleasures of nourishment and procreation and other things akin to them; or whenever we initiate action, do we do it with the whole soul in each of these different activities?" (436a-b). His answer to the question whether these three apparently different elements really are different is going to be that they are, and he arrives at it by the application of a psychological principle, which may be called the principle of conflict, illustrated by the case of a man who is drawn to action by one of his appetites (e.g. drawn to drink by his thirst) but who nevertheless refrains from that action because of some inhibiting factor (e.g. because his reason warns him against it). This principle is first stated in a very general form, and is illustrated by two examples, which are in fact unfortunately misleading. The general principle is: "It is clear that the same thing will not at one and the same time do (or suffer) opposite things in the same part of itself in relation to the same object" (436b). If a man is standing still and at the same time waving his hands about, we should say, not that the man is simultaneously motionless and in motion, but that one part of him is still and another part moving (436c). Again if a top is spinning on a single spot about a vertical axis, we should say, not that the top is both stationary and moving, but that its axis is stationary and its circumference is moving (436d-e).

The first example does illustrate the general principle that, if we can simultaneously say apparently contradictory things about an object (e.g. that the man is both motionless and in movement), we can dissolve the apparent contradiction by saying that one part of the man (e.g. his trunk) is motionless while another part (a hand) is in motion. But the second example does not: in the sense in which any *part* of a vertically spinning top is in motion, every part is; the fact that the top does not move from the spot on which it is spinning or incline out of its vertical axis does not mean that the *whole* top is not moving on that spot. Relativity of motion does not necessitate that different *parts* of the object are in motion and at rest respectively. The fact that the top does not move from the spot on which it is spinning does not mean that it is not moving on it. Furthermore, neither the general principle, nor the two illustrations of it, make any use of the notion of *conflict* which Plato requires for his psychological argument. And the fact that we can talk of a man's feet and his hands as being different *parts* of his body, or of a top's circumference and axis as being (in an extended sense) different *parts* of the top offers a misleading analogy for the soul, which Plato, believing it to be non-physical, cannot want to divide into parts in any literal sense. He does (although not until after his analysis of it) say that the soul consists of three parts (e.g. 442b), but what he wishes to mean by that is far from clear. It would have been better, on all counts, if he had omitted his general principle and his two physical examples, and had gone straight to the psychological principle of conflict itself; for the use which he makes of that is reasonably clear. He distinguishes appetite from reason by the example already mentioned, the conflict within a thirsty man when his desire for a drink is opposed by considerations of prudence. It does not matter to Plato's argument which of them overcomes the other, for all that he is concerned at this stage to bring out is that appetite and reason are in conflict with each other, and therefore cannot be the same as each other. His point that appetite and considerations of reason are of different orders from each other is a good one and important. There could be, and are, conflicts of appetite, but Plato would want to insist, and rightly, that they are different from a conflict between appetite and reason. Being thirsty and being offered a glass of milk, I might simultaneously both want and not want to take it, wanting to because it is a drink (a thirst-quencher), and not wanting to because I greatly dislike the taste of milk. But my desire and my aversion are related to different aspects of what I am offered (it as a thirst-quencher and it as having its particular taste), and both are explicable at a purely causal level. Such a conflict is quite different from Plato's, where I am pulled one way by an appetite (the thirst for a drink) and another way by reason, which recognises the imprudence of giving in to my thirst when it may be bad for me to do so.

It would be to misunderstand Plato to suppose that he is here opposing to each other Desire and Reason, and consequently to speak of what we have called the Appetitive element as the Desiring element. He is not saying at all the same kind of thing as Hume later said when he contrasted Desire (in Hume's terminology Passion) and Reason. According to Hume every action is motivated or initiated by desire, and the function of reason is purely informative, to tell us that the object of our desire is or is not attainable, or that the means which we propose to adopt for attaining it is or is not suitable for the purpose. Hume's point was that reason by itself can never induce us to do anything, or prevent us from doing it, and that in this sense reason is passive. In the absence of desire reason is powerless : I may know that by working harder I shall secure promotion or an increase in salary, but that knowledge by itself cannot spur me to work harder ; it is also necessary that I should want to rise to a better job or to a higher salary. However clear-headed or far-sighted I may be, this is of no practical use to me if I am also apathetic. Thus, because reason is entirely concerned with the facts of a situation, and desire or passion with what I want in the situation, there can never strictly be any conflict between reason and desire ; desire is the driving force, reason is the cool judge ; and the only thing that can conflict with a desire is a contrary desire. The desire to enjoy myself can conflict with the desire to get on in the world ; but the desire to enjoy myself cannot conflict with the recognition that this is not the way to get on in the

world. "Nothing can oppose or retard the impulse of a passion, but a contrary impulse. . . . We speak not strictly and
philosophically when we talk of the combat of passion and of
reason. Reason is, and ought only to be the slave of the passions, and can never pretend to any other office than to serve
and obey them" (Hume, *Treatise of Human Nature*, II. iii. 3).
For Hume, then, passion or desire is the conative element in
human nature, while reason is purely cognitive.

Plato's account differs from Hume's in two important
respects. His appetites do not correspond to Hume's passions
(desires, impulses), and his reason is not purely cognitive, with
the twin results that for him appetite and reason can conflict,
and that reason, as well as appetite, can motivate action. Thus,
the classification of psychological elements proposed by Plato
cuts right across the classification later suggested by Hume.
For Plato some desires, but not all, belong to the appetitive
element. The other two elements, spirit and reason, have
their own desires too, the desires of ambition and self-assertion,
and the desires of knowledge, and they, as much as our appetites,
impel us to action (580d). It may seem unfortunate that Plato
uses the same Greek word, ἐπιθυμία, sometimes to refer to
appetites in particular (and he called the appetitive element τὸ
ἐπιθυμητικόν), at other times to refer to desires in general, but
he nowhere confuses the two; and it is never difficult to tell
from the context which he means. The desires of appetite are
precisely specified at the outset as bodily desires (436a) and
"those akin to them", by which he means the acquisitive
desires for possessions and making money (580-581). The desires
of reason, on the other hand, are twofold. Corresponding to
the particular desires of appetite are the particular desires of
reason, to gain knowledge on a particular matter or in a particular field. The historian, the scientist and the philosopher
are moved to pursue their activities by their desire, which is a
desire of reason, to attain the truth and to achieve knowledge
in their subject. And their desires, because they are the desires
of reason, are of a higher grade and more to be admired, than
the desires of the appetitive or acquisitive man (581). But
over and above these desires of reason, which are desires for
its particular objects, there is another, and for Plato here more

important, desire of reason, viz. the desire of reason to control a man's soul, and consequently his life, as a whole in the way that is best. In this respect, it is the function of reason to "care for the whole soul" (441e). This is important for Plato, because, if reason just had its particular desires, they, while they might be more elevated than the desires of appetite or of spirit, would simply be in competition with them, with no authority for resolving or harmonising the competing interests. It is in its second capacity, as the overruling authority, caring for the whole soul, that reason has the function of controlling and harmonising the particular desires of all the elements (including its own). This is reflected in the life of the philosopher-Guardians, as eventually described, which is divided between the activities of philosophical research on the one hand, and on the other taking their turns in governing the city and maintaining its unity, i.e. caring for it as a whole. As philosophers they would prefer to devote their whole lives to the task of understanding reality, but as conscientious men they recognise that such activity must not be allowed to override the supreme task of harmonising all men's lives (their own included) in the life of the city. Reason is self-reflexive in a way in which appetite and spirit, just because they are not reason, cannot be.

Plato's definition of the appetitive element of the soul as that element to which bodily desires belong enables him to make a clear contrast between it and the rational element, but it does appear to be inconsistent with his belief, for which he argues in Book X, for the immortality of the soul. It is impossible to see what he can mean by 'soul', if he wishes both to say that the soul survives the death and decomposition of the body and to specify one of the elements of the soul as that which desires bodily pleasures. At one point in the *Republic* (518d-e) he shows some awareness of this difficulty himself, for he says that three of the four virtues are related to the body, wisdom or the virtue of pure reason being the only one that is free of it, although even it may be adversely affected by the soul's temporary conjunction with the body. But even there he does not seem to recognise the extent of the difficulty. It is one thing to say that the soul is separable from the body, while allowing that during its existence in the body it may be temporarily affected by its relationship with it.   But it is quite another thing to say both that the soul is separable from the body, and that some elements of the soul have desires for bodily experiences.   The latter claim involves an irresolvable contradiction between the account given of the soul and the proposition that it is immortal.   Indeed, it is difficult to see how Plato thought that what he says in 611c could be reconciled at all with his previous account of justice.   Nor is this a problem for Plato alone.   Many people, and most religions, sincerely believe that man possesses a soul which survives bodily death; and many people have been bothered as to what reason we can offer for accepting this belief as true.   But as the difficulties raised by Plato's account indicate, there is a still more fundamental problem, viz. that of understanding what this belief can even mean.   If the soul is to be immortal, it must not be characterised in a way which entails its connection with the body.

Having shown the difference between the appetitive and rational elements, Plato turns next to the spirited element in the soul (439e), and by a second application of the principle of conflict establishes two points: first that spirit, because it can be opposed to appetite, must be different from it, and secondly that spirit has an affinity with reason, being its ally rather than its enemy.   This again reflects the situation in the city where the Auxiliaries (its spirited element) have it as their function to assist the Guardians in maintaining the city's life. The difference between spirit and appetite is shown by the example of a man who suffers remorse or is angry with himself for indulging his baser appetites (439e-440a).   If I can be annoyed with myself for giving way to temptation, or if by pride or strength of will I can resist temptation, this shows that spirit is different from and ready to oppose appetite, on the side of reason.   In saying that spirit is the ally of reason (440b), Plato is not concerned to deny that we can be unreasonably angry.   Indeed he admits that we can, and uses the fact that we sometimes are for his final distinction, that between spirit and reason (441b).   What he means by spirit being the ally of reason he explains (440) when he says that we are never annoyed with ourselves for having done what we believe to be right. Here Plato is surely correct. We might regret having done something which was distasteful, because it hurt other people, or because it damaged some interests of our own ; but while we might wish that we had not had to do it, and while we might deplore the situation which made the action necessary, we could not, if we were convinced of the rightness and the necessity of our action, be angry with ourselves or reproach ourselves for having done it. For example, the Chancellor of the Exchequer may or may not be correct in believing at a given time that the country's economic difficulties call for drastic restrictions on purchasing power, say by an increase in taxation. But if he is convinced that that is the right course of action in the country's interests, then, while he may dislike having to interfere with the people's liberty of purchase, and while he may unhappily reflect on the adverse influence which his policy is likely to have on his own party's prospects at the next General Election, he cannot be angry with himself for pursuing that policy. Again, says Plato, the more honest a man is, the less likely he is to be angry when he believes himself to be in the wrong, and suffers for being so (449c). We are angry when we suffer injustice, but not when we suffer from what we believe to be justified. If I knowingly drive my car the wrong way down a one-way street and am caught, I am not angry with the policeman for catching me or the magistrate for fining me. I may be angry with myself for having been so stupid, but I cannot both acknowledge that what the policeman and the magistrate did "served me right" and be angry with them for having done it. If I am angry with them, it is because I think I have some reason for being angry — that the offence was so trivial (the street being empty at the time) that the policeman might have let me off with a warning, or that the fine imposed by the magistrate was excessive. But, if I do honestly admit that their action does serve me right, and that I have no reason for being angry with them, then I cannot be angry with them.

This brings out a point which Plato did not explicitly make, but which he could legitimately have made for his case for the affinity of spirit with reason. Anger is not the only manifestation of what Plato means by 'spirit', but it is the most striking and dramatic one. And when we are angry, we are always angry *with* someone and *for a reason*. If a man has an appetitive want, e.g. he feels thirsty, and if he is asked why he is thirsty, he will give a causal explanation of his being so, that he has had nothing to drink for a long time, or that he has become hot taking violent exercise. But, if asked why he is angry, his explanation, even if partly causal, will not be purely so. It will be an explanation that attempts to give a reason for being angry, i.e. that attempts to justify his being angry; what he is trying to do is to show that his annoyance is, in some degree or other, reasonable. We may not accept his reason as being a good reason, or a good enough reason, to justify his anger; nor indeed, on cooler reflection, may he, for he may come to admit that his emotion distorted his judgment. But at the time he will not think so; he is angry with the other person for having insulted him, or threatened him, or let him down. A man can be angry with himself; and he is, because he thinks his conduct has made himself look foolish, or has been unworthy of himself. Being angry involves consciousness of oneself as a person in a way in which feeling an appetite does not. It is a reaction to finding oneself placed, usually by the action of another, in a situation which he does not think is deserved or worthy of him, as is indicated by the etymology of the word 'indignation'. This provides the answer, on behalf of Plato, to those who suggest that he had no better reason for distinguishing the spirited element in the soul than his wish to balance a threefold soul with the threefold city: according to this objection, the soul should be divided into two, the rational and the irrational, and the expression of spirit is simply the emotional explosion from the conflict. Plato can reply that there is more to it than that, that we should not overlook that element in a man which makes him aware of himself not just as an individual among other individuals, but as an individual brought by the circumstances of human life into competition with them. Maybe, as Hume suggested, if the conditions of competition were absent, because either we lived in a world of such plenty that there was no occasion for it, or we were sufficiently benevolent or self-abasing by nature, the spirited element would atrophy. But life in fact is not like that, and any account

of human nature which ignored the threats to a man's integrity
and his human tendency to assert himself against the world,
would be to that extent deficient. Plato's attempt to distinguish
spirit from reason, on the ground that children have the former
but not the latter (441a), may be regarded as weak, because
we should say, not that small children have *no* reason, but that
in them reason has barely begun to develop. But the point is
still good, and could be applied to his other example, of non-
human animals (441b), that there is in them that self-assertive
and self-preservative tendency which expresses itself in anger
in the face of threats and frustrations. As Plato recognises,
spirit as the self-assertive element manifests itself, not only or
even mainly in anger, but also in fear, honour, ambition and
courage. That is why he regarded it as the prime function of a
child's education so to mould his character that he would fear
and honour the right things, have the right ambitions and have
the courage of his right convictions. It is the business of reason,
not only to keep self-assertiveness within the right bounds, but
also to head it in the right directions.

Having found the three elements in the soul, corresponding
to those in the city, Plato next proceeds to the assignation of the
virtues. And here, as already mentioned, it must be confessed
that his account is extremely sketchy. With regard to wisdom,
courage and self-restraint he merely repeats in summary
fashion (441-442) what he has already said of them as social
and political virtues, regarding it as obvious that they must be
the same on the small scale as they had been on the large.
This leads him, in the case of self-restraint, to skate rapidly over
some extremely thin ice. "Do we not call a man self-restrained
through the friendship and concord of these elements, when
both the ruling element and the two subject elements agree
together that reason should rule, and when these two do not
rebel against reason?" (442c-d). This is exactly the same
language which he has used when talking of the city (432a).
But, while it may have been appropriate there, it certainly is
not appropriate here; this is a case where the parallelism
between city and individual cannot be sustained. Given that
all three elements are to be found in each man's soul, it makes
sense to say that a member of the Economic Class, while

predominantly appetitive or acquisitive, has a sufficient degree of rationality to recognise that it is best that he should stick to his trade and leave government to men who are predominantly rational; and the corresponding thing may be said of members of the Auxiliary Class. But this thesis cannot be transferred to the soul itself, given Plato's account of it. For in it the appetitive element is purely appetitive and, as Plato himself says (439d7), has no reason in it. It might make sense to say that a man possessed the virtue of self-restraint if his reason controlled his appetites and his spirit (cf. 444b), but it makes no sense at all to say that reason controls appetite with the agreement of appetite that reason should be in control. That would be to assign to appetite some degree of reason which by definition it cannot possess. The only way by which the parallelism could be preserved would be to assign to *each* of the elements of the soul three sub-elements of reason, spirit and appetite. But this would be an untenable attempt at a solution, for it would make nonsense of Plato's whole psychology, and it would lead to a vicious regress. The consequence must be accepted that here we have at least one case where Plato's parallelism irremediably breaks down. If he had not been so brief and hasty in his account of virtues in the individual, he might have detected the inconsistency himself.

About the fourth virtue, justice, he does speak at slightly more length (443). Attempts, such as were made in Book I, to characterise justice in terms of a man's conduct are misguided and place the emphasis in the wrong place, for conduct is only a sign or "image" of character. A man is just when the three elements of his soul are in their correct harmonious relationship under the overall rule of the rational element. Such a relationship will manifest itself in just conduct. Conversely, the practice of just conduct, through moral training and example, will serve to produce and maintain the relationship, but should not be confused with it. In this contrast between conduct and the character of which it is, or should be, the expression, Plato is underlining a distinction which is central to ethics. Some of our moral judgments are judgments about a man's conduct, regardless of his motives or his reasons for acting so; and to this sphere belong especially words like 'right', 'wrong', 'ought'

and 'obligation'. We say that a man has done what was right
if his action conforms with what we accept as moral rules,
wrong if it violates them. For example, in the ordinary situation where no problems arise over which there is reason for
moral disagreement we may say that a man has done what was
right if, having made a promise, he keeps it, that he has done
wrong if he breaks it. If one man keeps a promise out of
respect for the sanctity of promises, and another keeps his
promise because he thinks it will pay him to do so, or that he
will suffer loss if he breaks it, we do not say that the first man's
action was right, but the second's was not. If it is right to pay
taxes and bills when they are due, to tell the truth when giving
evidence under oath, to obey traffic lights when driving a car,
to report for duty when called up into the army, etc., then
your conduct is right when it is of the prescribed kind. In
judging that what you did was right, or judging that you have
done what you ought, we are judging you for your conduct,
and are not interested in your motives or reasons. We shall
not withdraw our assertion that you did what you ought, if we
discover that your reasons for so acting were much less reputable
than we may have at first supposed. But belief and knowledge
about your reasons will determine a different kind of moral
judgment which we make, judgment about you as a man, or
about your conduct in relation to you as a man. And this is
the sphere to which the 'virtue' (and 'vice') words belong:
the general words like 'good' and 'bad' and the more specific
virtue words like 'generous', 'honest', 'courageous', 'conscientious', etc., and vice words like 'mean', 'malicious', 'un-
trustworthy', etc. These are the words which we use in
describing and assessing a man's character, and in appraising
his conduct when we are not simply judging it externally by
its conformity with (or violation of) a moral code of behaviour,
but are judging it in relation to the man's reasons and motives
for so acting. We approve of a man keeping his promise, whatever his reasons may be, but we shall not admire him if we know
that his sole reason was fear of the consequences to himself of
being caught breaking it. Plato's point is that in right conduct
as such there is no virtue. If a man sticks to his job, or stays
within his class, he is acting justly, but he is not on that account

a just man : he may be sticking to his job because he can make more money out of it than at any other, because of fear of unemployment if he leaves it, because he will lose his house if he leaves it, or because it has been made a legal offence to leave it. He will be a just man, or his conduct will display justice, only if it is the manifestation of his inner self or character, and only if that inner self consists of the three elements in their correct relationship; real justice, then, characterises, not a man's behaviour, but the state of his soul, which will naturally manifest itself in his behaviour. This raises the question whether, on Plato's account, everybody, no matter what kind of man he is (i.e. to which class in the city he belongs), is capable of being just. Although Plato has so far given no direct indication that justice is attainable only by a few, and although he even suggests in the present passage that it is obtainable by all (443e), the answer must surely be that, on his account, only very few men are capable of achieving it. For a man can be just only when each element in his soul keeps in its place under the overall rule of the rational element, the wisdom of which comes from the knowledge which it possesses. Therefore only that man can be just in whom the rational element is fully developed and possesses knowledge. This means that, in terms of the city, only the Guardians are capable of justice; and as will be seen later, they are capable of it, not because they are Guardians, but because they are philosophers. That true justice is the monopoly of philosophers may seem a surprising conclusion for Plato to reach, but it is inescapable. He cannot explicitly state it here, because he has not yet made his point that rulers must be philosophers, let alone given his reasons for making it. He therefore leaves us at this stage with the conclusion unstated, and perhaps with the vague impression that anybody can be just who has sufficient reason in him to keep his appetites and spirit in check, just as so far any city would be acceptable in which the wisest men wielded effective government. But later he has no hesitation in accepting the conclusion. When he returns to the question whether the just man will have the happiest life (583-587), his answer that he will depends on arguments from the claims of philosophy as a way of life. Commentators who complain that

Plato, by arguing that the philosopher has the happiest life, does not answer his own question, whether the just man has the happiest life, completely miss Plato's point, which by then he has made clearly enough, that only the philosopher is capable of being truly just, for he is the only man whose soul is informed by knowledge. The rest of us may lead decent, orderly lives, and our lives may be governed by our moral beliefs, so that in a limited sense we are capable of being just, but unless our beliefs are by philosophy transmuted into knowledge we necessarily fall short of justice itself (cf. 619c-d).

There remain two final matters for consideration : whether Plato thought of the soul as consisting of three *parts* ; and what he believed about the correspondence between the nature of a city and the nature of an individual. The first matter, while it has traditionally been treated as one of the central issues of Platonic interpretation, seems to us in itself to be of little importance, although it conceals something that is important. Hitherto, in expounding and commenting on Plato's analysis of the soul, we have, in order not to beg the question, avoided using the word 'part' at all, and have deliberately used indeterminate words like 'element' or 'factor'. And for this we have the authority of Plato himself, for he nowhere uses a Greek word which could be translated by 'part' until after his threefold analysis is complete. And even then the word μέρος, which first occurs at 442b11, while it can be translated 'part', does not have to be. All the words which he does use, even where they are psychological terms, are of a very general noncommittal kind, the most frequently occurring being γένος and εἶδος, meaning 'kind' or 'form'. (εἶδος does not yet bear the technical meaning which it acquires in the Theory of Forms, and γένος is the same word as has been used for a class of the city (cf. 434c2).) We cannot know how to respond to the suggestion that Plato divided the soul into three parts, until we know how 'part' is there being used. If it is being used literally, as when we use it of the spatially delimited portion of a physical object (the parts of a house, the three parts into which Gaul was divided), or of the temporally delimited portions of a physical process (the first part of a speech, the early part of a day), or of these two combined (Part I of a book), that is clearly not what Plato meant : the soul, for him, was neither a physical object nor a physical process. Again, we use 'part' in an extended sense (parts of an argument, parts of speech), but there is no reason to think that Plato meant anything like that. So, if Plato's soul has parts, it has so in a metaphorical sense ; and, until the metaphor is cashed into literal language, nothing is gained by asking whether Plato divided the soul into parts, while something is lost, because of the natural association of 'part' with physical division, which in the present context is grossly misleading. Clearly Plato's psychological talk is metaphorical, which is hardly surprising, for psychological talk nearly always is metaphorical, and Plato's was very early psychology. There is nothing inherently wrong with metaphor, which is frequently of great suggestive and illuminating value. But, if it is to be of such value, we must from time to time be able to cash it in non-metaphorical language. And here we are up against the great difficulty in Plato, that he nowhere does that. He should not be severely criticised for that, for he must have been aware himself of the enormous difficulty of doing psychology in language that was primarily designed, or had been mainly developed, for the quite different purpose of talking about the external world. With such a handicap, pioneer psychology is bound to fumble. To refer to the different elements in the Platonic soul as different tendencies, or springs of action, or even drives (in more modern psychological terminology), may not advance us much, but it does advance us in the right direction. To try to think of the soul as chopped up into parts does nothing to help us to understand what Plato was at, or even what we should be at instead.

But the upholders of the 'part' interpretation are on to one difficulty in Plato's account which does have serious consequences. On the one hand, he does think of the soul as a unity, as a whole comprised of related elements. On the other hand, he does think of our actions as arising from, or produced by, these elements, sometimes singly, sometimes in combination, sometimes in competition ; and, as we have seen, it is on what he regards as the introspectively observable fact of competition

between the elements that his doctrine of the divided soul depends. To use nouns like 'reason' and 'appetite' in talking of
a man's psychological make-up may be, for brevity's sake,
convenient, and to talk of reason conflicting with appetite,
and sometimes succeeding in controlling it, may be metaphorically acceptable. But such use of metaphor has its dangers,
from which Plato was not free, in particular the anthropo-
morphic danger of personifying the elements, factors, faculties,
or whatever we may choose to call them. If a man's soul or
self is composed of these three elements, how can he be anything over and above them? And if he is not, how can he be
held responsible, let alone morally responsible, for his actions?
If, on one occasion, my reason is strong enough to thwart my
appetites, what credit is that to me? If, on another, appetite
wins, how can I be blamed? Indeed, who is the 'I' to be
blamed? All we could say would be that, on the first occasion,
it was a good thing or a fortunate thing that reason prevailed,
and that, on the second, it was regrettable that appetite was
too strong; but I could not properly be blamed or criticised
on the second occasion, or praised on the first. For to do that
would be to imply that on either occasion I still had freedom
of choice; but if conflict, or moral conflict, is as Plato represents it, there would be no choice, and there could be nothing
to do the choosing. We are not, simply on this account, forced
to the conclusion that Plato's account was fundamentally
wrong. But we are forced to it, if we also insist on ever holding
a man responsible for his actions. In cases of abnormal psychology, such as neurosis or psychosis, an account something like
Plato's is now substantially accepted, even by the law under the
notion of "diminished responsibility", for in such cases the
claim is made and is frequently accepted that the man was so
far in the power of his mental disease (his alcoholism, klepto-
mania, or whatever it may be) that he could not help himself,
and therefore the attribution of blame would be out of place;
all that can be done is, in the short term to restrict his liberty
so as to protect himself and others from his weakness, and in the
long term perhaps to effect a cure by suitable therapeutic
treatment. There is even a tendency nowadays on the part of
some to interpret all cases of alleged "criminal responsibility"

K

in this way, as cases calling for treatment rather than punishment. But, unless this interpretation is correct, and unless the whole notion of personal responsibility is to be abandoned, the Platonic kind of analysis must be fundamentally mistaken — if we are correct in seeing in his analysis the tendency to personify the elements of the soul, and to regard the soul as something entirely comprised of these elements. Here Plato himself seems confused, and even to contradict himself. On the one hand, in Book IV of the *Republic* he does give predominantly the account which we have attributed to him. On the other hand, there are signs of his being at odds with his official account. As we have seen, his notion of spirit involves consciousness of self as something other than a union of elements. And he repeatedly insists that it is the function of the rational element to care for the soul as a whole (cf. 441e5, 442b6, 442c7). We must conclude that, even if the difficulties of his account of the soul were not clearly present to him, he was not entirely unaware of some of the considerations that would make them difficulties. But he shows no sign at all of having recognised the impossibility of squaring his account with the notion of personal responsibility. That in itself may be hardly surprising, for the idea of personal responsibility was hardly, if at all, current in Greek thought. But that Plato was not, and perhaps could not have been, aware of the philosophical problem raised by his theory of the self does not mean that the problem is not raised by it, nor that it is not still with us.

On the parallelism which Plato finds between soul and city we have two questions to answer. How close did he think it was? And what were his reasons for believing in it? On the first question, there seems no doubt that he believed the similarity to be very great, for, as we have seen, he draws it out in such detail himself. Not only does he divide both city and soul into three elements, but he throughout insists on a one-to-one correspondence between them, even when it involves him, as in the case of the virtue of self-restraint, in saying things about the soul that, on his own account, cannot be said of it. Everything that he first says about the three classes and the four virtues of the city is exactly matched by what he subsequently says about the soul. Furthermore, the whole original

enterprise, begun in Book II, of first finding justice on the large
scale in the city in order the better to be able to discern it on
the small scale in the individual, would have been entirely
pointless unless he had believed that city and individual were
structurally the same. And if he believes in this identity of
structure, why did he believe it? He can hardly have supposed that it was simply a gigantic coincidence, incapable of
explanation. Does he then argue from city to individual, or
from individual to city? Both views have been held, but there
seems to us no doubt which is correct, viz. the latter. It is,
of course, true that he gives his description of the city before
giving his description of the individual. But nothing can be
inferred from that, because frequently the order of exposition
of an argument is the reverse of the order of proof; such is a
perfectly legitimate procedure, and may often for clarity's
sake be preferable. If I wish to argue from a premise p to a
conclusion q, it makes no difference whether I present my
argument in the form $p \therefore q$ or in the form $q \because p$: each is a
different way of presenting the same argument. For instance,
I may say either that the barometer is falling and therefore we
may expect rain, or that we may expect rain because the barometer is falling. In either case I am offering the fact of the
barometer falling as a reason for expecting rain; which way
round I do it will be determined by convenience or context.
If we start by noticing the fall in the barometer and wonder
what that indicates, it would be most natural to argue $p \therefore q$. If
we start by wondering whether it is going to rain and then notice
the fall in the barometer, it would be most natural to argue $q \because p$.
Consequently, from the mere fact that Plato first states one
proposition (that the city has a certain structure) and then
states another (that the soul has an identical structure) we
cannot tell whether the two propositions are to be linked by
the $\therefore$ or by the $\because$ sign; we require further evidence to decide
the issue. Nor is the evidence provided by the fact that Plato
clearly regarded the city as being more important than the
individual; for that fact is equally compatible with either alternative. To say that the city is more important than the
individual is to make a judgment of value, that in a clash of
interests public interest ought to be preferred to private interest;

but that the city comes first in terms of value has no bearing
on the question of causal or even of logical priority. That Plato
believed that the argument is from individual to city is confirmed by the fact that, in at least two passages, he as good as
says so himself. In 435e he says that unless the same elements
.are to be found in each individual as have already been found
in the city, there can be no explanation of the city's having
them : where else could they have come from? And on the
preceding page he has emphasised that the account given of
justice in the city may have to be modified if we find that the
account to be given of justice in the individual does not entirely
square with it. We could hardly ask for clearer evidence as
to which was Plato's order of thought. This carries with it an
important implication for Plato's political philosophy, that his
was an organic view of the state, regarding it as a super-
individual of which individual men were members or even
servants, their function being to lead lives which contributed
to the total life of the state, much as the brain, limbs and muscles
of a man have each their own function to play in maintaining
his life. This metaphysical view of the state as a personality
may, as we are sure that it is, be grounded in logical confusion,
but it is emotionally of enormous power. It expresses itself in
the more misguided feelings of patriotism, it almost brought
ruin to civilisation under the Hitlerite version of it, and it still
bedevils international politics in the form of national pride.
It is because Plato committed himself to this view of the state
that he has been called, not unreasonably, the first totalitarian.
But it should be added that, while Plato was committed to
this view, and while he offered no clear or cogent reasons for
accepting it, he cannot be said to have clearly recognised the
implication himself. There are even occasional passages where
he writes the other way round, and speaks of the individual as
if he were a small-scale state; for example, the conflict of elements is once or twice referred to in political terms (cf. 440e5,
442d1), and injustice in the soul is described as civil war
(444b1). His use, in all these passages, of the political word
στάσις may be only a metaphor, but the fact that he found it
an acceptable metaphor perhaps indicates that his thought was
not entirely in the one direction. We should not, because we

find implications in a philosopher's thought, make the mistake of reading into his thought his own acknowledged acceptance of those implications. Equally we should not, because we cannot find in him acceptance of them, make the mistake of denying that he was committed to them.

Chapter 7

THE DISTINCTION BETWEEN THE
PHILOSOPHER AND THE
NON-PHILOSOPHER

By the end of Book IV the ideal state has been constructed
and justice examined both in the state and in the individual
soul. Socrates now proposes (at 445c) to review the various
forms that evil takes both in states and in the corresponding
characters of their citizens. At this point (449b-c) he is pulled
up by Adeimantus, who insists on being told more about the
proposed community of wives and children in the case of the
Guardians, which Socrates had touched on at 423e-424a. There
now follow the three "waves" — a metaphor used by Plato at
457b to describe the three contentious points with which he is
now engaged and which the argument has to breast. The
first wave (451b-457b) is concerned with the equality in education and public duties of female with male Guardians. Here
Plato relies mainly on an appeal to what is "natural"; at
455e ff. this equality is in accordance with human nature,
"every occupation is open to both women and men so far as
their natures are concerned", and it is also in accordance with
what happens in the natural world, since we expect this
equality of function in a pack of watch-dogs of which our
Guardians are the human counterpart (452d-e). The second
wave (457c-466d) provides the direct answer to Adeimantus,
and deals with the abolition of family life in the case of the
Guardians. For them wives and children are to be in common.
The motive for this is partly eugenic (459), but above all (as is
also the case with the abolition of private property for the
Guardians already outlined at 416-417) Plato's aim is to secure
unity in the state. In this latter connection, it is perhaps

sufficient to notice two points.   First, the passage from 462a-
466d deserves the closest attention, since here we have the
language of organic theories of the state (cf. Chapter 4, p. 76).
For example, in 462 there is the analogy with the human body :
if the finger is hurt the whole man shares in the pain ; and the
best ordered state will be that which most nearly resembles a
single person.   Secondly, Aristotle's criticisms in the *Politics*,
Book II, Chapters 1-5, of this way of attempting to attain unity
should also be studied.   It is here in Chapter 3 that Aristotle
points out how on Plato's proposals the words 'mine' and 'not
mine' would change their meaning and (in Chapter 4) makes
his well-known remark that "in a state having women and
children in common, love will be watery ; and the father will
certainly not say 'my son' or the son 'my father'.   As a little
sweet wine mingled with a great deal of water is imperceptible
in the mixture, so in this sort of community, the idea of relationship which is based on these names will be lost."   The second
wave is followed by a digression on war (466d-471c) in which
certain rules are laid down to humanise the strife of Greek
against Greek, and then (471c-474b) Socrates faces the third
and greatest wave, the question of the practicability of the
ideal state.

He begins by insisting on the importance of the ideal as a
pattern or model even if it should never be realised in practice.
We do not think any the worse of a painter who has painted
an ideally beautiful figure, if he cannot show that a person as
beautiful could exist.   Indeed the best we can hope for is that
practice should come as near the ideal as possible.   Given
these preliminary qualifications, Socrates then in 473 states
his solution of the problem of how, with the least possible
change in existing states, a state as close as possible to the ideal
might be realised.   It could be realised if philosophers became
the rulers, or if the present rulers became also genuine philosophers.   What is required is the union of political power with
philosophy.   Plato recognises that this must appear a paradoxical solution, and that to defend it he must make clear what
sort of people he means by his philosophers who are to have
political power.   Our own judgment on the practicability of
Plato's proposals will have to wait until he has done this.

Meantime there are one or two points of importance in the present section.

First it is worth noting the importance that Plato is attaching here to the ideal: he thinks it vitally important that we should possess ideals as standards or patterns, by which we can measure our actual human situation. Indeed at the beginning of 473 he insists that action or practice comes less close to truth than theory or thought: "Is it not in the nature of things that action should come less close to truth than thought?" (The word translated here by Cornford as 'truth' is the Greek word ἀλήθεια (*aletheia*) which in Plato comes at times to mean 'reality'. Lee's translation 'precision of theory' misses the point.) What Plato is suggesting is that what is revealed by thought or theory is in some way more true or more real than practice. He agrees that "people may not think so". They might rather take the view that it is experience, practice, that is the test of the truth of theory. But Plato, and Glaucon as a Platonist, take a different view; for them the world of thought or ideals is more real or more true than the world of experience or practice. When we come later to the Theory of Forms we shall have more to say about this; but meantime, even this early passage, where the reference is probably not explicitly to Forms, reveals Plato's predilection for the world of thought as against the world of experience or practice.

Secondly, in 472d, in defending the importance of ideal patterns, Plato takes a parallel from painting, and speaks of a painter as drawing "an ideally beautiful figure", "an idealised picture of a man"; and the implication is that the painter's ideal is not an imitation of any actual man, but surpasses any actual man, just as the ideal city surpasses any actual city. Now in Book X we find Plato maintaining that the artist is confined to imitation of the actual which, in turn, is an imitation of the Forms, and thus the artist's production is an imitation of an imitation. Plato might seem then in the present passage to be assigning the artist a higher and more important role than he is prepared to do in Book X; but probably too much should not be made of this, since the point is introduced in a fairly incidental way and without discussion. (The same applies to the simile of the artist-legislator at 500e ff., where again a higher role might be thought to be assigned to the artist.)

Lastly, in 473d-e, where Plato propounds his solution for realising the ideal state, namely that philosophers must become rulers, a point of some importance arises in the translation. To translate literally, what Plato says is that unless there is this union of political power and philosophy, "there can be no rest from troubles for states, nor yet, I think, for the race of men". Cornford translates, "there can be no rest from troubles for states, nor yet, as I believe, for all mankind", and Lee, "there will be no end to the troubles of states, or indeed of humanity itself". It will be noted that what in the Greek, literally translated, is simply 'the race of men' appears in Cornford as 'all mankind' and in Lee as 'humanity itself'. These two latter translations give the passage a particular colouring — they suggest that Plato is thinking of all mankind, that brooding over the evils men everywhere are suffering he propounds a solution which extends beyond the scope of the Greek city states he knew to humanity at large. In fact, however, it is not at all clear that the ambiguous phrase 'the race of men' will stand this interpretation. It could perhaps be extended in this way, but it could also simply refer to the individual citizens within the city, and recall the familiar contrast between city and individual, which appears for instance just below — "there is no other way of happiness either for the state or for the individual". It is in this latter way that Professor Popper in his book *The Open Society and its Enemies* understands the passage, and he protests against the former interpretation as an example of the "idealisation of Plato". He argues that in fact there is no evidence of humanitarianism in Plato, that is, of an interest in humanity at large. Rather, Plato is hostile to an equalitarian creed and to notions like that of the brotherhood of all mankind; and indeed the digression on warfare (469b-471c) which immediately precedes the present passage, however much in advance of its time it may be in regard to the treatment of Greek by Greek, still regards the non-Greek, the barbarian, as a "natural enemy" (470c). Popper's detailed discussion will be found on pp. 133-134 of the first volume of his book and especially in note (50) on page 237.   It is enough for us to note the point as an instance of how careful one must be to try to grasp what exactly Plato is saying without either over-idealising him or equally (as perhaps Popper is somewhat prone to do) under-idealising him. There is a further illustration of this within the present passage. After Plato in 473d has said that political power and philosophy must be combined, he goes on to say that the many people who now pursue either philosophy or politics to the exclusion of the other must be forcibly debarred from doing so.   That is, in Plato's state there will be no "pure" philosophers: there is only a place for the philosopher ruler, and anyone who wishes to pursue a life of pure philosophical study will be forcibly prevented from doing so.   Here again it is easy to miss the implications of this passage, or alternatively to mini- mise them.   But what Plato does in fact say is that the exclusive pursuit of knowledge just will not be allowed in his state.   We may set against this a passage from Kant (as rendered by Popper on p. 133 of his book referred to above): "That kings should become philosophers, or philosophers kings, is not likely to happen; nor would it be desirable, since the possession of power invariably debases the free judgment of reason.   It is, however, indispensable that a king, or a kingly, i.e. self-ruling people, should not suppress philosophers, but leave them the right of public utterance".   Plato has his reasons for his differ- ing view, and these should become clearer as we proceed. What is important is that what his actual view is should be plainly stated — in the present case, no pursuit of knowledge independently of taking part in the governing of the state — so that we may then go on to ask ourselves what merit or other- wise the view may have.

The Distinction between the Philosopher and the non-Philosopher (474b-480).   This is an important (and difficult) section in itself, and it also marks the beginning of the discussion of important philosophical topics that continues through Books VI and VII.   Socrates recognises that on the popularly accepted view of what is meant by a philosopher his proposition that philosophers must be kings can only incur ridicule.   He must then make clear what he himself means by a philosopher. The Greek word φιλόσοφος (*philosophos*) is made up from two other words, *philos* meaning 'loving' and *sophia* meaning 'wisdom', and the *philos* element appears in a number of other similar compounds, e.g. in 475 *philoinos*, a lover of wine, *philotimos*, a lover of honour. Socrates begins his explanation by arguing that since a lover of anything loves the whole of it, so a philosopher must love the whole of wisdom, must have a taste for every sort of knowledge, must be glad to learn and never satisfied, if he is to deserve the name of philosopher. Glaucon objects that this will include all sorts of dilettanti, lovers of sights and sounds, who never miss a theatrical or musical performance and so in this sense are glad to learn and acquire new experiences. These are strange people to class as philosophers. They are, in fact, counterfeit philosophers, Socrates replies; the genuine philosophers are those whose passion is to see the truth (475e). The rest of Book V is occupied with this distinction between the lover of sights and sounds and the genuine philosopher. The argument falls into two parts, (1) 475e-476d which is addressed to Glaucon, as one already acquainted with the philosophical view about to be developed and (2) 476d-480 which is addressed to a wider audience, and in particular to the lover of sights and sounds, the counterfeit philosopher. The outcome of the whole discussion is that the latter does not possess knowledge, does not really know anything, but has only belief (*doxa*), is a *philodoxos*, i.e. a lover of belief, whereas the genuine philosopher possesses knowledge, is able to apprehend the truth, and thus alone merits the name of philosopher. In both sections two parallel distinctions are brought out: (a) a distinction between the different sorts of objects with which the non-philosopher and the philosopher are concerned, and (b) a distinction between their different states of mind. The objects of the non-philosopher are appearances, of the philosopher reality; and with these two different classes of objects are correlated the two different states of mind to which we have already referred, namely in the case of the non-philosopher belief, and in the case of the philosopher knowledge. This part of the *Republic* is in fact primarily concerned with elucidating the distinction between knowledge and belief.

To return now to the actual argument, let us consider separately the two parts we have distinguished.

(1) 475e-476d. *The argument directed to those who already
accept the Theory of Forms.* As we have indicated, this part of the
argument is addressed to Glaucon, one who is already familiar
with and accepts a certain very celebrated philosophical view
of Plato, namely what is often known as Plato's Theory of
Ideas but is perhaps better described as Plato's Theory of
Forms. Chapter 8 discusses this theory at some length. It is a
good thing, however, before we come to this general discussion,
to plunge straight into the theory here and see something of
the actual use that is being made of the notion of a 'Form' in the
present passage. In the present passage, then, Glaucon accepts
at once and without discussion the view that, since for example
beauty and ugliness are opposites, they are two and each is
one, and so with justice and injustice, good and bad and so
on. There is then a single Form of Beauty, a single Form of
Ugliness, a single Form of Justice and so on. But each of these
single Forms, through its association with actions or with
material objects appears as many. Let us take two examples to
explain what Plato means. First take the case of beauty. We
might say a certain portrait was beautiful, a certain landscape
beautiful, a certain piece of music beautiful and so on. These
would all be for us beautiful things (in a wide sense of 'thing') ;
they would be in Platonic language "the many beautifuls" or
"the many beautiful things". But for Plato all these particular
beautiful things would be manifestations or appearances of the
single Form Beauty. Their beauty would arise from their relationship with the single Form. Within the present passage
Plato describes this relationship of Form to particular instance
in several ways — in 476a the Form "associates" or "combines
with" actions, etc., in 476c the particular is a likeness of the
Form, which is the reality of which the particular is a likeness
(in Cornford's translation the particular is a ' semblance ', the
Form 'the reality it resembles', in Lee the particular is an
'image', the Form 'the reality of which it is an image'),
in 476d the particulars participate in the Form (Cornford,
'partake of its character', Lee, 'share its character'). These
different ways of describing the relationship between Forms and
particulars should be noted. To take another example directly
related to the *Republic*, we judge this act or particular type of

act just, or that act or particular type of act just; Cephalus, for instance, thought it just or right to tell the truth and pay one's debts, and Polemarchus thought justice consisted in helping friends and harming enemies.   Here again Plato would maintain that there is a single Form of Justice or Rightness, which manifests itself in all the particular cases that we describe as just actions.   In this way the single Form of Justice appears to be a many or multiplicity, through its association with the many particular just actions which participate or share in its character.   Plato also refers here to the "associating" or "combining" of the Forms, not only with actions and material objects, but also "with one another".   This apparent reference to the combining of the Forms with one another has given rise to much discussion, and some scholars have tried unjustifiably to get rid of the reference by emending the text. The point is this.   In the earlier dialogues Plato seems to be primarily concerned with the relationship of the Forms to sensible things (using 'things' in a wide sense to cover actions as well as objects).   He thinks that we are able to call this thing beautiful, that thing beautiful and so on because these particular things share in the one Form Beauty, the Form combines with them and in this way each Form seems to be a many or multiplicity.   But now let us consider Forms by themselves.   Just as in the case of particular things we might want to call, for example, a picture beautiful, a statue beautiful and so on, so in the case of Forms we might want to say that, for example, the Form of Justice (Justice itself) was good, the Form of Temperance (Temperance itself) was good, etc., and here again if we followed the same sort of account as in the case of sensible things it would seem that we would be able to do this because these Forms all shared in the Form of Goodness. In this context then the Forms would be combining with one another.   In fact, however, apart from an implication in the final proof of immortality in the *Phaedo* (102a ff.) that one Form can participate in another, Plato does not explicitly discuss the combination of Forms with each other until the later dialogue the *Sophist*, and then his interest in doing so does not seem to be the same.   Hence the efforts of some scholars to emend the passage.   But, as we shall see later, apart from the reference we

have already made to the *Phaedo*, it looks as though the metaphysical views involved in Books VI and VII, and particularly
the place assigned to the Form of the Good, would imply this
sort of participation, and that we would have to be able to say
the Form of Justice is good and so on.   Thus there are no good
grounds for questioning the present passage.   It is true that
logically this notion of the combination of Forms as used in the
present context and exemplified in such propositions as that
Justice itself is good, Temperance itself is good, etc., is a very
difficult one.   One might raise the question whether logically
a Form, as Plato uses the notion, could ever be the subject of
predication, as it would be in such a sentence as 'Justice itself
is good'.   Discussion of this point must wait for the more
general discussion of the theory of Forms in Chapter 8 (cf.
especially pp. 194-195).   Meantime, to return to the main theme,
according to the view in the present passage, we would have two
broad classes of objects (again using the word in a wide sense).
We would have on the one hand the class of objects which
Plato calls Forms, and on the other hand the class of objects
comprising the many particular instances in which the various
Forms are manifested.] The Form would be the single unitary
entity, the reality, of which its many instances would be the
appearances : for example, the Form of Beauty would be the
single reality of which the many beautiful things would be
the appearances.   Given these two classes of objects, Plato
is now able to explain the difference between the counterfeit
philosopher, the lover of sights and sounds, and the genuine
philosopher.   The counterfeit philosopher is the man who is
content with the many beautiful things, the many just acts
and so on.   These are for him the reality, and it never occurs
to him that these are in each case merely appearances of a
single Form.   He mistakes the appearances (the many beautiful
things, the many just acts and so on) for the reality (the single
Form of Beauty, of Justice and so on) and thus (476c) he lives
in a dream.   In contrast the genuine philosopher is the man
who can distinguish between the appearances (the many particulars in each case) and the reality, in virtue of which in
each case the particulars are what they are.   Thus while the
lover of sights and sounds, the counterfeit philosopher, is living

in a dream, the genuine philosopher who distinguishes clearly between reality and appearance leads a waking life (476d). He, then, and he alone, has knowledge, since he knows the reality (the Forms) of which the many particulars are appearances. The non-philosopher, on the other hand, who is content with the many particulars does not have knowledge. His state of mind is one of belief. Beginning thus with two sorts of objects, Forms and particulars, Plato correlates with them two different states of mind, knowledge and belief, and then in terms of the latter distinguishes the genuine philosopher, the *philosophos* who has knowledge of the Forms, from the non-philosopher, the *philodoxos*, or lover of belief, who never rises above belief about particulars. The Greek word δόξα (*doxa*) which Plato uses to describe the state of mind of the non-philosopher, is a difficult word to translate. It is connected with the Greek verb δοκεῖν (*dokein*) 'to appear' or 'seem', which often occurs in constructions such as 'it appears or seems to me', 'it's my opinion or belief that', and with the verb δοξά-ζειν (*doxazein*), 'to believe or think or hold an opinion', which in 476d Plato directly associates with his use of the noun *doxa* — "so then would we not be right in saying that the state of mind of the philosopher is knowledge because he knows, while the state of mind of the other is belief (*doxa*) because he believes" (*doxazontos* from the verb *doxazein*). As Cornford points out on p. 176 of his translation, *doxa* is used in connection with seeming. It can be used of what seems to exist, sensible appearances, etc., or again of what seems true, beliefs, etc. It is often translated 'opinion', but again to follow Cornford, 'belief' is better, since the corresponding verb 'to believe' is in common use, whereas this is hardly so of the verb 'to opine'; and as we have seen we want a verbal form available as well as the noun. In fact, perhaps neither 'opinion' nor 'belief' are really adequate translations of what Plato means here by *doxa*. It will be noted that the verb 'to believe' regularly has a 'that' construction after it, i.e. I believe that such and such is the case, whereas Plato seems to be using the noun *doxa* to describe a state of mind that is concerned, in some cases anyhow, simply with an immediate apprehension of, for example, particular sounds, colours, etc. (476b — the lover of sights and sounds "delights in beautiful tones and colours" . . .), i.e. he seems to be using it of a state of mind that is simply an awareness of something (a sound, etc.) and not an awareness *that* something or other is the case. Hence the point made by Murphy (*The Interpretation of Plato's Republic*, p. 103) that "It seems quite inadequate to take it (*doxa*) as 'belief' or 'opinion' since it is chiefly represented here as a faculty of apprehending objects rather than of assent or dissent". He thus suggests that in certain parts of this section of the *Republic* Plato is using *doxa* in a specialised sense, "so that it no longer goes on all fours with the verbs *dokein* and *doxazein*", and translates 'acquaintance', 'unreflective acquaintance with'; yet at the same time he agrees that in this same section it is associated by Plato with these verbs, and that in this association "it seems to mean an unreflective intellectual condition not so much of acquaintance with objects as of uncritical belief about them". It is best then to retain our own translation 'belief' for *doxa*; and it should be added that behind these difficulties about translation there lurks an important philosophical point which is dealt with in the discussion of knowledge and belief in the next chapter (cf. especially p. 176). One thing that is clear about *doxa* is that when Plato uses it in contrast with knowledge it is always in some sense or other an inferior state of mind; in the present section it is inferior because, as we have seen, its objects are mere appearances or copies of the Forms, which are the objects of knowledge; and thus it itself is a dreaming state while the man who possesses knowledge is truly awake.

Plato then has distinguished to his own satisfaction and that of Glaucon the genuine philosopher who possesses knowledge from the non-philosopher who possesses only belief. This has, however, been done only to his own satisfaction and that of Glaucon, in that both of them accept the theory of Forms and the distinction has hinged upon that theory. At the beginning of the discussion it is simply accepted that there are Forms as well as particulars, and the rest of the argument, which establishes the correlations, Forms and knowledge, particulars and belief, depends on this. Anyone who rejects or doubts the theory of Forms will remain unsatisfied, and for this reason, in the second part of his discussion of the difference between the philosopher and the non-philosopher, Plato directs himself to a wider audience — he has to try to convince the non-philosopher himself of the truth of the distinction between knowledge and belief. One commentator has gone so far as to say that the propositions in this second part of the discussion "are not intended by Plato to depend on any theory not expressed in the passage but to be common ground for all schools". We shall see as the argument proceeds that this is perhaps an overstatement. But certainly in the earlier stages of the argument the theory of Forms as such is now much more in the background, and the distinction between knowledge and belief appears, initially anyhow, to be supported by arguments such as one who does not already accept the theory of Forms might be prepared to admit. That those arguments are in parts both difficult and unclear we shall see from their detailed discussion, to which we now turn.

(2) 476d-480. *The argument directed to a wider audience.* It is convenient to take the argument in three stages. (In what follows the expressions 'exists', 'is real', occur as synonyms. Now it could reasonably be objected that they are not in fact synonyms, since 'that x is not real' so far from entailing 'that x does not exist' in fact entails 'that x does exist' — it could not be not a real x unless it existed. Plato, however, does not make this distinction. He uses the Greek word εἶναι (*einai*) both where we would use 'to exist' and where we would use 'to be real', and is further prepared to talk in terms of degrees of existence and reality, i.e. to regard some things as more existent, more real, than other things; and this has an important bearing on his final epistemological and metaphysical views in the *Republic*.) (a) Plato begins with the point that when a man knows, has knowledge, his knowledge must be of something, and of something that exists. We could not have knowledge of the non-existent, the unreal. So knowledge is of the real or existent. With this he contrasts the opposite extreme to knowledge, ignorance, whose object would be the utterly non-existent. 'Ignorance' is introduced as a sort of ideal limit or imaginary extreme in contrast to knowledge — it represents zero on a scale of awareness, while knowledge represents the maximum (cf. the reference in 478e to the two

'extremes'). By it Plato means the complete opposite of knowledge, sheer blank ignorance, whose "object", so far as this notion had any meaning, would be sheer blank nothingness, the non-existent. Now if there is something that both exists and does not exist, then to correspond to this intermediate sort of thing that is partly real, partly unreal, we shall have to look for an intermediate state of mind, that lies between knowledge, whose object is the real, and ignorance, whose object is the totally unreal. In fact, there does seem to be such a state of mind, namely belief, which is a different "power" from knowledge, and whose objects therefore must be different. (b) At this point Plato breaks the argument in order to elucidate the notion of a "power" (*dynamis*), possibly because the use of the word in this sort of context was still unfamiliar at the time when he was writing. The word is usually translated 'faculty', but it simply means 'power' and the more general word 'power' is preferable as a translation. It would seem a pity to commit Plato at the outset to a theory about "faculties", since this apparently precise and explanatory concept has in fact usually caused trouble and shed little light on the problems it was supposed to explain. At the same time, as we shall see, Plato in fact develops the notion of a *dynamis* or power along the lines of the modern notion of a faculty, with consequent difficulties, and thus in the light of his own discussion the translation 'faculty' does little harm. He proceeds then (477c-d) to distinguish a power or faculty by two criteria — (i) by its field of objects, and (ii) by what it effects (in Cornford's translation, 'the state of mind it produces'. Lee's translation 'its function' is less clear. What is meant is that the power or faculty of knowledge, for example, effects or produces knowings or acts of knowing, the power or faculty of belief believings or acts of belief, etc.). The main thread of the argument is then resumed, these criteria for distinguishing a power or faculty having been made clear. It is agreed that knowledge is a faculty, the most powerful of all, and that belief is also a faculty and, as agreed at the end of (a) above, that it is a different faculty from knowledge; and the important point is now made that knowledge is infallible, while belief or opinion is fallible. It thus follows from the discussion of faculties above that, since knowledge and belief are different faculties, they must have different objects. What is known and what is believed cannot be the same. But the object of knowledge is what exists, the real, and thus the object of belief must be something other than what exists. At the same time it cannot be the completely non-existent, for a man who believes must be believing something — a man could not believe and yet believe nothing. Nothing, that which does not exist, is the object of the state of ignorance, which is as we have said a sort of imaginary extreme on the scale of awareness at the opposite end from knowledge. Thus the object of belief is neither what exists, the real, nor that which does not exist, the unreal, and belief is an intermediate state between know-ledge and ignorance, obscurer than knowledge but brighter than ignorance. It remains for us then to discover a field of objects that lie between what exists, the real, and the non-existent, the unreal, which will be the appropriate objects of the intermediate faculty of belief. (c) Plato now proceeds (479a) to the discovery of such intermediate objects. The non-philosopher, the lover of sights and sounds, denies the existence of Forms — he denies, for example, that there is a Form of Beauty, that remains always the same, and instead believes in a multiplicity of beautiful things. But, Plato says, there is none of these beautiful things that will not also appear ugly, and similarly no just or holy action that will not appear unjust or unholy. So again with the many things that are double, any of them appears just as much half as double, and similarly large things may just as much be called small things, or light things heavy things. No one of them is any more what it is said to be than it is not what it is said to be. They are ambiguous and remind one of riddles like that about the eunuch, who is both a man and not a man, and so on. They cannot be fixedly conceived as either being or not being, or as both being and not being, or as neither. They should then be assigned to an intermediate status between being and not being. Hence, then, we have discovered that the many conventional beliefs of the mass of people about beauty, etc. hover about as it were between the non-existent, the unreal, and the fully existent, the fully real. But we had already agreed that if we found any-thing of this sort, it would be the object, not of knowledge, but of belief; it itself, as intermediate between the existent and the non-existent, being apprehended by the intermediate faculty of belief. Those then who have eyes for a multiplicity of beautiful things or just acts, but cannot see the Form of Beauty or the Form of Justice, may be said to believe, but they have no knowledge of the objects of their belief. They are in fact *philodoxoi*, lovers of belief. In contrast, those who can see the Forms themselves in their unchanging reality have knowledge and not belief. They, then, are the genuine philosophers, the lovers of knowledge. Towards the end of the whole argument the theory of Forms has become explicit again, whatever appearance of independence of the theory the earlier part of the argument may have had. Thus once again the lovers of sights and sounds, the non-philosophers, are distinguished from the philosophers, in that the former have only belief, the latter knowledge; and once again, as in the first argument, this result is achieved by drawing the twofold distinction between, on the one hand, two states of mind, knowledge and belief and, on the other hand, two corresponding classes of objects, forms and particulars.

When we look at this more general argument from 476d-480 as a whole, the first stage in it, which we distinguished at (a) above, looks fairly straightforward (though, as we shall see in the next chapter, the straightforwardness is in important ways deceptive). The main point to notice is Plato's insistence that any state of awareness must have its corresponding object. When a man knows, he must know something, his knowledge must have some object, namely, the real. Even the imaginary extreme contrast to knowledge, ignorance, is assigned its object, nothingness. Similarly, if we find something that both exists and does not exist, then there will be some state between knowledge and ignorance of which it is the object. Plato often uses the Greek preposition ἐπί (*epi*) meaning ' upon ' or ' over ' to express this relation — a cognitive state is, or is set, "over" something, i.e. it has an object or field. When we come to the second stage of the argument ((b) above), this point about objects in the sense just explained becomes highly important.

Let us consider the two criteria which Plato gives at (b)

above for distinguishing different powers or faculties. He says they are to be distinguished (i) by their objects, and (ii) by their effects. Criterion (ii) is acceptable enough. Suppose someone asks me the answer to two times six, and I reply twelve, I would be said to know the two times table. But clearly I am not always answering questions about the two times table nor constantly rehearsing it to myself, and yet I would still be said to know it: if I am asked an arithmetical question about it I produce the correct answer. Philosophers have therefore often described knowledge as "dispositional" in character — it is a disposition which is evinced in use as occasion requires. In the *Theaetetus* (197 ff.), when Plato wants to bring out the distinction between knowledge as a disposition and knowledge in use, he begins with a simple example which may help to make the point clear. He says that a man may possess a coat, and thus have it, in the sense that he has bought it and it is his, but he may not have it with him, that is, he may not be wearing it here and now; and similarly that a man may possess knowledge (have it dispositionally) but may not have it to hand (that is, may not be using it here and now). Though we cannot pursue the topic here, it should be noted that this notion of knowledge as a disposition or, more generally, of words with a dispositional meaning, is of considerable philosophical importance. To mention only one example completely outside the present field of discussion, if we say rubber is elastic, it might be said that the word 'elastic' does not describe any feature of the rubber which is immediately present to our senses here and now, such, as, say, its green colour or its smooth texture or anything that is happening to it here and now, but that when we talk of the rubber as elastic what we mean is that, for example, if one were to pull it, it would stretch; i.e. that 'elastic' is a dispositional word or that elasticity is a dispositional property of the rubber, and thus unlike, for example, its smoothness or greenness which are non-dispositional properties. In fact, there are important and difficult philosophical problems involved here, but for our present purposes we can see that there is force in characterising knowledge as a disposition. We can also see that Plato, in describing knowledge in the present passage as a faculty or power, is, in part anyhow, noting the point about knowledge as a disposition; and though perhaps one might have hesitation about this, arising from an unwillingness to be committed to the view that there are mental acts of knowing, we can also for present purposes agree with him that we can distinguish or identify the disposition by what it effects, i.e. that we can identify knowledge as a disposition by the instances in which it is evinced. Further we could agree with the view at 477e that when we do know something, we cannot be mistaken, that knowledge is unerring, whereas this is not true of belief; and from this difference between knowing and believing we could then, using criterion (ii), infer that the faculty or power, which is responsible for cases where we know, is different from the faculty that is responsible for cases where we believe. Thus criterion (ii) works not unreasonably. On the other hand, even granted that we have established in the way just explained that knowledge and belief are different powers, it does not follow that their objects are different; or, putting the matter in the order in which it occurs in the text, it is not clear why, in suggesting criteria for distinguishing these powers of knowledge and belief, Plato should have put forward criterion (i), namely that they differ in their objects. Further, as we have seen from our summary of the argument, this criterion is of the greatest importance, since Plato, having satisfied himself in 477d and e that knowledge and opinion are different faculties, in that knowledge is unerring, belief not, then goes on to argue from the principle embodied in criterion (i) that they must have different objects: "it follows", he says in 478b, "that the objects of knowledge and belief must be different". This in turn leads him on his search for a separate class of objects which will be the appropriate objects for belief, and eventually thus to the establishment of two classes of objects, Forms on the one hand, which are the objects of knowledge, and particulars (the many particular beautiful things, etc.) on the other, which are the objects of belief. But while, as we have seen, there are considerations which lend plausibility to criterion (ii), Plato does not seem to have provided any arguments to persuade us of the truth of criterion (i) which he relies on in the subsequent discussion. Moreover, if, without any preconceived theories, we consider knowledge and belief, which are the two powers with which Plato is especially concerned here, we might well be inclined to think that criterion (i) causes a serious difficulty. Granted that we agree that knowledge and belief are different powers, it follows on criterion (i) that their objects are different, and this would imply that we cannot have belief and knowledge about the same object or thing. In fact, however, we tend to think that we can have first a belief, and then later knowledge, about the same object or thing, or that two different people can have one of them belief and the other knowledge about the same thing. We might want to say that the difference lies in the way of apprehending, and there is no necessary difference in the objects apprehended; indeed, it would seem that Plato himself was committed to the view that his Auxiliaries had true belief about the same things or objects of which his Guardians had knowledge, namely the maintenance of the ideal state. It is obvious that there is a trickiness here in the word 'object' of which we shall have more to say in the next chapter; but, even allowing for that, it seems a fair conclusion that Plato would have to produce arguments not present in this passage if he were to convince us that different powers must be concerned with different objects, or, more specifically, that the objects of knowledge must be different from the objects of belief. He himself, however, assumes that his readers accept that it is so and, in the third stage of the argument ((c) above), he claims to discover the appropriate objects for belief, namely the many beautiful things, just acts, etc., which occupy a midway status between what is completely real or existent and the completely unreal or non-existent, and which thus both are (exist) and are not (do not exist). He does this in the obscure and puzzling arguments which, it will be recalled, begin with the allegation that the world of the lover of belief, the *philodoxos*, is full of contradictions, that there is no particular beautiful thing that will not also appear ugly, and so on. What precisely is Plato saying in these arguments?

The predicates actually discussed at the opening of stage (c) of the argument (479a) at first sight fall into two groups. First there is the group consisting of predicates such as beautiful and ugly, just and unjust, holy and unholy, and secondly the

group consisting of predicates such as double and half, great
and small, light and heavy. These groups seem to be different
in that the second group is composed of predicates which we
would at once recognise as relational. Thus, double, we would
say, is a relational property — a piece of string two feet long is
double a piece of string one foot long; it has this property of
doubleness relatively to something else. Similarly, the same
piece of string two feet long is half a piece of string four feet long;
it has this property of being half relatively to something else.
Contrast this with, say, the colour of the string. If the string
is green in colour we think of the green as a property or characteristic of the string irrespective of its relations to other pieces
of string; or, putting it this way, it makes sense to say that the
string is green, in a way in which it does not make sense to say
simply that the string is double. In the latter case, to make
sense we have to specify that which it is double — it is double
this other piece of string, i.e. double is a relation holding
between two things, while green is a quality or characteristic
that can belong to a single thing, i.e. is a non-relational
property. It looks at first sight as if what we have described
as the first group of properties specified here (beautiful and
ugly, etc.) are of the non-relational type while the second
group (double and half, etc.) are clearly of the relational type.

Assuming this to be so, and beginning with the first group,
let us ask ourselves what particular consideration Plato may
have had primarily in mind in saying that there is no beautiful
thing that will not appear ugly (not beautiful), no just action
that will not also appear unjust, and so on, and why this should
then lead to the important conclusions he subsequently draws
about the semi-reality of particular beautiful things, etc. One
possible reason which might lead to the statement that there
is no beautiful thing that will not appear ugly would be the
fact of change. For example, someone might be beautiful in
youth and ugly in old age. This, however, would not seem a
case for philosophical puzzlement because we would simply
say that at one time or date X was beautiful, at a later time
or date X had changed, and was now ugly. It might be suggested, however, that what Plato had in mind here was change
in a much more radical sense. We know from other parts of

Plato's writings that he was much influenced by the views of
Heracleitus and Cratylus, two of his predecessors in Greek
philosophy. They held that everything is in a state of flux, of
constant change; and when this view if pushed far enough it
would mean that we can apprehend none of the things around
us, since in the very moment when we are trying to apprehend
them they are themselves changing, and thus any knowledge
of them would be impossible. One of the best places to see an
exposition of this view is in Plato's own dialogue, the *Theaetetus*.
The influence of the doctrine is clear in the dialogues he wrote
earlier than the· *Republic*, but it is in the *Theaetetus*, which is
probably slightly later than the *Republic*, that he examines it at
length. For example, at 157 in the *Theaetetus*, in discussing a
form of the flux theory, he points out that it implies that "the
verb 'to be' must be totally abolished" and that "we should
refer to things as 'becoming', 'acting', 'passing away',
'changing', for if you speak in such a way as to make things
stand still you will easily be put in the wrong", and again,
when later he returns (182d) to an extreme form of the theory,
he remarks, taking colour as an example, that on this extreme
view "there is flux even of the whiteness itself, which is passing
over into another colour", and he asks, "is it possible to give
any name to a colour which will properly apply to it?", to
which Theodorus answers, "I don't see how one could, Socrates,
nor yet surely to anything else of that kind, if, being in flux, it
is always quietly slipping away as you speak". Plato himself
is strongly influenced by this Heracleitean view in his own
attitude to the sensible world, i.e. the world revealed to us
through sense perception. He regards sensible things as constantly changing, as unstable, as coming into being, and passing
out of being, as not genuinely existing. Two of his favourite
ways of describing this changing world of sensible particulars
is to call it a world of 'appearances' (*phainomena*) or of 'things
that are becoming' or 'coming into being' (*gignomena*) —
'things that are becoming' in contrast to the Forms which
'are', i.e. are fully real. Is it then this feature of constant and
radical change that Plato has in mind in the present passage,
when he says that there is no beautiful thing that does not also
appear ugly, and so on? It is true that very shortly afterwards

at the beginning of Book VI (485b) when he is about to set out the various qualities required in his rulers in addition to their philosophical knowledge, he refers to one trait of the philosopher ruler as already taken for granted, namely "a constant love for such learning as will reveal to them something of that reality that exists forever, and is not driven to and fro by generation and destruction". The reference is clearly to the discussion in the present passage, and in the reference it will be noted that it is this idea of the sensible world as constantly coming into being and passing away that seems to be uppermost — indeed, the phrase 'generation and destruction' later acquires almost a technical use in this connection. Nevertheless, it does not seem that it is this that is uppermost in Plato's mind when he argues here that there is no beautiful thing that will not appear ugly, and so on. For one thing, there is no explicit reference to the doctrine of change and flux in the present passage. For another, if we now turn to the second group of predicates he discusses, double and half and so on, we can see that, if there is anything queer in describing the same thing both as double and as half, the queerness need not arise from the thing constantly changing; for it is obvious that quite apart from any question of change of any sort, a thing can be double and half: e.g. one piece of string is double another piece and half another piece without any question of its having changed arising. Plato, however, has himself made no distinction between the two groups of predicates (beautiful — ugly, etc., on the one hand, and double — half, etc., on the other), and it looks therefore as though whatever consideration it was that led him to see contradictions arising in the one group would also apply in the other group, and thus that it is not the argument from change that Plato has primarily in mind here.

Now there is a passage in Book VII of the *Republic* (522c ff.), which appears to have a bearing on the present passage. In the Book VII passage Plato is beginning to discuss the higher education of his Guardians, the education which will lead them to rise above sense perception and eventually to come to know the Forms; and he refers there to situations within sense perception where the mind is puzzled by what the senses seem to tell it and is thus led on to further investigation. The situations are those where, as he puts it at 523c, "perception yields a contradictory impression, presenting two opposite qualities with equal clearness". He illustrates what he means by the example of his three fingers — the middle finger, the third and the little finger. Sense perception tells us that they are fingers, and there is nothing here to cause a man to stop and ask himself what a finger is. But the case is different with, for example, the size of the fingers. If we look at our third finger it looks small compared with the middle finger, but large compared with the little finger. Thus the senses report the same thing (the third finger) to be both large and small; similarly with cases of thick and thin, hard and soft, light and heavy. Such reports, Plato argues, are strange or paradoxical. Our sense of sight seems to confuse together the large and the small, and our intelligence is thus compelled, in order to clear up the confusion, to sort out the large and the small as distinct things, and to ask itself what then are the large and the small. In this way we come to distinguish the objects of intelligence (the Large, Largeness, the Small, Smallness, etc.) from the objects of sight. It will be noted that here again, as in the Book V passage, Plato is referring to alleged puzzles that arise in sense perception, where the senses tell us that the same thing is both large and small, etc., and it will be also noted that in this Book VII passage it is puzzles arising from relational properties that he quotes, large and small, light and heavy, and so on, i.e. from the type of predicates that appears in the second group in the Book V passage. It would seem then that Plato believed that what we would call relational properties somehow generate problems within sense perception. It would also seem that in our present Book V passage he thinks these problems are such that we ourselves are thrown into confusion if we confine ourselves to sense perception, i.e. to the world of the lover of sights and sounds, to the world of belief, and that the reality of the sensible objects that display these relational characteristics is somehow called in question. It is difficult, however, for us to see why confusion should arise from the use of relative terms. The piece of string two feet long is double in length a piece one foot long, and half in length a piece four feet long; so, if you like, the same piece of string is both double and half, and no puzzlement or momentous consequences follow. Only, we must note, we would not ourselves say that the string was both double and half because this in itself would be an incomplete statement; we would have to specify what it was double and what it was half. Similarly, it would not make sense in itself to say a shilling was half and double, but perfectly good, and to us perfectly clear, sense to say a shilling is half a florin and double a sixpence. The same is true of the other cases, large and small, etc., for though it does look at first sight as though large, for example, was not relative in the same way, in fact it is, for a thing is only large relatively to something else: e.g. in Plato's own case the middle finger is large relatively to the other two fingers: it is larger than they are, though it itself is smaller than, say, a walking-stick. That is, half and double, large and small, and the other concepts in Plato's second group here are relational concepts, and as such require at least two terms — at least two terms, because some relations require more, e.g. the relation 'between' requires three terms. The point is that a relation holds between two (or more) terms and cannot be predicated of a single term (note that this is so even in the special cases of equal to, identical with, where we say that A is equal to itself, or identical with itself — even here we cannot simply say A is equal or A is identical). To predicate a relation of a single term, to say simply 'x is double', would be, we would say, to misunderstand the logic of relational expressions; and once we were clear about this the puzzle Plato finds would disappear. It would seem then that if we are right in thinking that this is Plato's argument here, it is a bad argument and nothing has been established about the self-contradictory nature of sense experience. That Plato found relational properties puzzling can be seen elsewhere in the dialogues as well. A good example occurs in the *Theaetetus* at the point where Plato is developing a relativist view of sense perception along Heracleitean lines, i.e. a view which would maintain that colours and other qualities are entirely relative to the observer and do not exist in things themselves. Apparently by way of supporting this theory and illustrating the difficulty of holding that qualities exist in the things themselves, he takes (*Theaetetus* 154c) the case of six dice, which are

more than four dice, i.e. half as many again, and at the same
time less than twelve dice, i.e. half the number, without anything having been added to or taken away from the original
six dice.   Again at 155b the example is used of Socrates himself, who may within a single year be at one time bigger than
the boy Theaetetus, and later, without himself having changed
in any way, be smaller than Theaetetus, who has grown meantime.   But how could he, without himself changing, be both
bigger than and smaller?   For our present purposes the interesting points here are first that, again, relational concepts are
being considered — half, double, bigger, smaller; that again
such concepts are found to be puzzling — Socrates refers to
such cases as puzzles and Theaetetus agrees that sometimes
when he considers them he feels "quite giddy"; and thirdly
that the puzzlement seems to arise from regarding these relational characteristics as though they were non-relational
characteristics.   To amplify the latter point, it looks as though
Plato does not distinguish here between relational concepts
like double and non-relational concepts like white.   Hence the
argument here seems to run like this; "it might be plausible
to say that a colour like, for example, white exists in the object,
and thus a relativist theory of sense perception, i.e. a theory
that said the colour does not exist in the object, but is purely
relative to the observer, would not be necessary.   But how could
you possibly say this in the case of double and half or in the
case of large and small, since in these cases, the same thing,
without changing, would have to be both double and half,
both large and small; but how could it?   These latter cases,
therefore, illustrate in a striking way the difficulty of supposing
that *any* qualities exist in the object".   This seems to be the
gist of the argument here, and if so, this *Theaetetus* passage
again illustrates Plato's failure to distinguish between two
different sorts of concepts, relational and non-relational, and
the unreal puzzles that are consequently generated.

Let us suppose then, following the clue supplied by Plato's
second group of predicates in the present Book V passage, that
it is by this, as we have seen unconvincing, argument from
relational concepts that Plato is seeking to generate puzzles
and contradictions within sense perception.   It will be recalled

that we said above that, since Plato himself makes no distinction between the two groups, it seems likely that he thought both groups led to contradictions in the same sort of way. What then are we to say of the first group of concepts, i.e. beautiful and ugly, just and unjust, and so on? It looks as though we will have to say that Plato here is regarding this set of concepts also as in some way relational. Again he has not made this clear, and certainly, at first sight, it looks as though, for example, the word 'just' behaves differently from the word 'double', in that to say 'x is double' is obviously an incomplete expression, there is something wrong with its logical grammar, whereas the same is not obvious in the case of 'x is just'. One possible way in which Plato may have regarded these evaluative concepts, just, beautiful, etc., as used in everyday life, as relational is suggested by, for example, the discussion of justice in Book I of the *Republic*. There, Cephalus holds that justice or right consists in telling the truth and paying one's debts, but Socrates at once points out (331c) that such an action would be sometimes right and sometimes wrong — wrong if, for example, we had borrowed a weapon and the friend from whom we had borrowed it meantime went mad. This would mean then that, if we confined ourselves to the world of particular acts, a particular type of act, such as returning what was owing, would be right in some circumstances and wrong in others. That is, there would be two factors involved, the act itself and the circumstances to which it was a response, and the notion of justice would be relational, in that it concerned the act in relation to the circumstances — we could not say simply "returning what we owe is just", but we would have to specify the circumstances — "when the friend is sane", etc. In many of the earlier dialogues Plato is concerned to show this relativity to situations of particular acts — e.g. in the *Euthyphro* the same sort of thing is done in the case of righteous or holy acts. Similarly perhaps in the case of beauty, Plato might have argued that (N. R. Murphy, *Interpretation of Plato's Republic*, p. 109) "The complexion that we would admire on Penelope would be as grotesque on the much enduring Ulysses as his on her. The complexion therefore is not intrinsically beautiful or it would always be so; its beauty lies in its suitable relation with the whole to which it belongs". No particular act then, is intrinsically just, no feature intrinsically beautiful, but the justice or beauty of particular things is relative. If this is correct, then in fact for Plato the two groups of concepts we have distinguished would in this way not be fundamentally different — they would both be groups of relational concepts.

Assuming then that this is so, we must repeat what we said above that relational concepts, when rightly understood, do not produce the puzzling situations of the sort Plato seems to envisage and to require in the present passage. Granted an act is just in this set of circumstances, and the same type of act unjust in different circumstances, or granted that the dice are double in relation to this number of dice and half in relation to that number, this does not establish that particulars have contradictory attributes, that returning what is owing is both just and unjust, or that six dice are both double and half — the contradiction disappears when the other term of the relational characteristic is specified. Yet the present argument would seem to require that one and the same particular act done in one and the same particular situation is both right and wrong, and so on with the other cases. Our conclusion then must be that, if we have interpreted the argument rightly, it fails in its ostensible purpose. It might perhaps be granted to Plato that relational characteristics do cause a certain puzzlement and stimulate thought in a way that non-relational characteristics do not; but if this is said, it must be made clear that the puzzlement is not of the extreme sort that Plato represents. It is not that we find particulars self-contradictory because of their relational characteristics, and thus are so completely baffled by them that we ask ourselves but how can what is right also be wrong, and so on. What would be meant instead would be this. In this circumstance and in that, returning what is owing is regarded as right, but in this different situation or in that, the same type of act is judged to be wrong. So while sometimes returning what is owing is right, at other times it is wrong. This may then lead us on to ask what then is rightness itself, which an act like returning what is owing sometimes seems to display and sometimes not. Clearly a type of action

like returning what is owing is not intrinsically right; if someone asked what is justice or rightness we could not answer
"returning what is owing" because there are cases where to
do this would be wrong; and similarly for any other type of
particular act; just as at 524, which we referred to above, sight
is said to perceive both large and small, only not as separate,
but in a confused sort of way, and we are thus prompted to ask
what is meant by largeness or smallness. In this sort of situation Plato sees the beginning of the search for the Forms — to
ask oneself what is justice itself as contrasted with particular
just acts which on occasion may be unjust, or to ask what is
largeness itself as contrasted with any particular large things
which on occasion relatively to certain other things may themselves be small. This, for him, is to ask about the unchanging
Forms, to whose presence in them particular things owe such
characteristics as they from time to time possess. It is the
beginning too of the corresponding transition from belief to
knowledge. The point then would be that on Plato's view
relational characteristics are particularly suited to stimulate
reflection — and this is, of course, the use they are put to in
the argument in the Book VII passage — and thus, as he believes, to lead us on to see the necessity for Forms and to pass
from belief to knowledge. While, however, they might thus
illustrate the need for further reflection on sensible particulars,
they would not, as seems to be claimed in the Book V passage,
show the sensible world to be self-contradictory.

Moreover, if our explanation of the present passage is correct, at best Plato would only have shown that it is particulars
with relational characteristics that cause perplexity, and thus
are objects only of belief; and nothing would have been said
to show that this is so in cases where there are no relational
complications. But it is clear from many places in Plato that
he would want the conclusion of the present passage — namely
that particulars are not fully real, and that they are the objects
of belief and not of knowledge — to apply to all particulars.
In fact, then, the argument from relational characteristics
would have to be supplemented from other sources, from, for
example, the argument Plato uses elsewhere, that sensible
things are in a state of constant change, to which we referred

earlier.   Again, there is an interesting passage in the *Phaedo* (74) which at first seems to follow the lines of the present passage.   Plato refers to things we call equal, e.g. two pieces of wood that are equal, and points out that the same pieces of wood may seem to one man equal and to another unequal, and thus these so-called equal things must be distinguished from the Equal itself (i.e. the Form of Equality).   He then goes on to say, and this is another important aspect of the theory of Forms, that the particular equal things fall short of perfect Equality, are inferior to it, are imperfect resemblances of it; they strive to be like the Equal, but fall short of it; and in 75 he says that all this just as much applies to Beauty itself, Good itself, Just itself, and so on.   This will mean then that in all these cases particular beautiful things, particular just acts and so on, are inferior to the Forms, fall short of them.   The Forms here are ideal standards of perfection, to which imperfect particulars approximate.   If we use this latter argument, then we could go on to say that, for example, any particular beautiful thing when compared to the ideal, i.e. the Form of Beauty, is not beautiful, is ugly, in as much as it falls so far short of perfect Beauty, the Form of Beauty.   The point then would be, as R. S. Bluck puts it (*Plato's Phaedo*, p. 178), that particulars "cannot strictly be said to possess any *distinct* character at all — compare the words in 479a, 'whatever any one of these things may be said to be can you say that it absolutely *is* that, any more than it *is not* that?' ".   Now it may be that in fact it is these other more general arguments, whether the Heracleitean form of argument from constant change, to which we have already referred, or this argument from imperfection just discussed, that are really behind the present passage in Book V.   Plato has not made the position clear.   Our own suggestion, using the Book VII passage (523-525) as a clue, has been that it is rather the argument arising from the alleged complications about relational characteristics that underlies what Plato says here, and we have tried to follow out and discuss the shortcomings of that argument.

We are not, however, out of the wood yet in this third stage of the present argument, for it will be recalled that Plato, having established to his satisfaction that there is no particular beautiful thing that will not also appear ugly, i.e. not beautiful, and so on, then appears to move from this position that a particular thing both is and is not such and such to the conclusion that therefore the thing itself both is and is not, i.e. both exists and does not exist, is both real and unreal. This move can be seen at 479c where Socrates asks, "do you know how to dispose of them [i.e. the particular things or acts] or can you think of a better position for them than to place them between being [or existence or reality] and not being [or non-existence or un-reality]"? And this move is necessary in order to provide objects for belief that occupy an intermediate status between the objects of knowledge, which are completely real, and the objects of ignorance, which are completely unreal. Now this argument seems to assume that when we say *s* (a subject) is not *p* (a predicate), e.g. when we say this act is not just, we are denying that *s* is in the sense of exists, just as it assumes that when we say *s* is *p* (e.g. this same act is just) we are assert-ing that *s* is, in the sense of exists. It is by this means that having established that *s* (a particular right act) is both *p* (just) and not *p* (unjust) we reach the conclusion that therefore *s* exists and does not exist. If this is Plato's argument here, and again it does seem to be, it is a bad argument, for to us it would seem to rest on a confusion between the use of 'is' as the copula or joining word, and the use of 'is' in an existential sense. To explain, and to take the existential use of 'is' first, this use is not very common in our language, but it does occur. Perhaps one of the most familiar cases is in the phrase 'God is' which means 'God exists', where 'is' is being used existentially — compare also Hamlet's 'to be or not to be', where 'to be' means to live or exist. For us, however, this is a somewhat unusual use of the verb to be — some philosophers would think a queer use. Contrast this with the common use in a sentence like 'the lemon is yellow', where 'is' here does not mean exists, but is a linking or joining word, by which we connect the attribute of yellow with the lemon. If the lemon is in a dish along with some oranges and walnuts we might say (1) 'The lemon is small compared with the oranges, but large (i.e. not small) compared with the walnuts', and here again 'is' would be being used as the copula. We could not then move from this sentence to (2) 'The lemon is both small and not small' and thence to the conclusion (3) 'the lemon both is and is not, i.e. both exists and does not exist'. In (2) we have now omitted to specify what the lemon is small or not small in comparison with and the contradiction is thus only apparent; and in any case at (3), leaving aside the difficulty about (2), we have passed from the use of 'is' as the copula, which was still the use in (2), to the existential use of 'is' equivalent to 'exists'. But if we say 'the lemon is yellow', 'is' is not being used here in such a way as to assert the lemon's existence, and similarly, if we say 'the lemon is not yellow', 'is not' is not being used in such a way as to deny the existence of the lemon. It has been thought that Plato could not have made such a "fantastic blunder" or "been so misled by current sophistries about negation, sophistries that he himself afterwards treated with contempt, as to suppose that in denying A to be B we are throwing doubt on A's existence"; and it has to be noted that in a later dialogue, the *Sophist*, Plato himself argued that when we say *s* is not *p* we are not denying existence to *s* but affirming *s* to be qualified by another predicate than *p*, i.e. affirming it to be other than *p*. It is not at all certain, however, that at the time when Plato wrote the *Republic* the confusion about negative judgment would in fact have been "a fantastic blunder". It is clear that about this time and a little earlier, many people, including Plato himself, were perplexed about predication, i.e. about how we are able to assign certain attributes to a subject, to say, for example, 'the lemon is yellow, bitter,' etc., and equally how we are able to deny attributes to a subject, for example, to say 'the lemon is not green, not sweet, etc.'. When one reads the *Sophist* one can see the effort that went into Plato's own solution to the problem of negative judgment, and the solution that 'is not *p*' is to be taken as 'is other than *p*' is obviously regarded as an important discovery. And rightly, since negative judgment does have problems with which philosophers still concern themselves. It should also be noted that while, as was remarked above, in English the verb 'to be' is not normally used meaning 'to exist', the Greek verb εἶναι (*einai*) can be regularly so used in addition to its use in predication; i.e. in Greek the same word *esti* is used in the sentence 'the man exists' and in the sentence 'the man is tall'; and this again makes it more difficult to see what is happening in a sentence like 'the man is not tall', and more easy to suppose that in the case of such a negative judgment one is somehow denying the man's existence. At any rate it does seem that in the present passage Plato has mistakenly assumed that a negative judgment such as 'this act is not right' involves the non-existence of the act itself. Once again we should note, however, that if in fact what Plato has in mind in the whole of the present passage is the more general arguments from the semi-reality of particulars to which we have already referred, the argument from change and the argument from imperfection, what we have just said would require revision; for now presumably he would not be seeking to establish the semi-reality of particulars from the alleged fact that they can bear contradictory attributes. He would instead be saying: because particulars are constantly changing and fall short of the perfection of the Forms, (a) they no more possess an attribute than they possess its opposite, e.g. a particular act is no more right than it is not right, and (b) they are to be assigned to an intermediate status between being and not being. The important word here would be the word 'and'; for in this case he would not be seeking to establish proposition (b) from proposition (a) in the way we have just discussed, but (a) and (b) would be two propositions that both derived from the general considerations about change and imperfection. But here again all one can say is that this does not seem to be the run of the argument in the passage. Instead, as explained above, Plato seems mistakenly to try to establish proposition (b) from proposition (a) and what seems to underlie proposition (a) itself is the alleged difficulty about relational characteristics.

It can be seen from our discussion that this part of the *Republic* from 476d-480 is puzzling and unsatisfactory — unsatisfactory because there is doubt about the actual arguments themselves, quite apart from the question of whether they are good or bad arguments. The attempt, however, to unravel them is well worth while since, even if at the end of it all we are still dissatisfied, we have learnt a good deal by the way. Also what emerges clearly from the whole passage 475e-480d with its two parts, 475e-476d directed to those who accept the theory of Forms, and 476d-480 directed to a wider audience, is the distinction between knowledge and belief, with the corresponding distinction between two different classes of objects, Forms which are truly real and are the objects of knowledge, and the many particular things and acts of the everyday world which fluctuate between existence and non-existence, are only semi-real, and are the objects of belief. Books VI and VII have more to say on these topics amongst others, and it may thus be helpful, before we return to a detailed examination of these later books, to pause at this point and devote a chapter to a somewhat more general consideration of knowledge, belief and the Forms.

Chapter 8

KNOWLEDGE, BELIEF AND THE FORMS

As we have seen, Plato, in order to distinguish between the philosopher and the non-philosopher, draws a distinction between knowledge and belief, and in doing this he makes a two-fold distinction between, on the one hand, two different states of mind, and on the other between two different sets of objects corresponding to these different states of mind. The philosopher's state of mind is knowledge and its objects are Beauty itself, Justice itself, and so on (i.e. the Forms); the non-philosopher's state of mind is belief and its objects are the many particular things, just acts and so on. We ought now to ask ourselves whether there is in fact a distinction to be drawn between knowledge and belief, and if there is, whether Plato's way of representing the distinction is satisfactory.

(1) *The distinction itself.* To say 'I know that such and such' is to say something logically different from 'I believe that such and such'. If I say 'I know that two and two are four', in saying 'I know' I am committing myself to the position that what I know is true, that I can't be wrong, i.e. that two and two cannot but be four. To put it generally, if I say 'I know that p' (where p is any proposition), then the statement 'I know that p' entails 'p is true'. Notice that it does not follow that p is in fact true. It may be that I have been mistaken in claiming to know that p, and thereby committing myself to the position that p is true: p may in fact be false. It is still true, however, that so far as I am concerned, by using the word 'know' I committed myself to the truth of p. If it turns out that p is in fact false, then my claim to knowledge was mistaken. Now contrast this with the use of the word 'believe' when for example, I say, 'I believe that the Prime Minister of Great Britain and the President of the United States met last June'.

In using the word 'believe' I do not commit myself to the position that I cannot be wrong about such a meeting. I have a certain amount of evidence about it.   I seem to remember reading about it in the Press or hearing something about it on the radio, and so I believe that such a meeting took place ; but I am prepared to admit that I may be wrong, that p may be false. Notice, too, that the strength of my beliefs may vary. I may very strongly believe that there was such a meeting because I clearly remember reading about it in *The Times* and seeing pictures of it on television and noting references to it since, or I may just believe there was such a meeting because I was out of the country at the time but seem to remember reading something about it in a foreign newspaper.   In the first case I have good evidence for my belief and hold it strongly, in the second less good evidence, and I hold it less strongly ; but in both cases alike, though in different degrees, I am pre- pared to admit that I may be wrong. Now contrast this with the use of the verb to know. If I say 'I know that the Prime Minister and the President met last June' I am excluding the possibility that I may be wrong, that p may turn out to be false. If, in fact, it is subsequently shown that the Prime Minister and the President were each in their own countries at the time in question, and could not have met, my claim to knowledge is seen to have been mistaken and I shall have to withdraw altogether my statement that I knew they had met. If, how- ever, all I said originally was that I believed they had met, there is no need to withdraw my statement that I so believed. What has happened is that my belief has been shown to be false. I believed, falsely as it turns out, that p.   The position can be brought out in this way.   In the first case, looking back on the whole situation, what we would *not* say is, 'so he knew falsely that p'.   What we have to say is 'so he did not know after all', i.e. he made a mistaken claim to knowledge.   In the second case, however, what we do say is 'so he believed falsely that p', 'his belief that p was false', and we would not say 'so he did not believe after all'.   Again, while, as we said above, the notion of degrees makes sense with a belief — a very strong belief that, a belief that, a weak belief that ('I believe there was a meeting though I may be mistaken') — such a notion does not make sense in the case of knowledge : i.e. we could not say 'he knows very strongly or confidently that', 'he knows less strongly or confidently that'. In the case of knowing you either know or you don't know. It is a knock-down business with no degrees in it.

It would thus seem even from these brief considerations that there are logical differences between the verb 'to know' and the verb 'to believe', or to put the matter in a more familiar way, that there is a distinction between knowledge and belief, and that Plato was correct in drawing a distinction between them; and further that, since the verb 'to know' is a powerful word — in Plato's language (477d) "knowledge is the most powerful of all the faculties" — the distinction is one of importance.

(2) *Plato's development of the distinction.* Granted then that it is important to distinguish between knowledge and belief, we have now to consider whether Plato's way of representing the distinction is satisfactory. As we have already pointed out he draws a twofold distinction; (a) a distinction between the two states of mind, knowledge and belief, and (b) a distinction between two classes of objects, Forms on the one hand, and the many particular things on the other, corresponding to these two states of mind. It will be convenient to consider (a) and (b) separately.

(a) *The distinction between knowledge and belief as states of mind.* It will be remembered that in the important passage 477c Plato described knowledge and belief as powers or faculties, but in other places he seems to be thinking of them rather as conditions or states of mind brought about by the exercise of the respective faculties, and later at 511d he explicitly calls them conditions or states of mind (*pathemata en te psyche*). For our immediate purposes, then, we can regard them as states of mind, and as such Plato points out at 477e that they are to be distinguished in that knowledge is infallible, cannot be mistaken, whereas belief is fallible, can make mistakes. In the present context this is all he has to say on the distinction between knowledge and belief as states of mind, and the rest of the passage is devoted to the development of the distinction at (b) above between the two different classes of objects corresponding to these two different states. From other parts of his

writings, however, we can add some further points. In the
Timaeus (51c), where incidentally as in the present passage of
the *Republic* Plato is arguing from the difference between knowledge and belief to a difference in their objects, he says that
rational understanding or knowledge and true belief differ in
that the former is produced by instruction, the latter by persuasion; the former can always give a true account of itself,
the latter can give none; and the former cannot be shaken by
persuasion whereas the other can be won over. These differences can be illustrated from elsewhere in the dialogues: the
"accountability" characteristic of knowledge, for example, is
illustrated later in the *Republic* itself at 506c where Plato distinguishes knowledge from true belief on the ground that the
latter is "without understanding", cannot, that is, in the
language of the *Timaeus*, give an account of itself. Similarly
in the *Meno* (98a) it is said that true beliefs are liable to run
away out of the mind of a man and thus not to be worth much,
until one binds them down "by a reckoning of the cause".
When they are so bound down they become knowledge and
remain stable. What Plato seems to mean is that unless you
understand why a statement p is true, then you do not know
that p, but have only a true belief; and in the *Meno* passage
the point is added that the latter is unstable, liable to change.
Thus Cornford and Lee are both somewhat misleading in their
translation of the passage at *Republic* 506c, since Lee represents
Plato as talking of "a true but unthinking opinion", and
Cornford translates "a true belief without intelligence", both
translations possibly suggesting that there is something silly
or stupid about a true belief; but Plato does not mean that.
The belief might be quite intelligent in our ordinary sense of
that word. Plato's point is that it remains only a belief unless
the holder of it has "understanding", i.e. grasps why it is true,
is able to give an account of it. Again the influence of persuasion on beliefs is brought out in the *Theaetetus* (201), where
knowledge is distinguished from true opinion on the ground
that a jury, though they do not have knowledge of some matter,
may nevertheless be rightly persuaded to form a true belief
about it and so reach a proper verdict. If we put all this together, Plato is then saying that we can distinguish belief from

knowledge as states of mind in that (1) (from our present passage 477e) belief is liable to error, knowledge not, and (from elsewhere) (2) belief can be produced and changed by persuasion, knowledge not, and (3) in the case of belief we do not understand why a proposition is true, whereas in knowledge we do. Now there may be points to disagree with here. It might be said, for example, that the approach is too psychological — that if one wants to distinguish between knowledge and belief one should think rather of the logical differences involved in the use of the verbs 'to know' and 'to believe', instead of becoming involved in attempting to discriminate between different states of mind. By and large, however, for our present purposes, we might say that the points Plato makes are not unreasonable. In particular his point in the present passage, which is the one with which we are directly concerned, namely that knowledge excludes error, whereas this is not so in the case of belief, and that they are thus distinguishable, is one that we ought to accept, even though we might want to frame it differently. We could then say that, so far, there is no reason for serious quarrel with the way in which Plato develops the distinction between knowledge and belief.

(b) *The distinction between knowledge and belief in respect to their objects*. It is when we come to this distinction that serious difficulties begin, difficulties moreover which raise points of much general philosophical importance. It is important, therefore, on both counts to spend some time on them. We said earlier (Chapter 7, p. 151), when we were discussing Plato's principle at 477d that different faculties are to be distinguished by the difference in their objects, that it seemed in fact that different faculties could have the same object, that for example one could come to know some thing or object about which one had previously only a true belief, or again that it could be said that the Guardians in Plato's own city had knowledge, and the Auxiliaries true belief, about the same object, namely the maintenance of the ideal state. At the same time we agreed that there was a trickiness in the word 'object' here, and it is time now to say more about this.

(1) If we consider the verb 'to know' there are two familiar uses of the word. (a) We may use it with a noun immediately

following which grammatically is the direct object of the verb. In this use we could speak of knowing a person, or a thing, or a place — for example, I know Jones, I know his yacht the *Sally Anne*, and I know the anchorage where he moors her. Here we are using 'know' to mean 'am acquainted with' — I have seen and spoken to Jones often, I've been on the *Sally Anne*, and so on. In this use of the verb 'to know' we can in ordinary speech sensibly talk of knowing things or objects. This notion of direct acquaintance with something, developed in a certain specialised way, has been prominent in many philosophical theories and has been given the label 'knowledge by acquaintance'. For our immediate purposes the important point is that there is a familiar use of the verb 'to know' with a noun or pronoun immediately following which is grammatically the direct object of the verb, such that we can speak of knowing things or objects. (b) There is also, however, a very familiar use where the verb is not followed directly by a noun, but instead by a 'that' clause: for example, 'I know that China is a large country', 'that swallows are migrants', 'that light travels at a speed of 186,000 feet per second', and so on. In this case I may never, for example, have been to China, have no direct acquaintance with it, but from reading books on geography, looking at maps and so on, I know that it is a large country. This is clearly a very important use of the verb 'to know', since when we reflect we realise that most of such knowledge as we claim to have takes the form of knowing that something or other is so and so. Again, for this use of the verb 'to know' philosophers have a label — 'knowledge by description'. The example just given about China will help in fact to explain the label: I have no direct acquaintance with China but have read descriptions of it, and so know it by description. Now in this case, unlike (a), what immediately follows the verb is not a noun or a pronoun but a 'that' clause. In this case then, what I know is not a thing or object in any ordinary sense; instead, what I know is that something or other is so and so. It would seem, then, that in this use of the verb 'to know' we ought to be very suspicious of talk in terms of 'knowing objects' or of 'the objects of knowledge'. We shall come back to this shortly.

Meantime (2) let us see how the verb 'to believe' behaves in this respect. What strikes us at once here is that there seems to be no use corresponding to the use of the verb 'to know' as at (a) above where the verb is followed by a noun or pronoun which is grammatically its direct object. We must not be misled by a sentence like 'I believe Jones'. This is not at all like 'I know Jones' — Jones is not grammatically the direct object and what we are really saying is 'I believe that Jones is speaking the truth', i.e. the grammatical object of the verb is really a 'that' clause. In fact it seems that there is no use of the verb 'to believe' corresponding to the use of 'know' at (a) above. When we believe, what we believe is expressed as a 'that' clause; that is to say, in this respect the use of the verb 'to believe' follows the use of the verb 'to know' at (b) above. Thus if we were to talk about the 'objects' of belief, again we would be using 'object' in the highly suspect way to which we have already referred. But before we discuss this further there is a third point to notice.

(3) If we consider again the distinction Plato draws at 477c between knowledge and belief — knowledge is infallible, unerring, whereas belief is not so, can make mistakes — two points arise. In the first place, the sense in which knowledge is unerring should be the same as that in which belief is liable to error. We have, however, seen at (2) that in the case of belief, what we believe is expressed in a 'that' clause, and in this case error must arise when the 'that' clause is false. Thus the error here is related to the truth or falsity of the 'that' clause. Similarly then in the case of knowledge, the unerring nature of knowledge should be related to the truth or falsity of the 'that' clause which expresses what we claim to know — in the case of a correct claim to knowledge the 'that' clause must always be true. It is, however, only in the use of the verb 'to know' at (1) (b) above, i.e. where we are talking about knowledge by description, that this arises, and once again this is the use of 'know' where we have already questioned talk about 'objects' of knowledge. Indeed, secondly, even apart from this, the criterion that knowledge cannot be mistaken does not easily fit the use of 'know' at 1(a) above, i.e. knowledge by acquaintance. It seems as though in the case of knowledge by acquaintance you are either acquainted with a

thing or are not acquainted with it, and in neither case does the question of truth or error arise. Alternatively, if a place were sought for error by saying that sometimes one might fail to recognise subsequently something one was already acquainted with, then this would be to allow that knowledge by acquaintance could be mistaken. The case is quite different with (1) (b) above, where questions of truth and error are in order, since in (1) (b) what one wants to say is that in claiming to know that something or other is the case, one is claiming that the 'that' clause is true, and thus knowledge is in this way unerring, excludes the possibility of mistake. But this again leads us back to knowledge that, as opposed to knowledge of things or objects.

(4) It is time now to return to the consideration of the use of the notion of 'objects' in connection with knowledge and belief. When Plato asks at the very end of 476 whether a man who knows knows something or nothing we are inclined to agree with Glaucon's answer that he knows something. Similarly Plato's remark (at 478b) that a man cannot believe and yet believe nothing (the 'in' in Lee's translation 'believe in nothing' should be omitted) seems innocuous enough. It looks then as though we would all agree that when a man knows he knows something, and similarly when he believes he believes something. The trouble lies in the ambiguity in the word 'something'. This can be seen in the discussion in the text, since Plato there proceeds to argue that in the case of knowledge the something that is known must be something that is real, and that in the case of belief, while the something believed cannot be real, as in the case of knowledge, it must nevertheless have some sort of reality, cannot be completely unreal — if it were the latter then in belief we would be believing the completely unreal, i.e. nothing. Hence then the subsequent argument by which Plato seeks to show that the objects of belief are the many particular things which occupy a half-way position between the completely real, which is the object of knowledge, and the completely unreal. In both cases, then, Plato is committed to a search for appropriate objects and in both cases the objects must have some sort of reality. Now if we consider knowledge by acquaintance at (1) (a) above, it is plausible to say that if I am acquainted with something, there must be a

real something for me to be acquainted with.   If I know Jones
i.e. am acquainted with him, then there must be a real person
Jones for me to know — I can see him and hear him and touch
him.   Similarly, if I know his yacht, there must be a yacht
which I can see and touch and climb aboard and so on.   In
this context then it is plausible to talk in terms of real objects
or things — if there were no such real objects then there would
be nothing to be acquainted with.   The situation, however, is
quite different, in the case of knowledge by description at
(1)(b) above, and with belief at (2) above.   In both these
cases, as we have already agreed, what we know or believe is
that such and such is so and so.   The 'object' then, if we were to
use that word, that we know or believe in these cases appears
in the form of a 'that' clause. But in these cases what are we then
to make of Plato's argument that the 'object' must have some
sort of reality, that otherwise we would not know or believe
at all ?   Suppose I believe that there is a desk in the next room.
Following Plato's line of argument the 'that' clause will be the
object of my belief.   It seems clear that it is a mistake to raise
questions about the reality of this sort of object as we could
raise questions about the reality of what we familiarly call
objects, such as desks or chairs.   To ask whether 'that there
is a desk in the next room' is real or unreal or semi-real is to
ask a question that is void of application.   Whether there really
is a desk next door or not, my belief is still the same.   Only, if
there is no desk next door, the belief is false.   For this latter
reason it is clear, too, that it is not possible to hold that the
'object' of a belief, meaning by this the 'that' clause, must have
some sort of reality in the sense that what I believe to be the
case must in some sense be the case ; for when I believe that
something is the case, as we have already seen at (3) above,
nothing follows about the truth or falsity of what I believe :
what I believe may be the case, but it may just as well not be
the case, i.e. my belief may be false.   Our conclusion then from
this must be that while it is in order to talk of objects and the
reality of objects in the case of knowledge by acquaintance, in
the case of knowledge by description and of belief such talk is
mistaken or at best highly misleading.   Moreover, in the present
case it has the very important consequence that Plato uses it in

establishing a wide-reaching metaphysical view which distinguishes between two classes of objects, Forms on the one
hand and sensible particulars on the other, and two levels of
reality or existence, that of the Forms, which are completely
real or existent, and that of the sensible particulars, which are
semi-real, partly existent and partly non-existent.

(5) Finally, it is worth asking why Plato should have become
involved in these difficulties, and here two points suggest themselves.   (a) It is true that when Plato is considering knowledge,
or belief, or indeed thinking generally, he tends to take as his
model sense-awareness, i.e. our apprehension through our sense
organs of the world surrounding us, and particularly the model
of sight and touch.   For example, in the *Republic* itself at 476b
the lover of sights and sounds cannot "see" the nature of the
Beautiful itself (where the "seeing" is not seeing with the eyes
but seeing so to speak with the mind's eye), and so again at
479e; again at 511a the Forms are "seen" by thought (compare 533d 'the eye of the soul'); or again 511b, reason
"grasps" the first principle of everything (where the Greek
verb means ' to lay hold of ', 'grasp', 'touch', and Lee's translation 'reached' somewhat obscures the point).   There is a
passage in the *Theaetetus*, 188e ff., where Plato is discussing
false judgment, which brings this out strikingly.   There it is
argued that it is not possible for a man to see something and
yet see nothing — if he is seeing any one thing he must be
seeing a thing which is (i.e. exists), and similarly with hearing
and touching.   Similarly, then, a man who is judging some one
thing is judging something which is (exists).   A man who
judged something which is not (i.e. falsely) would be judging
nothing, and a man judging nothing would not be judging at
all.   Plato is not content to accept this argument and proceeds
to try to account for false judgment in several different ways.
None of these accounts, however, is really successful, and the
whole section in the *Theaetetus* again shows the influence on
Plato of the model of awareness through the senses, i.e. through
sight, touch, etc., when he comes to consider knowing, believing, and so on.   Hence it has been said that Plato tends to
regard thinking as a sort of ghostly sensing.   The influence
on Plato of the analogy from sense-awareness, from seeing,

touching, and so on, when he is discussing knowledge and belief can be overstressed. For example, so far as language is concerned, we ourselves very frequently use the language of sight and touch in the same context ('he grasped the solution', 'he saw the answer', etc.); and again, there are elements in Plato's thought that point in a different direction. Still, it is true that when he is talking of knowledge and belief the model of seeing or touching does seem to be prominent. Now, of course, in the case of sight and touch, the notions of acquaintance (in the fairly wide sense in which we have been using it), of objects, of the reality of the objects, all have a place. If I am seeing or touching something, then I am immediately aware of, directly acquainted with, a thing or object, and it must be a real thing or object — there must be something there that I am seeing or touching. If then we take sight or touch as our model when we come to discuss knowledge or belief, it is natural to find a parallel in knowledge by acquaintance, and then to suppose that somehow knowledge that and belief can be made to fit into the same pattern and that talk in terms of objects and the reality or non-reality of these objects is in order here too. Enough, however, has perhaps been said, for it to be realised that the analogy with seeing or touching can be fundamentally misleading in the case of knowing that and belief. It may be then that some of the difficulties in Plato arise from his being over-ready to accept this analogy. It is certainly true that he is not clear in his thinking about the difference between acquaintance and knowledge that, and we have already pointed out earlier (Chapter 7, pp. 143-4) that it might be said that there is the same ambivalence about his use of the Greek noun δόξα (*doxa*) which we translate as 'belief' — that there are times here too when he seems to mean by belief some sort of immediate awareness, whereas he also clearly uses it elsewhere to mean belief that. (b) It is also probably true that in his theory of knowledge Plato was influenced by his metaphysical views — or perhaps it would be better to say that his theory of knowledge and his metaphysics had a reciprocal influence on each other. He wanted to hold that the familiar world, the world of particulars revealed to us through sense perception, was in various ways an unsatisfactory world, and that there was another permanent unchanging world, the world of Forms, which transcended, lay behind the familiar world, and was superior to it in status — it was this latter world alone that was truly real, while the familiar world was only partly real. Certainly one of the reasons which led Plato to this two-world view was that he thought it was demanded by the difference between knowledge and belief: i.e. as in the present arguments in Book V of the *Republic*, his epistemological views led to the two-world view. At the same time Plato had other reasons, some of which should become clear later, for his two-world view. It might be said then that because in any case he believed his metaphysical two-world view to be correct, he was perhaps over-ready to make his arguments from the side of theory of knowledge fit in with his metaphysics.

Two points of warning should be added to conclude this discussion. First, in it the reader has been introduced in a general way to the distinction between knowledge by acquaintance and knowledge by description, and it has been indicated that important use has been made in philosophy of this distinction. It should be noted, however, that while we have talked above about knowing an object by acquaintance, where 'object' could mean an object in the familiar sense, such as a yacht or a desk or a chair, in the specialised sense of knowledge by acquaintance that has been used for example in fairly recent philosophy, it would not be said that we could be acquainted with an object like a desk or chair. Instead it would be said, for example, that we have knowledge by acquaintance only of "sense data", and that our knowledge of a physical object such as a desk is knowledge by description. Clearly, beyond issuing this warning we cannot pursue the matter here. A good place to see the use made of the acquaintance-description distinction is for example in Bertrand Russell's *Problems of Philosophy*, Chapter V. The second warning relates to Plato himself and it is perhaps unnecessary to give it since the point should already be clear; but it is a point of much importance in understanding Plato. We said above that in the case of knowledge by acquaintance it was plausible to hold, as Plato said, that there must be a real object there with which one is acquainted, just as when we touch something,

for example, the desk, there must be a real object there to be
touched.   When, however, Plato says that knowledge is of
what is real he means by 'real' something different from what
we would mean if we spoke of desks or chairs as real.   He would
say that the desk as a particular sensible object is only half
real.   He would also say that there can only be belief about
the desk, never knowledge of it.   Knowledge can only be of
the Forms and the Forms alone are truly real.

This brings us to the second topic of the present chapter.
We have seen in the preceding chapter something of the use
Plato makes in Book V of the notion of 'Forms' and we have
just been discussing the role of these Forms in his theory of
knowledge.   It would seem helpful now at this stage to take a
more general look at the theory of Forms, partly by way of
amplifying what we have already learnt, and partly to provide
a background for the subsequent discussion of Books VI and
VII.

A very great deal has been written over many years about
the theory of Forms, and it is quite impossible in a narrow
compass to be other than arbitrary in one's way of presenting
the theory.   What we shall do here is, after one or two preliminary remarks, to collect, mainly from the *Republic* and from
the dialogues whose date of composition is recognised to be
earlier than that of the *Republic*, some examples of some of the
various roles played in Plato's philosophy by the Forms, and
then add one or two brief comments.

The first preliminary remark is concerned with the label to
be used in English in connection with the theory.   When Plato
himself wants to refer to Beauty as opposed to the many particular beautiful things or Justice as opposed to the many particular
ust acts, he very frequently does this by the use of the Greek
word for 'itself'.   Thus Beauty is *auto to kalon* (literally 'the
beautiful itself'), Justice is *auto to dikaion* (literally 'the just
itself'), and so on.   He also, however, uses the two Greek
words εἶδος (*eidos*) and ἰδέα (*idea*) in this connection, apparently
completely interchangeably.   Thus instead of speaking of 'the
Beautiful itself', etc., he will speak instead of 'the *eidos* of the
Beautiful' or 'the *idea* of the Beautiful'.   The English word
'idea' is an exact transliteration of the Greek ἰδέα, and hence

as we noted earlier (Chapter 7, p. 140), English commentators speak of the 'idea' of Beauty, etc., in Plato, and more generally of Plato's Theory of Ideas. This, however, is an unfortunate rendering of the Greek. The English word 'idea' tends to carry with it the notion that ideas exist only in the mind, that they are only thoughts of ours, that questions can be raised about how far they represent reality, that they are only "subjective", what we think, as opposed to what is "objective", what is really the case independently of our thinking, and so on. It should be clear from what we have already seen, and it should be still clearer from what will be said later, that all these notions are quite alien to Plato's intentions when he talks, for example, of the *eidos* or *idea* of Beauty. This is for him another way of referring to Beauty itself and for him it is Beauty itself that is truly real, that is the object of knowledge ; and whatever ideas (in the familiar use of that word) we may have about Beauty, there is a real unchanging Beauty there for us to grasp if we can, and which is what it is quite independently of any ideas of ours. If we are still to use the word 'idea' in connection with Plato's theory, then it must be neutralised and these familiar associations it has must be forgotten ; and since it is not easy to do this the translation 'idea' is undesirable. In fact, though there has been controversy over the precise reasons which influenced Plato in his choice of the Greek words *eidos* or *idea* in this context, the words themselves meant originally 'visible shape' or 'form' and, more widely, 'form', 'nature', and then 'form', 'type' (as for instance in the phrase 'forms or types of disease'). The English word 'form' keeps near to the meaning of the Greek words, and is also free from the misleading associations of the word 'idea'. For these reasons then it is proposed to keep to the terminology we have already been using and to refer to Plato's theory as the Theory of Forms.

The second preliminary point is concerned with what is known as the 'Socratic problem', i.e. the question whether we are to take the views attributed to Socrates by Plato in the dialogues as having been actually held by Socrates himself, or whether Plato attributes to Socrates views which the historical Socrates never expressed and which are in fact Plato's own. In particular, there has been much dispute as to whether the

theory of Forms is Socratic or whether it is primarily a theory
which Plato himself developed. However, for present purposes
it does not seem necessary to go into this question, nor to be
over-anxious about distinguishing Socratic and Platonic elements within the theory of Forms. It will be enough for us to
look in a general way at the theory as it is exhibited in the
Republic and the dialogues composed by Plato earlier than the
Republic, and to this we now turn.

In illustrating some of the roles of the Forms in Plato's
theory, we may begin with what we have already learnt from
Book V, and for convenience we will tabulate the various
functions of the Forms as we go along, even though some of the
tabulations may be misleadingly brief. The list we will produce is not meant to be exhaustive nor to be arranged in any
order that would suggest that one function of the Forms is
more important for Plato than another.

(i) *Forms as the objects of knowledge.* This is familiar from the
end of Book V. Knowledge and belief are different powers
in that the former is infallible, the latter not. Their objects
then are different and the objects of knowledge are, as we find
in the subsequent discussion, the Forms.

(ii) *Forms as what is real.* For Plato the reality of the Forms
follows from their being the objects of knowledge, and with
this again we are familiar from Book V, cf. 476e-477a, where it
is argued that if a man knows, there must be something that
he knows and that "something" must be real. We have also
seen that in Book V Plato argues that sensible particulars, the
many beautiful things and so on which the lover of sights or
sounds sees or hears or touches, are not perfectly real: they
are only semi-real and occupy an intermediate position between
what is completely real (the Forms) and what is completely
unreal. They are then appearances of the underlying reality,
the objects not of knowledge but of belief.

(iii) *Forms as ideal standards.* This again we have met in
discussing Book V, since in examining the argument there
(see Chapter 7, p. 161 ff. above) which purported to show that
particulars were only semi-real we suggested that possibly
what Plato had in mind was the notion of the Forms as ideal
standards of perfection to which particulars only approximate.

As we indicated, the best place to see this aspect of the Forms is in the *Phaedo*, 74-75. It is connected there with the doctrine that learning is recollection, that we had knowledge of the Forms before we were born into this world, but lost it at birth, and then are reminded of it again by our experience of the sensible world, so that we are enabled to judge the latter against the standard of the perfect Forms. A short quotation from 75b of the dialogue sums up this role of the Forms : "I suppose then that we must have acquired knowledge of the nature of the Equal itself before we began to see and hear and to use our other senses, if we were going to refer to that criterion things that appeared to the senses equal, on the ground that they all do their best to be like it, though they are inferior". And Plato makes it clear immediately after (75c-d) that the same holds also for the Forms generally, for the Beautiful itself, the Good itself, and so on. The doctrine of recollection is in itself an interesting link in Plato's whole attempt to account for *a priori* knowledge. For our immediate purposes, however, what we have to note especially in this section of the *Phaedo* is how the Forms function as criteria or standards — Justice itself (the Form Justice) is the perfect exemplar or instance of justice against which we must measure the imperfection of our own just acts. The latter "do their best to be like" perfect justice but fall short, fail to be themselves perfectly just.

(iv) *Forms as universals*. What we mean by this should become clear as we proceed. Let us illustrate this function of the Forms by two quotations. The first is from Book X of the *Republic*, where at 596a Plato says, "Well then, shall we proceed as usual and begin by assuming the existence of a single essential nature or Form for every set of things which we call by the same name?" The second is from the earlier dialogue, the *Meno*, 72a ff. Meno has been asked to say what he thinks virtue is and has replied by giving a list of particular manifestations of virtue — the virtue of a man is to administer the state, of a woman to order her house, and so on. Socrates then goes on, "How fortunate I am, Meno! When I ask you for one virtue you present me with a swarm of them, which are in your keeping. Suppose that I carry on the figure of the swarm, and ask of you, What is the nature of the bee? and you answer that there are many kinds of bees, and I reply: But do bees differ as bees, because there are many and different kinds of them; or are they not rather to be distinguished by some other quality as for example beauty, size or shape? How would you answer me? *Meno*: I should answer that bees do not differ from one another, as bees. *Soc.*: And if I went on to say: That is what I desire to know, Meno; tell me what is the quality in which they do not differ, but are all alike; — would you be able to answer? *Meno*: I should. *Soc.*: And so of the virtues, however many and different they may be, they have all a common nature [an identical Form] which makes them virtues; and on this he who would answer the question, What is virtue? would do well to have his eye fixed; Do you understand?" (Jowett's translation.) Socrates subsequently illustrates the sort of answer he wants by taking the example of figure or shape. Here again if asked what is figure it will not do to reply, for example, roundness, for roundness is only *a* figure, and there are many other figures, e.g. squareness, etc., and Socrates goes on, 74d, "And suppose that he were to pursue the matter in my way, he would say: Ever and anon we are landed in particulars, but this is not what I want: tell me then, since you call them by a common name, and say that they are all figures, even when opposed to one another, what is that common nature which you designate as figure — which contains straight as well as round, and is no more one than the other — that would be your mode of speaking?" It will be noted from these passages that the Forms are being used to account for the fact that things in the world go together in groups or kinds, that for example there is a group of particulars which, though they differ from one another individually, e.g. some are bigger, some smaller and so on, nevertheless still form a group such that they are all bees; or, again, to take another example, that there is another group of particulars such that, though again they differ in certain ways from one another, they are all chairs, and so on. Plato is suggesting that in each case there is a group or kind because there is a single characteristic, namely the one Form (e.g. Beeness, Chairness), present in all the many particular instances (of bees, of chairs) within the group. There is, that is, a one over the many in each case.

He is also saying that it is because of this that we are able to use general terms, or, as he calls them, 'common names' — e.g. 'bee' is not the name of one particular bee, but has general application to any of the particulars within the group, so that we can say this is a bee, that is a bee, and so on. In philosophy the term 'universal' has been used of that which is common to a group of particulars or again from the side of language as that of which a general term is the name. Hence then our use of the word 'universal' at the beginning of this paragraph.

(v) *Forms as "causes"*. This function of the Forms is best seen at 100c-d of the *Phaedo* where Socrates says "I no longer learn about, and cannot understand . . . these other subtle 'causes', but if anyone tells me that anything is beautiful, as having a bright colour or a special shape or anything of that sort, I dismiss the other 'reasons' — all the others confuse me — and purely and simply and perhaps naïvely keep to this, that the only thing that makes it beautiful is the presence of, or its participation in — or whatever the relationship may be — that 'Beautiful' [the Form of Beauty]. I do not now insist upon any particular relationship, but only that all beautiful things are beautiful simply *because of* the Beautiful" (Bluck's translation). Here then the Forms are "causes". It is important, however, to recognise that the Greek word αἰτία (*aitia*) which Plato uses here is a tricky word — perhaps even trickier than our own word 'cause'. Without going into the difficulties that surround it, we might say for our present purposes that by 'cause' here is meant something like a necessary condition. This is why we have put the word in quotation marks, letting it take its colouring from the context.

Now when we look at the various jobs of the Forms listed above, it is obvious that the theory of Forms has a very wide range. This is why Professor Cherniss entitled an article which he contributed to the *American Journal of Philology* (*A.J.P.* Vol. LVII, 1936) 'The Philosophical Economy of the Theory of Ideas'. He argued there that by one single unifying theory, namely the theory of Forms, Plato was able to solve outstanding problems in ontology, in ethics and in epistemology; and he thus commended the theory for its philosophical economy. About the alleged economy of the theory we will say something later. Meantime it may be useful to say a little about the theory under the three heads listed by Professor Cherniss.

(a) First, then, from our list above we can see that the theory of Forms is an ontological theory, i.e. a theory concerned with being or existence. This is clear from (ii), (iii) and (v) above and is also involved in (iv). In its ontological aspect, what the theory of Forms is maintaining is that there is a world of permanent, unchanging and perfect entities which are un-affected by variations in circumstances or conditions and which comprise reality. It is they that are "real" or, as Plato some-times says, "completely real" or "truly existent". The ordinary, everyday, sensible world, on the other hand, is not completely real: it is only semi-real: it is the world of appearance as opposed to the world of reality, namely the Forms; and further, it owes such reality as it does have to the Forms. The theory of Forms then is a metaphysical theory, in that it claims to be telling us something that is true about what there is indepen-dently of human beings and minds. To use a phrase used by Socrates in the later dialogue, the *Parmenides* (132d), the Forms are "as it were patterns fixed in the nature of things", i.e. they are the permanent furniture of the universe. There are various difficulties in this ontological aspect of the theory of Forms, but one word of caution may be relevant. The theory main-tains that our ordinary, everyday objects, for example the chair I am sitting in, are not "real" or "really real", but are in a sense only appearances; and the unphilosophical reader may be tempted to reject out of hand a theory which denies the full reality of the chairs he sits in, the houses he sees when he goes out into the street, and so on. Now Plato may be mistaken in what he is saying, but his view cannot be rejected in this out-of-hand way. For one thing, many philosophers besides Plato have held that the everyday world is a world of appearances, and have contrasted it with a reality beyond appearances; and if the unphilosophical reader is unmoved by this consideration, he must be asked why he himself calls the chair he sits in real, as opposed to a hallucinatory or dream chair. In fact he will find that the word 'real' is a very tricky word. It might be suggested that when he calls the chair he is sitting in real, as distinct from a hallucinatory or a dream chair, he is employing certain criteria, not in themselves easy to formulate, which he regards the "real" chair as satisfying. One such criterion, for instance, might be that the real chair is in some sense or other more permanent than the hallucinatory chair. Moreover, the word 'real' seems in addition to have a commendatory or preferring force : because the object satisfies these criteria, he singles it out for preference or commendation by calling it real (cf. the use of the word 'real' in an argument whether or not, for example, Britain is a "real" democracy). Now a philosopher might want to suggest either that the criteria we ordinarily employ in using the word 'real' are too un-exacting or that sensible objects when carefully considered do not in fact adequately satisfy even our existing criteria, or he might want to suggest a combination of both. That is, in one way or another he might want to shift the use of the word 'real', so that everyday sensible objects no longer counted as "real" or as "completely real". This is what Plato is doing when he says that only the Forms are completely real whereas the sensible world is a world of appearances, only semi-real. As we have said, this may be a mistaken move. The arguments behind it may not be sound, it may lead to more confusion than it is worth, and so on. The point however is that it cannot be rejected out of hand simply because it denies the "reality" of our everyday world.

(b) Secondly, the theory of Forms figures prominently in Plato's ethical views. Here all five functions of the Forms that we have listed are really involved, but perhaps the third (Forms as ideal standards) has a special relevance. We have already mentioned (Introduction, pp. xiii-xiv) the moral problems that faced Athens at the end of the fifth century. It was in fact a time of much questioning of the traditional morality, and the notion that moral standards were a matter of convention, that there was no absolute right or wrong, gained considerable currency. This was a notion to which Plato was violently opposed, and the theory of Forms in its ethical aspect is an attempt to account for absolute moral standards. The theory holds that there are Forms of moral characteristics (e.g. of goodness, justice, etc.) as well as of non-moral characteristics. Indeed, it seems probable that, at any rate at the beginning,

under the influence of Socrates, the former were Plato's primary
concern, though mathematical Forms (Equality, etc.) had also
already become prominent in certain of the dialogues earlier
than the *Republic*. Now granted that there are Forms of moral
qualities, when we look at our list of the various jobs the Forms
do, we can see how Plato regarded his theory as providing an
answer to any relativist view of morals. For example, in our
list the Forms again function as objects in the case of our knowledge of moral truths (i) ; they are real, are what they are
quite independently of what we may think or say (ii) ; and
they are perfectly that to which imperfect particulars only
approximate (iii). Thus, for example, the Form Justice is a
perfect, unchanging pattern or model or standard, there to be
known, given that men, or some men at least, can be brought
to know it, and just conduct then is no matter of convention,
but a matter of conforming to the ideal standard of Justice
which like the other Forms is part of the nature of things. It
can be seen then that Plato's ethical theory is interlocked with
his epistemology and his metaphysics ; his is certainly an ethics
that has a metaphysical basis. It can also be seen how his
political theory in the *Republic* in turn interlocks with these.
For Plato absolutely certain knowledge is possible, in morals as
elsewhere. As we shall see, it requires men of special ability to
reach it, and even they can only do so after a long and arduous
training. When they have reached it, however, they have
arrived at absolute truth : in the moral-political sphere they
just know wherein the good life consists. On Plato's view then
they alone are fit to rule and it is plainly to the benefit of the
mass of the citizens that the few who have this knowledge
should guide their lives for them. It is this interlocking of
different facets of his thinking that makes Plato's political theory
especially important. If we find the political theory repellent,
it is not merely enough to dismiss it as a product of anti-
democratic bias. If we think it is mistaken, we have to show
why it is mistaken ; and just because, in Plato's thinking, it is
tied in with, amongst other things, his ethical, epistemological
and metaphysical views, we have to have them too under
consideration if we are criticising his political theory. There
is one further point we ought to add. This relates to a develop-

ment in his thinking which we shall find when, in the next chapters, we are studying Books VI and VII of the *Republic* (cf. especially Chapter 10, pp. 260-261); for in these books a special status is assigned to the Form of the Good as the supreme Form, and Plato suggests that the notion of the reality of the Forms (and this would apply to all Forms) cannot be separated from the notion of their goodness, or that, to use somewhat grandiose terms, reality and value coalesce.

(c) Thirdly, the theory of Forms is very much concerned with epistemological issues, i.e. with questions concerning the nature of knowledge, its distinction from other types of cognition, and the objects of the various types of cognition. Since these issues are particularly prominent in Books VI and VII of the *Republic*, it may be useful to say rather more on this matter than we said on (a) and (b), and here we shall have particularly in mind the role of the Forms at (i) (Forms as objects of knowledge) and at (iv) (Forms as universals) in our list above. Let us begin then with (i). Plato is convinced of the fundamental difference between knowledge and belief. Knowledge is unerring, infallible. What is known remains true always. Beliefs, on the other hand, are always liable to error and subject to alteration. Further, he believes that given the proper training, the philosopher can attain to this infallible knowledge, can attain, that is, to truths that remain true always. But now to use the 'object' talk which we discussed above, it follows that granted the existence of knowledge as described it must have appropriate objects, i.e. just as knowledge itself is stable and unchanging, so its objects, what it knows, must also be stable and unchanging. At the same time Plato is convinced, and in Book V we considered some of his arguments for this, that the many particulars of the sensible world cannot satisfy this requirement. They are in a state of constant change, are now this and now that, are imperfect, and have none of the stability and permanence required if they are to be objects of knowledge. But knowledge does exist and Plato has no doubt of that. It follows then that its appropriate objects must exist, namely objects that are permanent and unchanging, i.e. what Plato calls Forms. This argument for the Forms is implicit in Book V of the *Republic*. It is put clearly and explicitly in the

Timaeus (51d) (the *Timaeus* has usually been regarded as a late dialogue but may in fact have been the crowning work of the *Republic* group of dialogues. See G. E. L. Owen, *Classical Quarterly*, N.S., Vol. III). "My own verdict, then, is this. If intelligence and true belief are two different kinds, then these things — Forms that we cannot perceive but only think of — certainly exist in themselves; but if, as some hold, true belief is in no way different from intelligence, then all the things that we perceive through the bodily senses must be taken as the most certain reality. Now we must affirm that they are two different things, for they are distinct in origin and unlike in nature" (Cornford's translation). Plato then thinks that the existence of knowledge requires that there should be Forms, since they alone provide the appropriate objects of knowledge. We have already in the earlier part of this chapter discussed the difficulties that arise over this notion of "objects" of knowledge. It is important, however, to recognise that when Plato makes his Forms perform the role of objects of knowledge, he is attempting to answer a genuine and serious philosophical problem. There are some propositions which we are all inclined to regard as true, come what may, that is, as necessarily true. For example, within Euclidean geometry we would say that we know that triangles on equal bases and between parallels are equal in area, and that this is a truth that holds always. It is not that we have found this true in some particular case or even that we have considered many cases and never found a contrary instance. Rather we know this to be true for any triangles whatsoever. Triangles on equal bases and between parallels must be equal in area, and no particular instances in the way of diagrams or models that we can see or touch could ever falsify this. Contrast a proposition like 'jet engines are noisy'. It may well be that in our experience this has always so far been true. Yet clearly this has been a matter of experience and the possibility is open that on some further occasion we may come across a jet engine that is not noisy — indeed it might be that some invention would make jet engines completely silent. Or again the difference between our two propositions, the triangle case and the jet engine case, can be brought out by considering how we would verify them. In the case of

'jet engines are noisy', experience is clearly relevant. It would
be relevant to the truth of this proposition to go to airfields
and listen to jet engines, and it would, up to a point anyhow,
be sensible to suggest that even though all the jets on this air-
field are noisy, it would be worth going round some other airfields to check that the jets there are noisy too. But clearly in
our triangle case there is something entirely wrong with the
notion that even though the proposition about the equality of
the triangles holds in this particular case and that particular
case, it might nevertheless be wise to go on looking at more
cases to make sure there was no mistake. Given an understanding of Euclidean geometry, we know that this proposition
must always be true of all cases. It is a necessary proposition,
could never be false, whereas the jet case is one which may be
true for all the instances we have come across, but could in
principle be falsified. In contrast with the triangle type of
proposition, which is a necessary proposition, it is convenient
to call the jet type of proposition a contingent proposition : it
happens to be that way but it could be different. Necessary
propositions are also often called *a priori* propositions, i.e.
propositions such that no experience could falsify them and
which in that way come "before" sense experience ; and the
knowledge involved in knowing them is labelled *a priori* knowledge. Contingent propositions, on the other hand, are often
called *a posteriori* propositions, in the sense that their truth or
falsehood is dependent on sense experience and thus they come
"after" sense experience. Now what account to give of necessary propositions or, if we prefer it, *a priori* knowledge is a
philosophical problem which has long exercised the minds of
philosophers, and still does. What we must note for our present
purposes is that the theory of Forms is an attempt to account
for necessary propositions or *a priori* knowledge, and this is
why above we said that in his theory Plato is attempting to
answer an important problem. What he is saying is that if we
are to account for necessary propositions we must look beyond
the sensible world. Sensible objects are subject to change —
what is true of this particular object now may not be true to-
morrow or even the next moment ; the features they appear to
possess are subject to all sorts of conditions : e.g. colour is

subject to the intensity of the light, the observer's eye, etc., the shape of an object to the distance we are from it and so on ; in various ways they are imperfect and imprecise — the triangle we draw or model is only an imperfect representation of what a mathematician means by a triangle, and can never be perfectly triangular. It is impossible then, Plato thinks, to frame a precise statement about any particulars that will hold always ; in fact necessary statements cannot be concerned with the sensible world. The objects then that we are thinking about when we do make necessary statements must be different from the objects of the sensible world : they must be permanent and not subject to change, they must retain a fixed nature independently of the conditions under which they are apprehended, and they must be perfect. Only granted such objects can we account for necessary truths and for the possibility of *a priori* knowledge. It would take us too far afield to discuss Plato's argument in any detail here. What has been said earlier in the chapter in the discussion on knowledge and belief (cf. particularly pp. 173-176) may suggest to the reader that Plato is over-influenced in all this by the model of knowledge by acquaintance. Nevertheless his solution of the problem of necessary truths has, with various modifications, found support among many philosophers; W. D. Ross, for example, in recent times, in his book *Plato's Theory of Ideas*, p. 225, in expressing approval of the theory of Forms says, "In reason we have a faculty by which we can grasp universals [he is referring here to Plato's Forms] in their pure form and to some extent see the relations that necessarily exist between them".

It will be noticed that in thinking of examples of necessary propositions in what we have just been saying, the example we actually used was a geometrical one; and, in fact, mathematics is the field that we tend to think of when the question of necessary propositions is raised. There does seem to be a difference in kind between mathematical propositions like two and two make four or our triangle case, and most other sorts of proposition that we can think of. Two and two, we think, from the nature of the system of numbers must always be four, and similarly triangles on equal bases and between parallels must always be equal in area from the very nature of our geometrical system. Nothing could possibly upset these propositions, and they thus seem to have a special status. Now Plato was the first philosopher who clearly recognised the special status of mathematical propositions as necessary propositions, though he also believed that the field of necessary propositions extended beyond mathematics. Indeed, as we shall see in detail in the following chapters, he was not prepared to allow that the mathematician has knowledge in the full sense. On the other hand, he was equally clear that there is a certainty about mathematical propositions that is quite absent from the propositions which we merely believe (i.e the sort of everyday propositions that the lover of sights and sounds of Book V entertains). Thus he describes the mathematician's state as one intermediate between belief and knowledge in the full sense, and gives it the name 'thinking' (*dianoia*). Similarly, on the object side, he is clear that the objects about which the mathematician thinks are not the changing, unstable objects of the world of sense perception, but must belong to the intelligible world. Whether Plato regards them as Forms or as a special class of mathematical object, is again a point to be discussed in the following chapter. What is clear beyond any doubt is that they belong to the intelligible, not to the sensible, world, and in this allocation Plato is showing that he recognises the special character of mathematical propositions which we have just been discussing. This is why too in the higher education of the Guardians in Books VI and VII it is the various branches of mathematics that are the essential preliminaries to the study of philosophy. In the latter alone, Plato thinks, full knowledge is attained, but mathematics is the essential bridge-study which introduces the mind to the intelligible world, the world of stable, permanent objects about which alone certainty is possible. This recognition by Plato of the special status of mathematical propositions and the emphasis that he puts on mathematics is clearly of great importance in the history of thought, when we consider how fundamental a part mathematics has played in the subsequent development of western civilisation.

The function of the Forms as universals ((iv) on our list) is of course closely connected with what we have been saying.

It has an ontological or metaphysical side as well as an episte-mological side. (a) On the metaphysical side Plato thinks the Forms are necessary not only to account for such existence as particulars do have, but to account also for the fact that they go in groups or sets, e.g. one group all of which are square in shape, another group circular in shape, another group (of par-ticular acts) all of which are just, another group comprising unjust acts, and so on. He thinks this grouping of particulars by kinds can only be explained by, in each case, a common Form which is somehow present in all the particulars of the group, or which they all somehow share (cf. on this latter point the language in the *Phaedo* quotation at (v) in our list). (b) On the epistemological side not only are the Forms necessary if we are to get beyond belief to knowledge — the point we have just been discussing above — but also to account for the experi-ence we do have of the world. There are two connected features of the latter that are relevant here. (i) We experience things in the world as belonging to kinds — we are constantly noting similarities between things and thus classifying them (e.g. these shapes are all similar and we classify them as square — this is square, that is square, etc.). (ii) This is reflected in the language we use, for by far the greatest part of our language is made up of general words, e.g. 'square' is not a word that we use only of the shape of the top of the table in our own dining-room, but of the tops of many other tables which in this respect are similar to our own table. Indeed, the point of using the word 'square' of our own table is to relate it to the many other tables — they are all square tables. Both (i) and (ii) Plato thinks can only be accounted for by the existence of the Forms: we experience things in groups and are able to classify them accordingly because of the presence of a common Form in the group (the metaphysical counterpart noted at (a) of this classifying activity of ours); and the occurrence of general words as a feature of our language is explained by supposing that their reference is to the Form present in the many instances of which they are used: i.e. if for the moment we regard 'square' as a name, then it is not the name of the shape of my table-top nor of yours but the name of the Form common to them, i.e. when we call them square we are referring to the common Form Squareness present in them. This problem of how we are able to use general terms has become known as the problem of universals, and any discussion of it as such lies beyond our present scope. At the moment it must suffice to say that Plato holds what is called a realist view of universals. We have already seen that the Forms are entities that exist in their own right, independently of any thinking of ours, and we have just seen that Plato uses them to account for our classificatory activities and consequent use of general words, i.e. as a solution to what might be described in a very unsatisfactory way as the problem of universals. Plato's, then, is a realist view because he believes that universals are real entities which are what they are quite independent of the existence and nature of human or other minds, and of which general words are the names. For difficulties in this realist view and for other possible views of universals the reader may be referred to A. D. Woozley's *Theory of Knowledge, An Introduction*, pp. 70-101. The whole problem of classification and the use of general terms is one which has recurred constantly in philosophy. Thus this aspect of the theory of Forms, which seeks to provide a solution to this problem, is of the utmost importance; and this is so, even if one finds more difficulties in the solution than W. D. Ross does when he writes (*Plato's Theory of Ideas*, p. 225) "the essence of the theory of Ideas lay in the conscious recognition of the fact that there is a class of entities, for which the best name is probably 'universals', that are entirely different from sensible things. Any use of language involves the recognition, either conscious or unconscious, of the fact that there are such entities; for every word used, except proper names — every abstract noun, every general noun, every adjective, every verb, even every pronoun and every preposition — is a name for something of which there are or may be instances."

Finally, having now looked at the various functions of the Forms in relation to Plato's metaphysical, ethical and epistemological views, let us come back to Professor Cherniss's commendation of the theory for its philosophical economy. Certainly if it worked over all the areas we have mentioned, it would be an extremely economical theory. Indeed, one of the troubles with the theory, one is inclined to think, is that it is too economical, that the Forms are set to perform too many tasks, some of which are incompatible. We can do no more than illustrate this very briefly here. Consider the function of the Forms at (iii) on our list (Forms as ideal standards). Now as an ideal standard the Form is perfectly that to which imperfect particulars in varying degree approximate: for example, no particular act is perfectly just — only Justice itself (the Form) is perfectly just. It follows from this, first, that the Form becomes a sort of ideal particular, i.e. it is the perfect instance of that of which it is the Form, and it then becomes appropriate to predicate a Form of itself, i.e. to say Justice is just, Holiness holy (and Plato does say precisely this at *Protagoras*, 330c-d); and secondly, that the tendency when regarding the Forms as ideal standards, as the perfect exemplars to which things in our world can only approximate, will be to push them right out of our world, to regard them as quite separate and apart from particulars. Now difficulty arises when we consider the first point in relation to the function of the Forms at (iv) (Forms as universals). At (iv) the problem is how we are able to predicate the same general term of a number of particulars, and the answer to it is that we are able to do this because the general term refers to a property or attribute which is common to the particulars (i.e. to a universal). The Form then is the common attribute of a group of particulars and is predicated of the particulars, but, of course, is not itself a particular, but belongs to a totally different logical category. Indeed, one of the great achievements of the theory of Forms in this respect is that it points to the important distinction between attributes (or universals) and substances (particulars) of which the attributes are predicated. On the other hand in (iii), as we have seen, the Form itself becomes a subject of predication in that it becomes an ideal particular of which it is then itself predicated — Justice is just, Holiness holy. It is quite clear that the "economy" of the theory has led here to a very serious difficulty. In answer to this it has been suggested by some commentators that it is incorrect to think of Plato's Forms in the way in which we think of universals — that really the Forms should not be regarded as universals at all. This is a controversy which, unfortunately, we cannot pursue here, but it may be remarked that the reader who does pursue it for himself will find it philosophically interesting and rewarding. Again, the second point we raised above, namely the tendency towards separation of Form and particular which results from the function of the Forms as ideal standards ((iii) in our list), causes difficulty when we consider the functions of the Forms at (iv) and (v). In these latter functions the forms make particulars what they are, and here what seems important is that the Forms should be present in the particulars, and not separate from them. Once more the "economy" of the theory seems to create difficulty. The quotation from the *Phaedo* in (v) of our list may suggest that Plato himself felt some difficulty about the relation, as may the discussion in the first part of the later dialogue, the *Parmenides* (130-135), which everyone who is interested in the theory of Forms ought to read. Again, however, it has been argued that the difficulty arises from misunderstanding the nature of the Forms, and again it is impossible here to pursue the point. The reader, however, should bear in mind this problem of the relation between particulars and Forms when reading Books VI and VII, to which we now turn. He will also find some further points about the theory of Forms in Chapter 12, pp. 284-287.

Chapter 9

SUN, LINE AND CAVE

At the end of Book V, arising out of Plato's statement at 473d-e that philosophers must be rulers, the philosopher has been distinguished from the non-philosopher. The latter is, to use Plato's words at the beginning of Book VI, "lost in the maze of multiplicity and change", while the former is "able to grasp the eternal and unchanging", i.e. the Forms. Thus the philosopher alone has knowledge of Justice itself (the Form of Justice), and so with the other virtues. Plato in Book VI, in the passage running 484a-502c, is first (484a-487a) concerned to show that the philosophic nature also involves the other characteristics requisite in a ruler, and these are conveniently summed up at 487a: the philosopher requires to have a good memory, he is quick to learn, magnanimous, gracious, a friend and kinsman of truth, courage, justice and temperance. In fact, in all respects, philosophers are the only completely suitable persons to whom to entrust the state. Secondly (487b-497a), Adeimantus objects that the facts are at variance with this conclusion: as things are, even the best of the philosophers are regarded as useless and most of them are thoroughly vicious; and Plato argues that this arises, not through the fault of philosophy, but because of the corrupt societies in which philosophers have to live. Finally (497a-502c), the discussion returns again to the practicability of an ideal state in which philosophers are kings.

There are only one or two points that call for special comment here. (1) Plato lists as one of the qualities belonging to the philosophical nature "truthfulness" — the philosopher "will never tolerate falsehood, but will hate it and love the truth" (485c). This characterisation of the philosopher has to be considered against the background of what Plato says

196

elsewhere. When he says here that the philosopher "will never voluntarily tolerate falsehood", falsehood here is the "ignorance in the soul" of Book II, 382b. In that passage Plato makes a distinction between "ignorance in the soul" which, he says, "really deserves to be called true falsehood", and spoken falsehood, which is "not pure unadulterated falsehood". Adam, in a note on this latter passage, says "the distinction between veritable and spoken lies . . . enables Plato to call his ideal archons [rulers] ideally truthful, even when practically they tell lies, and it is with this object in view that the distinction is introduced". What Adam has in mind here is the provision at 389b-d that while, if any of the other members of the ideal state are caught lying they must be punished, the rulers are permitted the use of the "medicinal" lie "for the good of the city"; and in fact at 459c ff. we have a good example of this sort of medicinal lie, when the rulers administer "a considerable dose of fiction and deceit" to secure eugenic breeding. Thus when Plato in the present passage describes the philosopher as a lover of truth, this is for him still compatible with the proposal that the philosopher-ruler may use deception as an instrument of government, and criticism of the latter proposal remains unaltered. This is why Professor Popper (*The Open Society and its Enemies*, Vol. 1, p. 121), with the earlier passages in mind, in which lying is forbidden to the rest of the citizens, but permitted to the ruler for the good of the city, comments on the present passage that "only in this slightly unexpected sense is Plato's philosopher king a lover of truth".

(2) The second part of this section (487b-497a), where Plato is discussing the alleged uselessness or worse of the philosopher, is important as showing his attitude to the Athenian democracy, the democratic politicians, and indeed the whole of contemporary Athenian society. In the simile of the ship, 488a ff., the master, who is a bit deaf and shortsighted, and knows little or nothing of navigation, is the Athenian people, and the sailors are the demagogues. The whole aim of the latter is to get control of the ship by any means they can, although in fact they themselves have never been taught navigation and indeed deny that it can be taught. Thus they

have no use for the true navigator, the man who by study is
alone properly equipped to command a ship, and they regard
him as an idle talker and a star-gazer. If we cash the simile,
Plato is saying that the art of ruling is something only to be
acquired by such studies as the philosopher undertakes, and
his quarrel with the Athenian democracy and the democratic
politicians is that they fail to recognise this. They are, in fact,
to use the language of 484c, like blind men cut off from the
knowledge of reality and with no clear pattern to guide them
in laying down rules for the state. The same point comes out
again a little later in the present section at 492a ff., where
Plato is describing the corrupting influences that assail the
philosophic nature. The arch corrupter is the Athenian people
itself, clamouring its approval or disapproval in the assembly
(the Athenian "parliament") or elsewhere, according to its
moods and desires, and forcing everyone to accept its own
notions of right and wrong. The so-called teachers of wisdom,
the sophists, merely study the moods and desires of the "huge
and powerful beast" (the Athenian people) and, without really
knowing which of these is good or bad, right or wrong, employ
all these terms in accordance with the beliefs of the great beast.
Neither the sophists nor the politicians nor the Athenian
democracy have any awareness of the distinction between
Beauty itself, Rightness itself, and so on, and the many particular beautiful things, right acts, and so on. Thus they have
no use for the philosopher and can never themselves be philosophical (494a).

Plato's antipathy to democracy as he knew it thus emerges
clearly in this section. No doubt his anti-democratic attitude
is a product of various complex factors, but what should interest
us here is the philosophical ground for his condemnation of
democracy. As a philosopher he holds that knowledge and
belief are distinct, that knowledge is concerned with the real,
the Forms, and belief with the world of appearances, the many
particulars. He also holds, and we shall hear much more
about this shortly, that a long and arduous intellectual training,
of which only a few are capable, is necessary if knowledge is to
be reached. Thus only a few, the philosophers, can attain to
knowledge, and thus only a few know the real nature of Good-

ness, Justice, and so on. It is then only these few who have a
true standard or pattern by which to live; the rest are lost in
the shifting and changing world of belief, unless they are prepared to listen to the philosopher and let him mould their lives
for them in accordance with true Goodness, Justice, and so on,
of which he alone has knowledge. As Adam says, "the theory
of Ideas is not a democratic philosophy". What is important
is to note how Plato's philosophical views in the *Republic* and
his political views fit into one another. Thus if we feel that
his present condemnation of democracy is harsh and mistaken,
we must also be prepared to suggest what is wrong with the
philosophical views which lie behind it.

(3) Lastly, when in the final part of this section (497a-502c)
Plato is again discussing the practicability of the ideal state, he
is less hopeful than in the earlier books — even in Book V at
470e, it was still to be a Greek city, and at 473b he was still
talking in terms of the least change in existing cities that would
lead to a city approximating to the ideal. In the present passage, however, 499c, its realisation depends on "some happy
circumstance", "some chance" compelling philosophers to be
kings or "some divine inspiration" leading some of the present
kings or rulers to philosophy; and when ("in the infinity of
time, past or future") or where ("in some foreign region far
beyond our horizon") this is likely to happen is left in doubt.
Plato returns again to this question at 592a-b with an even
increased pessimism — the ideal city there "is perhaps laid up
in heaven as a pattern for him who desires to behold it, and
beholding it, to found it in his own heart".

Having then come to the conclusion, though with diminished optimism, that the notion of a philosopher king could be
realised in practice, Plato now proceeds to the training appropriate for such a ruler. This part of the *Republic* marks the
transition from the earlier discussion of rulers, ideal state, and
virtues, outlined in Books II-IV, to a new discussion at a
different level. Plato himself marks the transition at 503a-b
where he refers to the earlier discussion of the rulers in Book
III. It will be remembered that in Book III, 412b-414b,
from amongst those who have been educated in music and
gymnastic those are to be chosen as Guardians or rulers in the

full sense who under every sort of trial preserve a true belief about their duty to the state. The mark there of the ruler was true belief. Now, however, the position is changed. True belief is not enough. There must, as is said at 497d, be some authority in the state with the same idea of its constitution, the same understanding of it, as Glaucon and Plato, the original legislators. That is, the rulers must have knowledge, must in fact be philosophers. Thus Books V-VII provide a new discussion of the ruler from this new aspect of knowledge, an aspect which Plato here says he had evaded earlier; and the immediate question with which the present section begins is the studies which the future ruler must undertake. This new approach to the rulers and their training can be seen again as soon as discussion begins (at 504) of what these studies are to be. Socrates says that in addition to moral qualities, the future rulers must have the endurance to pursue the highest kinds of knowledge, and on being asked what these are he answers by referring back to something he had said in Book IV. It will be remembered that in Book IV, after having discovered justice and the other virtues, Socrates proceeds to the examination of the individual soul, the result of which is to establish that the soul also, like the state, is tripartite and exhibits virtues corresponding to the virtues already found in the state. At 435d, just before he embarks on this examination, Socrates remarks "it is my opinion that we shall never reach an accurate answer to this question by such methods as we are now using in our discussion, for the road which leads to it is another one, longer and more difficult". In the present passage (504b) Socrates recalls these words — "You remember", he says, "we said that for it to be possible to see them at their clearest there was another, longer way round, although it was possible to give an account of them on a level with our previous argument"; these two passages have already been discussed in Chapter 6, pages 112-115. The "longer way" is the way of Books VI and VII, and the difference between the two ways lies in this. In Book IV the method employed in studying the virtues was a psychological method, or perhaps it might be better to say that in Book IV Plato is concerned with what we might call moral psychology, and that he seeks to exhibit the virtues in terms of the three aspects of the soul he distinguishes and the relations between them. In Books VI and VII, however, he has moved from the plane of moral psychology to philosophy, and is asserting that if the virtues are to be fully understood, this can only be achieved by a rigorous philosophical training, which the future rulers in the state must undergo. Thus the earlier psychological or moral psychological approach gives way to a new philosophical approach involving questions of epistemology and metaphysics.

Plato's next task then is to explain what he means by the "highest kind of knowledge" (504) involved in this new approach, and this he does in three connected similes, the simile of the Sun (505a-509c), the simile of the Divided Line (509c-511e) and the simile (or, more properly, the allegory) of the Cave (514a-521b). These similes, particularly the two latter, have caused a great deal of difficulty, not least because it is not at all easy to be clear what precisely Plato intended to convey by means of them, and more has probably been written on them than on any other specific part of Plato's work. All that can be done here is to indicate briefly some of the difficulties and some of the ways in which they have been interpreted, and to suggest preferences of our own which, given the limitations of space, will be bound to seem dogmatic.

We begin then with the simile of the Sun. At 505a Plato explains that he means by the highest kind of knowledge which the Guardians must attain knowledge of the Form of the Good. It is from the Good, he says, that both right acts and everything else derive their usefulness and value. He rejects the suggestions that the Good might be pleasure or knowledge. What the Good is is clearly a matter of much dispute, yet it is the end of all human endeavour and something about which the Guardians of the state cannot be left in the dark. When challenged as to what he himself thinks the Good is, Plato says (506e) that a direct answer to this question is beyond the scope of the present inquiry, but that he is prepared to talk about what he regards as the offspring of the Good and most like to it. He now repeats the distinction with which we are familiar from the end of Book V, between the many particular good things or beautiful things and so on, and the single Form in each case of Goodness, or Beauty, and so on. The latter, the Forms, are objects of thought but not of sight; the former, the many particular things, are objects of sight but not of thought. He then proceeds to differentiate the sense of sight from the other senses on the ground that if the eye is to see and the object is to be visible, a third thing is required, namely light, and the source of this light is the Sun. Thus the Sun through its light enables the eye to see and the object to be seen. The Sun then, Plato says (508b), is the offspring of the Good, occupying in the visible world a position analogous to that of the Form of the Good in the world of Forms. The Sun simile then is an analogy, illustrating, by the role of the Sun in the visible world relatively to sight and the objects seen, the role of the Good in the intelligible world relatively to knowledge and the objects known (i.e. the Forms). The terms of the analogy are fairly straightforward and the principal equations are as follows:

$$
\begin{aligned}
\text{Visible world} &= \text{Intelligible world (the world of Forms)} \\
\text{Sun} &= \text{Form of the Good} \\
\text{Light} &= \text{Truth} \\
\text{Objects of sight} &= \text{Objects of knowledge (the Forms)} \\
\text{Sight} &= \text{Knowledge}
\end{aligned}
$$

Just as, then, in the visible world the Sun is the cause of light which enables visible things to be seen and of sight which enables the eye to see, though it itself is neither light nor sight, so in the intelligible world the Form of the Good is the cause of truth, which enables the Forms to be known, and of knowledge, which enables the mind to know, though it itself is neither truth nor knowledge (508e). Further (509b), just as the Sun not only enables visible objects to be seen, but causes the processes of generation and growth, though it itself is not such a process, so the Good not only enables the objects of knowledge to be known, but is the cause of their being and reality, though it itself is not being, but surpasses even being in dignity and power.

Plato then, using an analogy with the Sun in the visible world, is seeking to illustrate the special position which he believes the Form of the Good to occupy in the intelligible world relatively to the other Forms. Without the Good the other Forms would not be known; and indeed, more than that, their very being or existence is in some way derivative from the Good. We shall return later to what Plato says here about the Good. Meantime, it seems wise to look first at the two other figures of the Line and the Cave. All these figures are connected — note how in 509c the Line simile, which Plato is just about to begin, is represented as "completing the comparison with the Sun" — and thus it might be hoped that the two later figures would throw further light on the Sun analogy which we have just been considering.

The Line simile takes the form of a diagram. Plato begins at 509d by recalling the distinction in the Sun simile between the visible world, ruled over by the Sun, and the intelligible world, ruled over by the Form of the Good. We are now asked to take a line and divide it into two unequal parts, the one part representing the visible world and the other the intelligible; and then again to divide each of these two parts in the same proportion, the proportion representing degrees of clearness and obscurity. We thus have a diagram of the following sort:

where the original line AB is divided into two unequal parts AC and CB, and each of these parts is again divided, at D and

E respectively, in the ratio AC : CB. That is AD : DC = AC : CB, and CE : EB = AC : CB. It follows then that AD : DC = CE : EB. There are two further features of the diagram which should be noticed. Both follow mathematically, given that the diagram is constructed in the way just described, and the mathematically-minded can be left to work out the proofs. (1) The first is that it follows from the ratios already given that CB : AC = EB : DC, and that CB : AC = CE : AD. These ratios Plato explicitly uses later at 534a. (2) It also follows, given that the diagram is constructed in the way described, that the two middle segments DC and CE are equal. Now, as we shall see shortly, on one view of what Plato intends to convey by his diagram, the four segments of the Line are each meant to stand for an increasing degree of clarity and reality, and some commentators who take a different view of the Line have called attention to the equality of the two middle segments. They have drawn the inference that Plato in constructing his diagram deliberately intended this equality, and that thus the different segments of the Line cannot stand for increasing degrees of clearness and reality. Against this it must be noted that Plato himself makes no mention of the equality of the two middle segments. Given that he wanted to sub-divide the two segments AC and CB in the same ratio in which he had divided AB, the equality of the two middle segments DC and CE was an unavoidable consequence. His silence about this equality suggests that he did not intend it to be taken as significant, and it may be indeed that he himself failed to notice that it was a consequence of the construction that he had adopted. At any rate, in interpreting the Line, we shall take no further notice of the equality of the two middle segments.

Such being the diagram in outline, the next thing is to see how Plato fills it in. We have already been told at the end of 509 that the lower main segment, i.e. AC, represents the visible world, and we are now told at the beginning of 510 that the lowest sub-segment, i.e. AD, stands for "images . . . shadows . . . and reflections . . . and everything of that sort", while the next sub-segment, i.e. DC, stands for the originals of which the images, i.e. the shadows and reflections in AD, are likenesses. These originals are said to comprise "the living things about us and plants and all manufactured objects". Plato now asks us to agree that the visible world (i.e. in our diagram AC) has been divided in respect to degrees of reality and truth (the Greek word here is the single word ἀλήθεια (*aletheia*)) in such a way that as the sphere of belief is to the sphere of knowledge (i.e. as AC is to CB) so is the copy to the original (i.e. so is AD to DC). This is an important passage to which we shall return; at the moment it is enough to notice that whereas hitherto AC in our diagram has been described as representing the visible world, in the ratios which Plato now draws here it is referred to more widely as representing the world of belief (*to doxaston*).

So much then for the two sub-segments of AC. When Plato turns to the main upper segment of the Line, i.e. CB, which we have already at 509 been told represents the intelligible world, he adopts a different procedure. Instead of distinguishing between CE and EB by assigning them different objects, as he had done in the case of the two lower subsegments, he distinguishes them rather by the different methods of inquiry the mind uses in each of them. These methods of inquiry, he tells us at 510b, differ in two respects. (1) In the first upper sub-segment, i.e. CE, the mind proceeds by using as images the objects of the preceding sub-segment, i.e. the objects of DC, which, it will be remembered, were themselves originals relatively to the shadows and reflections which formed the content of AD; whereas in the second upper sub-segment, i.e. EB, the mind makes no use of such images but conducts its inquiry solely by means of Forms. (2) In the first upper sub-segment, i.e. CE, the mind begins from hypotheses or assumptions and proceeds not to a first principle but to a conclusion, whereas in the second upper sub-segment, i.e. EB, the mind proceeds to an unhypothetical first principle. At the end of 510b Glaucon protests that he has not fully understood, and the rest of 510 and most of 511, as far as 511d, are taken up with a fuller explanation of these two methods of inquiry. This passage is of the greatest importance, and we shall be considering it in detail shortly. At present, it is enough to note that it becomes clear from it that Plato is contrasting the method of the mathematical sciences (in CE) with what he

believes ought to be the method of philosophy (in EB). Next
in 511d he proceeds to assign to the four sections of the Line
four corresponding states of mind, intelligence, νόησις (*noesis*),
to the highest section (EB), thinking, διάνοια (*dianoia*), to the
next (CE), belief or commonsense assurance, πίστις (*pistis*), to
the next (DC), and illusion, εἰκασία (*eikasia*), to the lowest segment of all (AD). Again we shall have to return to these states
of mind later and attempt to justify the English meanings we
have assigned here to the Greek words Plato uses. Finally, in
the very important closing sentences of Book VI, he bids us
arrange these states in terms of a proportion, attributing to
them such a degree of clearness as their objects have of truth
and reality.

This concludes the Line simile. Before we look at it in
detail we ought to have some idea in outline of the Cave
simile which immediately follows. This simile takes the form
of an allegory, concerned, as Plato tells us at 514, with the enlightenment or lack of enlightenment of our human condition.
He asks us to picture an underground Cave with a long steep
passage opening eventually to the daylight, though because
of the length and steepness of the passage no daylight enters the
Cave itself. At the lower end of the Cave are men who have
been there from childhood, chained in such a way that they
face the end wall of the Cave and can see only what is in front
of them, because their chains will not let them turn their heads.
Higher up the Cave a fire is burning, and between the prisoners
and the fire there is a track across the Cave with a parapet
built along it, like the screen at a puppet show. Behind this
parapet and screened by it are men passing along the track,
some of them talking to one another and carrying all sorts of
manufactured objects — statues of men and animals — which
overtop the parapet and cast their shadows on the end wall
of the Cave which the prisoners face. This, Glaucon interjects
at 515a, is a strange picture and these are strange prisoners,
and Plato answers, in a very important phrase, that the
prisoners are like ourselves. Chained as they are, they can
only see the shadows of themselves and of the objects carried
past by the men behind the parapet thrown by the fire on the
wall of the Cave. Again, if they could talk to one another,

their talk would be about the passing shadows, and if any of the people behind the parapet spoke, the prisoners would suppose the sound, reflected from the wall of the Cave, to come from the shadows before them. The prisoners then would recognise as reality nothing but the shadows.

Plato now, from 515c ff., describes the release of a prisoner and the curing of his lack of wisdom. First, he is freed from his chains and forced to turn round and see the objects (the statues, etc.) whose shadows he had formerly seen on the wall, and the fire itself. This is a painful process : he is dazzled and cannot see clearly, and he believes the objects he now sees to be less real than their shadows with which he was familiar before. Next he is dragged up the entrance to the Cave to the sunlight. This again is a painful process, again he is dazzled, and at first finds it easiest to look at shadows and reflections in the outside world. Later, he is able to look at the things themselves, the heavenly bodies by night, and last of all at the Sun itself (516b). The prisoner so rescued pities his fellow-prisoners in their cave-dwelling and would be prepared to endure anything rather than return to his old beliefs and his old life (516d) ; and if he had to return to the Cave and discriminate once more between the shadows, it would take some time to become accustomed to the darkness there, and he would cut a poor figure among his fellow-prisoners, who would say that his sight had been ruined by his ascent to the daylight, and would be ready to kill anyone who tried to set themselves free. Finally, in 517a-c we are given instructions as to what we are to do with this allegory. We are to apply, or attach, or connect it with what was said before ; and Plato then goes on to mention particular points of connection whose detailed consideration can be left for the moment.

Having now looked in outline at these two similes of the Divided Line and the Cave, we turn now to the vexed question of their relation to one another and to the simile of the Sun, and of how in general they are to be understood. As we have already said, there has been a great deal of discussion on these similes and there is a variety of divergent interpretations. Such being the position, it may be helpful, by way of giving some indication of the matters in dispute, to state briefly two well-known interpretations which are widely divergent. One of these is what we might call the orthodox or traditional interpretation, the other a more recent interpretation particularly associated with the name of Professor A. S. Ferguson. By discussion of these two widely differing interpretations we may also be able to give some indication of some intermediate positions that have been adopted, and suggest some conclusions of our own.

There are two points that are central to the orthodox view. (a) In the first place this view holds that the Line symbolises four mental states arranged in an ascending scale of clarity, with, corresponding to them, four classes of objects arranged in an ascending scale of truth or reality. If we look back at our diagram, then, the lowest segment of the Line, AD, represents a state of mind that has a low degree of clarity, and whose objects correspondingly have a low degree of reality. DC represents a state of mind that has more clarity than that represented by AD, and whose objects similarly have more reality than the objects in AD, and similarly again with the segment CE, until finally we come to the topmost part of the Line EB, where the state of mind represented has the maximum of clarity, and whose corresponding objects have the maximum degree of reality. The Line then represents four degrees or stages of insight, representing the stages through which the human mind must pass if it is to reach perfect knowledge of that which is completely real. There is a progression from each stage to the next, and all four sections of the Line represent actual stages in the mind's development, each stage having its corresponding object of thought. Hence R. L. Nettleship in his *Lectures on the Republic* called his chapter on the divided line "The Four Stages of Intelligence". (b) The second point that is central to the orthodox view is that it holds that the Cave simile has to be applied to the Line simile in the sense that a parallelism holds between the two. We might say that the Line is a map of the country through which the human mind must travel as it progresses from a low degree of intelligence to the highest, while the allegory of the Cave pictures to us the actual journey through the country mapped out in the Line. On this view then we would expect to find four stages in the journey corresponding to the four levels of intelligence indicated in the Line, and again, as with the Line, each stage of the journey would represent an actual stage in the progress of a human mind from darkness to enlightenment.

Now this orthodox view, when closely examined in the light of what Plato actually says, is by no means without difficulties, and some critics have considered these difficulties to be so great that they have felt obliged either to modify it quite considerably, or, as in Professor Ferguson's case, to abandon it completely. Some of these difficulties will emerge in more detail as our discussion proceeds, but putting the matter fairly generally at the moment, Professor Ferguson's position is that the orthodox view misunderstands Plato's intentions and misrepresents his symbolism. He further holds that this becomes all the clearer when we attempt to work out the orthodox view in detail — that, for example, we can find no philosophically significant actual level of apprehension to correspond to the lowest segment of the Line, that we cannot find stages in the Cave corresponding to the four sections of the Line, and that in particular the attempt to make the initial state of the prisoners in the Cave parallel with the lowest segment of the Line breaks down altogether — that in fact the Cave just will not fit the Line if we attempt to take the similes in the way recommended by the orthodox view. For these reasons the Ferguson view takes a radical way with the orthodox view, by denying outright the two points described above as central to that view. (a) In the first place Ferguson denies that the Line represents a fourfold classification of mental states according to clarity and a corresponding fourfold classification of objects according to their reality, with the attendant notion that there is a progression from one state to the next. Instead he maintains the following view. The Line simile is a continuation of the Sun simile — and we noted above that at 509c Plato explicitly introduced it as "completing the comparison with the sun". Now in the Sun simile what was brought out was the analogy between the special position of the sun in the visible world and the special position of the Form of the Good in the intelligible world. Plato in the Line simile continues the comparison with the Sun in order now, to use Ferguson's own

words, "to illustrate how two successive methods of studying
the intelligible may lead to knowledge of that transcendent
Good, still using the convenient symbolism of the visible"
(Ferguson, *Classical Quarterly*, Vol. XV, 1921, p. 136). Both
the Sun simile and the Line simile and, as we shall see, the
Cave simile as well, are all, in this view, really parts of one
simile which Ferguson calls the simile of Light. Thus in the
Line simile an illustration is again being used from the visible
world to bring out the difference between two methods, namely
that of mathematics and that of philosophy, which are used in
the study of the intelligible world. These two methods are
represented by the two upper segments of the Line: i.e. in
terms of our figure, CE stands for mathematics and EB stands
for philosophy. The whole lower Line, i.e. AC, represents
simply and solely the visible world (not, as the orthodox view
holds, the whole world of sensible things, the objects of belief),
and is itself sub-divided into the two segments AD, standing
for shadows and reflections, and DC, standing for the originals
which cast the shadows; and its function is simply and solely
to symbolise the relationship between mathematics and philosophy represented in the two upper segments of the Line. What
is being said in the Line then is that as shadows and reflections
are to their originals in respect of clearness, so is mathematics
to philosophy: i.e. as AD is to DC so is CE to EB in respect
of clearness. Putting it more generally, Plato is calling attention in the lower Line to a familiar situation in the visible world
illuminated by the Sun, namely the situation of seeing shadows
and reflections, e.g. the reflection of a tree in water, and seeing
the originals which cast the reflections, e.g. the tree itself. The
original is clearer than the shadow. He is then inviting us to
take this as an illustration of the relationship between mathematics and philosophy: as images are less clear than their
originals, so mathematics is less clear than philosophy, and
the same ratio in respect of clarity holds between each of the
two pairs. The important point to grasp then is that the
function of the whole lower Line is purely illustrative — it
illustrates by the distinction between images and originals the
relationship of mathematics to philosophy. As Ferguson puts
it, "Once the logos [ratio] has been given, there is nothing

further to say about these images and originals. They are used
here, as they are used outside the cave, to furnish an analogy
for grades of intelligibles; and they are not used here any more
than the objects outside the cave, for any other purpose"
(*Classical Quarterly*, Vol. XXVIII, 1934, p. 200). (b) The
second main point which we described above as central to the
orthodox view was the parallelism between the Line and the
Cave. This, too, Ferguson denies. For him the Cave allegory
"is not framed to exhibit how opinion mounts by a graduated
ladder to knowledge. It is not even primarily concerned
with the relation of the sensible to the intelligible" (*Classical
Quarterly*, Vol. XVI, 1922, p. 15). Instead it introduces a new
point. It is a political allegory whose purpose is to contrast
two ways of life: on the one hand, in the Cave, the life of
politics, and on the other hand, outside the Cave, the life of
theory, or, we might say more generally, the life of philosophy.
The prisoners in the Cave represent men engaged in the activities of the Greek states of Plato's own time. As we saw earlier
in Book VI, Plato regards contemporary politics as perverted
and corrupt and its ends as false, and he thought this inevitable
so long as political power was divorced from philosophy. Only
if the rulers in a state knew the true end of life, the Form of
the Good, would the state itself be good; but the Greek states
of his time, he thought, were controlled by men who despised
philosophy and who, therefore, had no knowledge of the real
end of human life. Hence their values, and the values of the
whole state, were false and perverted. This state of affairs,
Ferguson argues, is what the Cave allegory is intended to
represent. The whole machinery of the Cave, firelight instead
of sunlight, manufactured objects instead of real things, and so
on, is meant to convey the warped and corrupting atmosphere
of contemporary society. The state of mind of the prisoners
in the Cave is not even one of belief but one of perverted belief.
Their life is contrasted with the life of the philosopher in the
sunlight outside the Cave. The outside of the Cave picks up
again the symbolism of the sunlight, which we had both in the
Sun simile and in the lower Line, and the whole Cave allegory
is to be attached (517a) to what was said before, i.e. to both
the Sun and the Line similes, the point of attachment being

the visible region outside the Cave. In a later article (*Classical Quarterly*, Vol. XXVIII, 1934, p. 209) the application of the Cave allegory is made even more general, and Ferguson paraphrases the words in 517a, "apply this allegory as a whole to what we said about philosophers in politics". To sum up this Ferguson view then, the whole lower segment of the Line represents only the visible world, and uses from that world the relation between shadows and originals to illustrate the relation between mathematics and philosophy symbolised in the whole upper Line; the Line and the Cave are not parallel; and the Cave itself, still using the general simile of light, but this time the artificial light of the fire, contrasts by this means the corrupt and false life of the states of Plato's day, with the life of the philosopher in the sunlight outside the Cave.

There is no doubt that Ferguson's treatment of this part of the *Republic* has contributed greatly to our understanding of it. There are, however, reasons, some of which may be briefly mentioned, which make both of his main contentions as set out at (a) and (b) above dubious.

(a) Ferguson's first contention is that the whole of the lower Line stands merely for the visible and serves a purely illustrative purpose. Against this, (1) if Ferguson were right, Plato would have made his intention clearer, by using two parallel lines, one for the visible, the other for the intelligible. Instead he uses one continuous line. (2) Plato stresses at 510b, 510e, 511a, that the mathematician uses as images what in the preceding sub-section served as originals: i.e. mathematics represented by CE of the Line uses as images the objects belonging to DC of the Line, which, in their turn, are the originals of the shadows and reflections at AD. This suggests that just as there is continuity in the symbol Plato uses (a single continuous line), so there is continuity between all the four subsections of what is symbolised, and that thus the four states of mind symbolised by the four sub-sections of the Line are on a common scale of clearness just as their objects are on a common scale of truth or reality. If this is correct, then the purpose of the lower Line cannot be confined solely to that of illustrating the relationship between the two sub-sections of the upper Line. (3) At the end of Book VI, 511e, after the four states of

mind — intelligence, thinking, belief, and illusion — have been
assigned, each to their sub-section of the Line, we are then
explicitly told to arrange them in a proportion "attributing
to them such a degree of clearness as their objects have of
truth or reality": i.e. Plato seems to be explicitly saying that
just as there is a common scale of clearness applicable to the
four states of mind, so there is a common scale of reality applicable to their objects. For this a single continuous Line is an
appropriate symbol, and again the inference is that the lower
Line cannot be merely illustrative of the upper Line. (4) On
the view that the lower Line is merely illustrative, it stands
for the visible world, and the visible world only — it illustrates
the relation between mathematics and philosophy from the
visual situation of seeing shadows, etc., and seeing the originals
which cast the shadows. Now at 509d, consistently with this
view, Plato refers to the whole lower Line (AC) as representing
to horaton or *to horomenon*, i.e. the visible world; but at 510a
(though Ferguson understands the passage differently — cf.
Classical Quarterly, Vol. XV, 1921, pp. 143-144), the whole lower
Line seems to be referred to as the sphere of belief (likeness
stands to original as belief to knowledge), where instead of *to
horomenon*, i.e. the visible, the wider Greek word *doxaston* is
used, i.e. the world of belief, which would comprise the whole
world of particulars and would in fact be the world of the non-
philosopher with which we are familiar from the end of Book
V. Further, the term 'belief' is again used of the lower Line
at 534a; and in 511d (cf. also 533d) in describing 'thinking',
the state of mind of the mathematician, Plato refers to it as
being something between belief (*doxa*) and intelligence, where
'belief' again seems to refer to the whole lower Line. It would
seem then from Plato's own use of language that he intended
the lower part of the Line to stand for more than merely the
visible world, that in fact it stands for the world of the many
particulars, the whole world of the non-philosopher of Book V,
and for his state of mind, belief. Apart from their linguistic
significance the two passages at 511d and 533d also reinforce
our earlier arguments, for they imply that belief (represented,
if we are right, by the whole lower part of the Line), thinking and intelligence form a series such that, as 533d tells us,

thinking is clearer than belief, but dimmer than knowledge. Thus the states symbolised by the Line would be being evaluated on a common scale, and thus what was symbolised by the lower Line would not have merely illustrative significance.

(b) Ferguson's second contention is that the Line and the Cave are not parallel. Here again, in the same summary way, we will mention four considerations which weigh against this contention. (1) 517a-c contains Plato's instructions as to what we are to do with the allegory of the Cave. The first few lines of the instructions are particularly relevant to our present discussion, and translated literally they run as follows: "Now, my dear Glaucon, I said, you must apply this simile in its entirety to what we were saying before, comparing the region revealed through sight to the prison-dwelling, and the light of the fire in it to the power of the sun; and if you take the upward ascent and the sight of things in the upper world as the ascent of the soul to the intelligible region, you will be in possession of my surmise, since that is what you wish to hear". In these instructions the phrase 'what we were saying before' is in itself quite general — it could refer to the Line simile or to both the Sun simile and the Line simile (as Ferguson held in the earlier article already mentioned), or even more widely (as he held in the later article) to the discussion in Book VI, 488 ff., on the gulf between philosophers and politicians. Advocates of a parallelist view, taking 'what we were saying before' to refer to the Line, have also understood the Greek word translated by 'apply' to mean 'apply' in a quasi-mathematical sense of finding a one-to-one correspondence between the stages in the Cave and the divisions in the Line. In fact, however, the Greek word is not used by the mathematical writers in this sense, and Ferguson is justified in his earlier article in suggesting a wider meaning of 'apply' as simply 'attach', or, it might be suggested, 'connect', or again 'link on to'. The point here is that the Greek word does not in itself commit one to finding some one-to-one correspondence. So far then there is nothing in the language of Plato's instructions which would debar the Ferguson view. It is with the word in the next clause, translated 'compare', that serious difficulty arises. On Ferguson's view the Cave simile introduces a new point, the contrast between the debased world of politics with its perverted beliefs, inside the Cave, and the sunlit world of the philosopher outside the Cave. He has then to understand 'compare' in the instructions as 'compare and contrast' — as he says in his earlier article "the visible region, held together by sunlight, is compared and contrasted with a wretched place where the light is a fire and the place a prison". Now the Greek word ἀφομοιοῦν (aphomoioun), translated here as 'compare', means literally 'to make like' and then 'to liken to' or 'compare', but not 'to contrast', and thus the Ferguson interpretation of the word as 'compare and contrast', which is necessary to his view of the Cave, will not stand. What we are being told to do rather is to compare or liken "the region revealed through sight", which was symbolised by the whole lower Line, with the Cave: i.e. the whole lower Line then is parallel with the Cave. Further, though in the Line nothing is said explicitly of "an ascent of the soul to the intelligible" the notion is implicit in the language used there — at 511d "intelligence" is assigned to the "highest" sub-section, "thinking" to the second, and so on — and thus it is reasonable to take the next clause of the instructions, which bids us take the upward ascent from the Cave as the ascent of the soul to the intelligible world as again referring back to the Line. (2) At the end of 533, after having explained the role played by the mathematical studies in the rescue of the prisoners from the Cave, Plato returns again to the diagram of the Line, recalls the names he gave there to the four states of mind represented by the four divisions of the Line, and mentions various ratios involved. The implication of the passage is that the Line diagram is applicable also to the Cave, and thus that Cave and Line are parallel. (3) In the Line Plato makes extensive use of the shadow-original relationship. He does the same in the Cave. This surely must mean that there is a clear correspondence between the two similes. Mr. Murphy, in arguing for the application of the Line to the Cave, remarks (*Classical Quarterly*, Vol. XXVIII, 1934, p. 213) that "even if Plato had not intended it, yet the 'Line' may be said to apply itself; it sets up a general thesis about the ratios of intelligibility as between shadows and their originals, and the situation within the cave is in fact (even if

Plato hadn't noticed it!) a case in point". (4) On Ferguson's view the Cave represents perverted belief, the corrupt world of contemporary Greek politics. Now if Ferguson were correct about this, it would seem that once the ideal state had been established, there would be no Cave world. In fact, however, at 519-520 (cf. also 539-540) Plato envisages his philosophers descending in turn to the Cave to take their part in the unenviable task of ruling, and it is clear that he regards the Cave as a permanent feature even of his own state. Thus the Cave cannot represent an unnatural, perverted form of belief; rather it represents the world of the ordinary non-philosopher, the world of belief, which, if we are right, is also symbolised in the lower section of the Line. Thus again in this respect Cave and Line would correspond.

There are then, as can be seen even from these summary remarks, reasons which make it doubtful whether Ferguson's two contentions, (a) that the whole lower section of the Line is illustrative only, and (b) that the Cave itself is not parallel with the Line, should be accepted. Two points, however, arise. First, part of the Ferguson case was that no other interpretation would work at all satisfactorily. Thus, even granted the difficulties for his view mentioned above, it might be that one might still have to accept his interpretation on the ground that any other involved still greater troubles. It is incumbent on us then to attempt to produce some other interpretation which, while avoiding the difficulties of the Ferguson view, makes sense of the similes. Secondly, it does not follow that if the Ferguson view is rejected we are necessarily committed to the orthodox view, and in fact other interpretations have been offered which, while agreeing with us in rejecting Ferguson's two contentions, nevertheless differ considerably from the orthodox view. One of the most attractive of those intermediate views is what we shall call the 'tripartite' view, a form of which has been advocated by Mr. Murphy (*The Interpretation of Plato's Republic*, Chapter VIII, pp. 151-164). This view agrees that the whole main lower Line (AC) is not merely illustrative. The whole main lower Line, it argues, stands for belief, and in this respect it agrees with the orthodox view. Where it disagrees is in holding that the sub-division

within the sphere of belief between shadows and reflections on
the one hand, and the originals which cast the shadows on the
other, is purely illustrative. What it is saying then, in terms of
our diagram, is that AC stands for the sphere of belief, but
within the whole sphere of belief the familiar relation of shadows
(represented by AD) to originals (represented by DC) is picked
out to illustrate the relation between the whole world of belief
and the intelligible world, i.e. between AC and CB; i.e. as
shadows are to their originals so is the sensible to the intelligible.
The sub-division then within the main lower Line has purely
illustrative significance, though the whole main lower Line has
a genuine philosophical content and stands for belief. Similarly, in the case of the Cave it agrees with the orthodox view
in holding that the Line and Cave are parallel, but disagrees
in that it argues, following on its position about the Line, that
while the whole of the Cave stands for belief, the first advance
within the Cave of the prisoners from the shadows to the
artificial objects which cast the shadows is again purely illustrative, illustrating the advance from the sensible to the intelligible, i.e. from the Cave to the world outside the Cave. The
whole Cave, then, is parallel with the whole lower Line and
represents belief, but again in the Cave simile the shadow-
original relation is picked out within the Cave to illustrate the
advance from sensible to intelligible. It follows then that we
should be wrong in attempting to supply a philosophically
important content for the first section of the Line, and wrong
in supposing that the first advance in the Cave had in itself
a philosophical significance. In both cases the significance is
purely illustrative.

Now, in fact, it is the difficulties which the orthodox interpretation has with the sub-division of the main lower Line
and with the first stage of advance in the Cave that have provided one of the main reasons both for the more radical Ferguson view and also for the intermediate tripartite view just
discussed. The orthodox view, it would be said, cannot assign
any convincing philosophical significance to the sub-division
within the main lower Line, nor make it fit with the Cave.
We must then return to the orthodox view to see what can be
said for it on this score. At 510a Plato tells us that the lower

sub-section of the Line (AD) stands for images, and he explains
that he means by images "shadows . . . reflections in water
and everything of that kind", while the upper sub-section
(DC) stands for the actual things of which the first are likenesses; and later, at 511e, he assigns a state of mind which he
calls εἰκασία (*eikasia*) to the lower sub-section (AD) and one
which he calls πίστις (*pistis*) to the upper sub-section (DC).
It may be helpful for us to try to decide what exactly Plato
means by εἰκασία. Here Greek linguistic usage does not help
us much. The Greek word in itself could mean simply 'the
state of mind concerned with images' or it could mean 'conjecture', and it is such a comparatively rare word that we can
draw no reliable conclusion from its use elsewhere. This is
the more unfortunate in that the translation 'conjecture' produces an ambiguity. If we describe the state of mind of the
man looking at shadows and reflections as 'conjecture', we
might mean by this, (a) that from the shadows, etc., he makes
guesses or conjectures about the originals that cast the shadows;
or (b) we might simply mean that within the world of shadows
he makes guesses or conjectures about the relations of the
shadows to one another, i.e., that his conjectures are confined
to the shadow world. The importance of this is that if we
accept (a) as the correct way to understand Plato's use of
eikasia here, then the state of mind represented by the lowest
section of the Line will not fit in with the state of mind of the
prisoners in the Cave; for it will be remembered that in his
description of the Cave Plato takes pains to emphasise (514a)
that the prisoners cannot turn their heads, and so have no
notion that there are originals which cast the shadows. Thus
there is no question of the prisoners conjecturing from the
shadows about the originals which cast the shadows. In point
of fact, at 516c-d Plato does represent his prisoners as making
conjectures (though he does not actually use the noun εἰκασία
or the related verb), but they do so in the sense at (b) above,
i.e. they make guesses about which shadows will follow which.
If, then, we wish to maintain that Line and Cave are parallel
(and we have seen reasonable grounds for this), and if we also
wish to maintain that the parallelism is exact, in the sense that
the first section of the Line corresponds to the state of mind of

the prisoners in the Cave (and so far anyhow this is a more disputable matter), we must understand *eikasia* in some other sense than 'conjecturing about originals through their reflections', i.e. 'conjecture' in sense (a) above. Now linguistically, as we have already noted, there is no objection to this — the word can mean simply 'the state of mind concerned with images', 'apprehension of images', 'imagination' (provided the latter word is understood in the sense of imaging, and not with the sort of connotation it has in, for example, 'a writer (or poet etc.) of great imagination'). We could then, working back from the Cave and insisting on close correspondence, decide at once for this latter meaning. Since, however, we are still uncertain how far we are justified in pressing such a close correspondence, it would be desirable, if possible, to produce some independent ground for advocating our understanding *eikasia* in the sense of 'imagination' just explained. That there is some independent ground for this is perhaps suggested when we look back first to 476c, where Plato — contrasting the non-philosopher who believes in the existence of beautiful things, but not of Beauty itself, with the philosopher who knows Beauty itself and the other Forms — describes the former as leading a dreaming life. He there explains what he means by 'dreaming' as 'thinking what is like something not to be like it but to be the thing itself, which it is like', i.e. taking a likeness for the original. Next, at 533b the mathematician, in his attitude to his hypotheses or assumptions, is described as "dreaming about being". We shall have to say more about this when we discuss mathematics in the next chapter, but meantime for our present purpose, if we follow what was said at 476c about dreaming, the mathematician's state of mind will be one in which in some sense or other he too takes a likeness for the original, not realising that it is a likeness. Finally, in the mechanics of the Line, the division representing the mathematical studies (CE) is related to the lowest division of the Line (AD) (see the ratios drawn at 534a), and this suggests that as the mathematician in some sense takes likeness for original, not realising that it is a likeness, so the man in the state of *eikasia* does the same. This would mean then that the state of mind represented by the lowest division of the Line is not one of guessing at originals through their likenesses (conjecture in that sense), but one in which likeness is accepted as reality, without any realisation that it is a likeness, i.e. one concerned solely with likenesses or images; and it would then be parallel to the state of mind of the prisoners in the Cave.

Granted then that we understand *eikasia* in this sense, can we assign to it any convincing philosophical significance? In attempting to answer this question we may first recall that we have agreed that the whole lower Line represents more than simply the visible world, that it stands for the whole world of belief. In seeking some content for *eikasia* we are not then confined simply to the visible. If with this in mind we look at 517d, we find that Socrates there, in describing the plight of the philosopher who is compelled to return to the Cave, represents him as having to contend in the law-courts or elsewhere "about the shadows of justice or the images [i.e. in the allegory, the statues, etc.] which cast the shadows"; and again at 520c the politicians in the states of Plato's time are described as "fighting with one another about shadows and struggling for power". It might be suggested then that the shadows on the wall of the Cave and the shadows and reflections of the lowest section of the Line would in part symbolise the imitations of justice, goodness and so on, created by the rhetoricians and sophists and politicians in the law-courts or in the assembly. These would be representations of what was just or good, designed to achieve one's immediate end — the winning of one's case in the courts, the gaining of one's way in the assembly. That in fact they misrepresented justice, etc., that they were merely shadows of them, would not in the least matter, provided they were presented with such rhetorical skill as to persuade the jurors or the assembly into unquestioning acceptance. Correspondingly, the state of mind that accepted these representations at their face value, not realising that they were mere imitations of the real thing, would be *eikasia*. The second section of the Line and similarly the second stage in the Cave, when the released prisoner looks at the originals (i.e. the statues, etc.) which cast their shadows on the wall, would, by contrast, represent the state of mind of the man who looks at the facts for himself and reaches his own conclusions about

what is right or good. The contents of this state of mind would
be first-hand opinions, as opposed to the second-hand opinions
purveyed by the rhetorician and politician, who put shadows or
semblances between men's minds and the facts. The man in
this state of mind would still be far from philosophic insight,
would still be in the realm of belief, but nevertheless would
have advanced significantly beyond the stage of unquestioned
acceptance of the semblances presented to him by the rhetorician. It may be objected that, apart from the fact that this is
to read a good deal into what Plato actually says, in any case
the state of mind that accepts second-hand opinions for the
real thing is not a separately identifiable state meriting a distinct section of the Line and a distinct stage in the Cave to
itself; nor is the advance from this to first-hand opinions, to
decision about the facts for oneself, an advance meriting the
importance that Plato apparently attached to it. Here, however, we have to remember the attitude that Plato displays
throughout his dialogues to the sophists, rhetoricians and politicians. It is clear throughout that he regards them as a sub-
stantial threat to the living of the good life. We have only to
look at 492-493 of the *Republic*, where Plato is describing the
corruption of the philosophic nature in contemporary society,
to see this. It is true that there it is the Athenian populace
"crowding together at meetings of the assembly or in the law-
courts or at the theatre" that is the arch-corrupter, but the
role of the sophist and politician is also clear. They pander
to the unthinking tastes of "the great and powerful beast" (the
mob), and without in the least knowing which of its humours
and desires are good or bad, just or unjust, they simply fit
these terms to the reactions of the great beast, calling what it
likes good, and so on. The same view of the danger of the
sophist and rhetorician can be seen in the earlier dialogue, the
Gorgias, for example, at 464-465 (cf. the proportions drawn in
465c — "as the art of adornment is to gymnastic, so is sophistry
to legislation" and "as cookery is to medicine, so is rhetoric to
justice"). In the dialogues later than the *Republic* the same
antipathy is seen. In the *Theaetetus*, for example, at 172 ff.,
the "free man", the philosopher, is contrasted with the man
of affairs, for example the pleader in the law-courts, who has

to learn how to flatter his master (the court), and whose "apprenticeship in slavery has dwarfed and twisted his growth and taken away his free spirit, driving him into crooked ways" (173a). Again, the whole of the dialogue the *Sophist* is, nominally anyhow, concerned with defining the sophist and revealing his true nature as an impostor, as an imitator of that of which he has no knowledge (267). His art (and that of the demagogue too) is a branch of the human art that is concerned with the production of images, and this in turn takes two forms, one (*eikastike*) the production of genuine likenesses, and the other (*phantastike*) the production of mere semblances. It is with the latter that the sophist is concerned — he is a mere maker of semblances or appearances (*phantasmata*), 266 ff. It will be noticed here that in the language used there is at least an echo of the *Republic*, and some, e.g. Adam, have thought that the objects of the two arts of likeness-making and semblance-making clearly belong to the lowest section of the divided Line. How far this can be pressed is perhaps doubtful : there are, for example, complications about divine image-making in the *Sophist* which make direct application more difficult. What is true, however, is that the *Sophist* again illustrates the importance Plato attaches to the sophist and demagogue as influences for evil ; and it is also true that there are passages in the *Sophist* that certainly make us think of the *Republic*, and particularly of the Cave allegory, for example the passage at 234 which describes how the young can be imposed upon by means of images of all things conveyed by words, and how all these illusions created by words are upset by the realities encountered later in life.

There is reason then for believing that, in Plato's view anyhow, the imitations of goodness, justice and so on embodied in the words of the sophist, the rhetorician and the demagogue constituted a serious menace to a good society, and that men were only too ready to be beguiled by them and to accept second-hand opinions as the truth. It may be thought that Plato over-emphasises the danger. Yet when we think of our own society and consider how many of our own beliefs and value judgments are second-hand and have been accepted by us unthinkingly when they have been presented to us by others

through the press or television or other means of mass com-
munication, we may begin to see Plato's meaning. It may be
an exaggeration to say, as, on our interpretation, he does, that
the prisoners in the Cave are "like ourselves", i.e. that most
men without knowing it live in this sense in a shadow-world,
but it is an exaggeration that has some point to it ; and for the
same reason the orthodox interpretation of the Line and the
Cave, which understands Plato to be saying this, is also not
without point. There is in addition another class of "imitations" which the orthodox view would assign to the lowest
division of the Line, namely the imitations produced by the
painter and the imitative poet. Plato discusses the work of the
painter and the dramatic poet in the early part of Book X of
the *Republic* (595a-602b) and the view he takes there is that
their products are like mirror-images (596d), "thrice removed
from reality, nothing more than semblances" (599). The
word *eikasia* does not occur in the discussion in Book X, but it
is not unplausible to assign the semblances or imitations created
by the artist to the lowest division of the Line, where they too
will be among the objects of *eikasia*. Moreover at 598c Plato
remarks that a skilful painter could deceive children or simple
people into thinking his picture of a carpenter to be a real
carpenter, i.e. they take the imitation to be the real thing,
whereas, as he says at 598d below, they have been tricked by
an illusionist and imitator. This might be regarded as some
confirmation of the interpretation offered above of *eikasia* as a
state of mind that accepts a likeness as the original, not realising
that it is a likeness. For art and its possible connection with
eikasia compare also in the discussion of "music" in the *Laws*,
666 ff., the reference to the "eikastic" arts (667c) and the
remark at 668b that "all musical compositions consist in imitation and representation" where the Greek word for the latter
is ἀπεικασία (*apeikasia*), which again might be taken to have
some bearing on the use of *eikasia* in the *Republic*. Moreover,
it is clear both from the *Republic* and from other dialogues that
Plato regarded the imitations of the artist as potentially dangerous. It is therefore not unplausible that he should have wished
to mark off these imitations, as well as those of the sophists and
rhetoricians, from the real things of which they were mere

images, and that similarly he should have regarded it as a distinct and identifiable (and dangerous) state of mind where
likeness was taken for original and men were deceived by
imitations.

The traditional orthodox view then can put up a fair case
for taking the lowest sub-division of the Line as of philosophical
significance, at any rate in relation to Greek society as Plato
knew it, and can understand the Cave allegory in such a way
as to fit in with this. It should, however, also be obvious to
the reader, even from the brief account above, that there is a
great deal of divergence of opinion amongst commentators on
the interpretation of this part of Plato, and it seems doubtful if
any final and definitive interpretation is likely to be reached.
(See also the note at the end of this chapter.) As J. E. Raven
has argued in an article on *Sun, Divided Line and Cave* (*Classical
Quarterly*, N.S., Vol. III, 1953), what seems to have happened
is this. Plato begins this whole section of the *Republic*, which
comprises the three inter-connected similes of Sun, Line and
Cave, by using the visible world and the position of the Sun
in the visible world to illustrate the intelligible world and the
position of the Form of the Good in the intelligible world.
Sight then is analogous to intelligence. Now, as we noted
earlier, the Line simile is introduced at 509c as a continuation
of the Sun simile, and here again it appears that the visible
world, represented by the whole lower Line, is to serve as an
analogue for and to illustrate the intelligible. At the same
time, however, we have to remember the fundamental contrast
in Plato, which we have seen at the end of Book V, between
the world of belief or opinion and the intelligible world, the
world of Forms, and we have to remember that when he is
making that contrast, the visible world constitutes part of the
world of belief. Thus when he is thinking along these lines,
so far from the visible world serving as an analogue for the
intelligible, it is sharply contrasted with it. At the beginning
of the Line simile then, as in the Sun simile, it appears that the
visible world is to be used for the purposes immediately in
hand as an analogue for the intelligible; but as the Line and
Cave similes develop, the standing contrast between the world
of belief (including the visible world) and the world of intelli-

gence begins to emerge again, so that at the end of the three
similes we are back again at the old contrast of Book V, where
now once more the Cave, as representing the world of belief,
is contrasted with the region outside the Cave representing
the intelligible world. Thus, to quote Raven (p. 32), "the
Divided Line has in fact — and herein lies its difficulty — a
dual function to perform. It sets out not only, as Plato tells
us, to complete the analogy between the two worlds, visible
and intelligible, but also to prepare us for the return, effected
by the time we come to the Cave, to the old contrast between
opinion and knowledge." It seems then that too much has
crept into Plato's similes, that they begin with analogy and
end with contrast, and that thus their interpretation has been
made extremely difficult. As Raven says, "at some point in
the mere three pages [in Plato's text] devoted to the Divided
Line the transition has to be effected from temporary analogy
back to habitual contrast, and the question at issue is thus
reduced to the question of where that point lies". We have
seen that the Ferguson view, in stressing the analogical or
illustrative role of the visible world in the similes to the point
of excluding any element of contrast between visible and intelligible, encounters considerable difficulties. At the same time,
the work of Ferguson and others who have followed a similar
line has made it clear that, on any interpretation, part of what
Plato is doing is to illustrate features in the intelligible by
means of the visible. This is what makes some form of the
tripartite view, which we referred to earlier, attractive, in
that the tripartite view both recognises the illustrative role of
the visible in the first two sections of the Line and the first two
stages in the Cave, and yet at the same time finds a place in the
lower Line as a whole, as contrasted with the upper Line, and
in the Cave as a whole, as contrasted with the world outside
the Cave, for the familiar contrast between belief and knowledge. Nevertheless, as we have tried to indicate, there are
some grounds for thinking that Plato would not have wished
the sub-division of the lower Line, and the change from shadows
to originals in the Cave, to be understood as merely illustrative,
and thus perhaps some grounds for in the end holding to the
traditional view of four philosophically significant levels in the

Line and four stages in the Cave. Only, if we do take this view, we must also recognise the illustrative element in the sub-divisions both in the lower Line and the Cave. This is particularly so in the case of the Line, since it is clear that there Plato's main interest is in the difference between mathematics and philosophy, and that the sub-division in the lower Line, whatever other role it may also have, is intended to illustrate this difference.

This chapter has, unfortunately but unavoidably, been concerned in large part with questions of scholarship and not with philosophy. In the next chapter, while clearing up a few further points of interpretation, we shall be mainly concerned with the philosophical implications of the three similes we have been considering. Meantime, in concluding this chapter, it may be well, in the light of what we have said, to consider the English translations we are to adopt for the two Greek words εἰκασία (*eikasia*) and πίστις (*pistis*) which Plato uses for the states of mind represented by the lowest sub-section (AD) and the second sub-section (DC) respectively of the Line. Earlier we said that *eikasia* linguistically could mean simply 'the state of mind concerned with images', 'apprehension of images'. We subsequently argued that Plato intended the word to signify the state of mind in which a person accepted a likeness or imitation for the original, without any inkling of the fact that it was only a likeness. In the light of the whole discussion, it might be suggested that 'illusion', which is the rendering used by Lee in his translation, might be adopted for *eikasia*, though as we have already said it is extremely difficult to find a really satisfactory translation, and in fact the word 'illusion' itself could have logical implications that are alien to Plato's intentions. The usual rendering of *pistis* is 'belief', and perhaps that is as near as we can get to what Plato means. We want to convey the difference between the state of mind involved when we are dealing with things at second hand, with imitations or likenesses, and the state of mind involved when we are dealing directly with things themselves. In the latter case there is a greater security or grasp or assurance — and 'commonsense assurance' might be a possible rendering for *pistis* — which is lacking in the former. This would not mean, on our understanding of *eikasia*, that the man in that state actually felt any insecurity. As W. D. Ross says (*Plato's Theory of Ideas*, p. 67), "εἰκασία and πίστις as used here by Plato are distinguished not by a smaller or greater feeling of security, but by a smaller or greater actual security in their grasp of reality". An objection to adopting the rendering 'belief' for *pistis* in the present context is that we have also been using the word 'belief' in the discussion of the contrast between belief and knowledge at the end of Book V, and we have also described the whole lower Line and the Cave as representing the world of belief. The Greek words Plato uses in this latter context are δόξα (*doxa*) and the verb δοκεῖν (*dokein*). These could be translated as 'opinion' and 'to opine', but in commenting on Book V (Chapter 7, p. 143), we explained why the renderings 'belief' and 'to believe' were to be preferred. The use of the same English word 'belief' both in connection with the whole lower Line (AC) and in connection with the upper segment of it (DC) need not cause trouble, provided that we keep the contexts clear. When, then, we are talking of the whole lower Line we will take it as representing opinion or belief (*doxa*), where belief is being contrasted with knowledge, and when we are talking of the second sub-division of the lower Line we will take it as representing belief, where now in this context belief (*pistis*) is being contrasted with illusion (*eikasia*).

Note.—Perhaps not surprisingly, the one section of the *Republic* on the interpretation of which the authors have found themselves unable to agree is that comprising the Line and the Cave, especially the latter. In this chapter four stages have been found in the Cave, corresponding to the four sections of the Line, and the prisoners in their initial condition are taken to be in the state of *eikasia*. This can be argued for, not only in terms of symmetry with the Line, but also on the ground that the prisoners are said by Plato to be looking at *shadows*, which he had mentioned as one of the defining objects of *eikasia* in the Line (510a). But it seems to one of us that (quite apart from the interpretation of *eikasia* as 'illusion', which is open to question) this view has its own considerable difficulties, chiefly two: (a) that Plato describes the initial state of the prisoners as being the normal condition of man, which (in terms of sight) is certainly *pistis* rather than *eikasia*; (b) that Book VII, to which the Cave is an allegorical introduction, is concerned with two stages of higher education, first that by which, through the mathematical disciplines, a man can attain *dianoia*, and secondly that by which, through philosophical study, he can attain *noesis*; this is the topic of our next chapter. All that Plato, then, is here interested in is the transition from the sensible to the intelligible world, i.e. from *pistis* (or *doxa* in general) to *dianoia*, and then within the intelligible world the transition from *dianoia* to *noesis*. Thus, he has no need in the Cave to distinguish *pistis* from *eikasia*; not that he would deny the distinction, for he has already insisted on it in the Line, but that it plays no part in the Cave. This interpretation cannot be further argued for here. But, on it, the prisoners in their initial state represent men in the condition of believing that the world with which they are familiar through their senses is all the reality that there is. To convince them that this is not so, and that the nature of their own experience presupposes that it is not so, is, says Plato, one of the hardest tasks of education; for it has to be carried out against the opposition of fixed ideas and prejudice. This is represented in the Cave by the reaction of the prisoner who is forced to turn round and look straight at the models, whose shadows are all that he has previously seen. He is being forced to recognise that his own so-called "real world" depends on another; he is being forced to recognise, in fact, that particulars require Forms. He has advanced a step in his education. He has not reached reality yet, but he is nearer than he was. He gets there when he emerges from the cave into the sunlit world (attains *dianoia* in the full sense); and his liberation is completed when finally he can gaze on the Sun/Form of the Good (attains *noesis*). A merit of this interpretation is that it emphasises what Plato wants to emphasise in Book VII, viz. the importance of mathematics as a bridge-study between the sensible and the intelligible worlds.

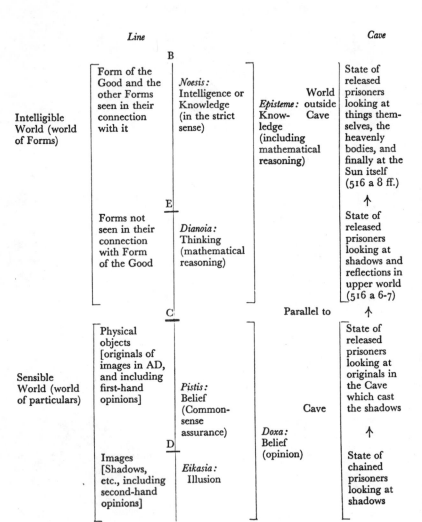

Line   Cave

B

Intelligible World (world of Forms)

Form of the Good and the other Forms seen in their connection with it — *Noesis:* Intelligence or Knowledge (in the strict sense) — *Episteme:* Knowledge (including mathematical reasoning) — World outside Cave — State of released prisoners looking at things themselves, the heavenly bodies, and finally at the Sun itself (516 a 8 ff.)

↑

E

Forms not seen in their connection with Form of the Good — *Dianoia:* Thinking (mathematical reasoning) — State of released prisoners looking at shadows and reflections in upper world (516 a 6-7)

C   Parallel to   ↑

Sensible World (world of particulars)

Physical objects [originals of images in AD, and including first-hand opinions] — *Pistis:* Belief (Common-sense assurance) — Cave — State of released prisoners looking at originals in the Cave which cast the shadows

↑

D

Images [Shadows, etc., including second-hand opinions] — *Eikasia:* Illusion — *Doxa:* Belief (opinion) — State of chained prisoners looking at shadows

A

Chapter 10

MATHEMATICS AND PHILOSOPHY

WE begin this chapter by recalling in a summary way what we have learnt about the Sun, Line and Cave similes in the preceding chapter. The Sun simile we might set out in an abbreviated form as follows:

SUN				GOOD
in				in
VISIBLE WORLD				INTELLIGIBLE WORLD
by its		analogous to		by its
LIGHT				TRUTH
cause of				cause of
SIGHT				KNOWLEDGE
and of existence of objects of sight				and of existence of objects of knowledge (i.e. Forms)

The Line and Cave similes we might attempt to represent diagrammatically as on the opposite page, adopting the interpretations suggested in the last chapter. It will be noticed that in the diagram two stages are now discriminated outside the Cave, corresponding to the two upper divisions of the Line. Here again there has been controversy, but on this it may suffice to say that the stages in the diagram are based on 516a, where in lines 6-7 Plato describes the released prisoner in the upper world as first looking at shadows and reflections. That this is intended to be taken as one distinct stage is suggested by the use of shadows and reflections also to distinguish the lowest section of the Line. In 516a8 the second stage begins with the prisoner subsequently looking at the things themselves and being led thence finally (516b4) to look at the Sun itself. It will also be noticed that in the diagram contents have been assigned for the two upper divisions of the Line — Forms not seen in their connection with the Form of the Good as the contents of CE, and the Form of the Good and the other Forms seen in connection with it as the contents of EB. The discussion which follows gives reasons for this. A last point about the diagram, of which the reader who has considered all the arguments of the preceding chapter needs scarcely to be reminded, is that it represents in schematic form only one of the many possible interpretations of this difficult section of the *Republic* — it may be indeed that in the light of the further discussion in the present chapter some readers may be inclined to return to some one of the other possible interpretations which we have outlined.

In the present chapter we are concerned primarily with Plato's views on the relationship between mathematical thinking (symbolised in the Line by the lower sub-division CE of the upper Line, and in the Cave by the contemplation of shadows and reflections outside the Cave) and philosophy or dialectic (symbolised by the higher sub-division EB of the upper part of the Line and by the contemplation of things themselves, the heavenly bodies, and finally the Sun itself outside the Cave). In the previous chapter, while we argued that the relationship between mathematics and dialectic was not Plato's sole interest in this part of the *Republic*, we nevertheless agreed that it was a main interest, and it consequently requires a proportionate amount of our attention. The most important sections of the text for our present purpose are 510-511 and 531-534. In these sections Plato calls attention to two features which he regards as distinguishing the method of the mathematicians of his time from that of philosophy as he thinks philosophy ought to be practised. First, the mathematician uses sensible images, and second, he is compelled to employ assumptions which remain unproven assumptions. These Plato regards as defects in mathematical method which the philosopher, pursuing his method of dialectic, is able to avoid. The position will be found stated succinctly at 510b, and the whole passage 510b to the end of Book VI is of the greatest importance.

To begin, then, with the mathematician's use of sensible images: in the scheme of the Line these sensible images, i.e. the diagrams or models (a wooden triangle, square, etc.), which the mathematician uses, themselves belong to section DC of the Line: i.e. they are visible objects, which may in turn have reflections or shadows of themselves, which would belong to the lowest section AD of the Line. At the same time Plato is clear that, though the mathematician uses these sensible aids in doing mathematics, he is not thinking about them, but about those objects of which these are copies, namely "the square itself and the diagonal itself". This is stated clearly at 510d-e. Thus the contents of DC of the Line, which were originals relative to the shadows and reflections which were their images and formed the content of AD, now in turn serve as images for the mathematician, and are copies relative to the originals which the mathematician studies; and as we noted in the last chapter, this continuing image-original relation suggests that the two lower sections of the Line are not solely illustrative of the two upper sections, but that there is a continuity between all four sections. Plato holds then that the mathematician (and he has the geometrician particularly in mind, though the same would apply to other branches of mathematics too) makes use of sensible diagrams or models, but nevertheless his thinking is not concerned with these, but with objects of a different sort. Let us consider three points arising from this.

(i) First let us ask what are the objects with which Plato does think the mathematician to be concerned. Thinking, the state of mind of the mathematician, is assigned to the upper half of the Divided Line, i.e. to the half which symbolises the intelligible world. Its objects, therefore, one would expect to be intelligible objects, i.e. objects not apprehended by the senses of sight, touch, etc., but by some form of non-sensuous apprehension; and granted this, there are two candidates for the role, namely Forms, with which we are familiar from Book V as objects which are non-sensuously apprehended, or alternatively some other class of intelligibles. Now there are

considerations that might incline one to the view that in fact
Plato intended as the objects of this third section of the Line
a special class of intelligibles other than Forms. Let us take a
case from geometry, and let us suppose that the geometrician
is concerned with demonstrating some proposition about, for
example, two triangles — for instance that two triangles on
the same base and between the same parallels are equal in
area. But what are the two triangles involved? For Plato
they cannot be the two triangles the geometrician draws.
These are particular sensible figures, and as such, as we have
learnt from the theory of Forms, they are impermanent and
subject to change, whereas the proposition, once proved, holds
always; and again, drawn figures are only approximations
to the perfect figures the geometrician has in mind — no drawn
circle is ever perfectly circular, no straight line ever perfectly
straight. Thus, as Plato tells us in the present passage, it is
not about his sensible diagrams that the mathematician is
thinking — these are merely aids in his thinking. On the other
hand, we can see from the present example that there is a
difficulty in saying that it is Forms that the mathematician
has in mind. Certainly Forms are permanent and unchanging
and (if we ignore the confusion between universal and ideal
particular mentioned in our discussion on the theory of Forms
in Chapter 8, especially pp. 194-195) perfect, but they are
unique. That is, there is only one Form of Triangle, one of
circle and so on, and it is explained at 597c of the *Republic* why
this must be so. In our example, however, two permanent,
unchanging, and perfect triangles are required, and the same
point would arise if our demonstration were about two inter-
secting circles, or two straight lines, or two squares, and so on.
Thus, given the general setting of the theory of Forms, what
seems to be required is a class of geometrical objects intermediate between sensible things and Forms which, like sensible
things, are many, but, unlike sensible things, are perfect, eternal
and unchanging, and as such belong, not to the sensible world,
but to the intelligible world. Arithmetic may not present
quite the same case as geometry. In geometry it is clear that
no drawn figure satisfies our geometrical requirements: the
drawn circles or squares are only imperfect approximations,

and the geometrician's demonstration thus clearly cannot be
about these. It has frequently been argued, for example by
W. D. Ross in an excellent short discussion of the topic in his
edition of Aristotle's *Metaphysics*, Volume 1, pp. liii-lvii, that
this same difficulty does not arise in the case of arithmetic:
"Every pair of things is a two; it may be designated from
another point of view by another number as well (just as what
is one week is also seven days), but this does not prevent it
from being fully and perfectly a pair". Thus in respect to the
imperfection of the sensible instances the argument for an intermediate class of objects may be less strong in the case of arithmetic. Yet here too we can see an argument that when the
arithmetician claims that two and two make four, he is not
thinking about, for example, these two particular oranges and
these two particular oranges as making four oranges. He is
not thinking of any particular impermanent and changing
instances; what he is maintaining is that two and two will
always be four. At the same time he cannot be talking about
the Form Twoness — there is only one Form of Twoness, and
even apart from this it would make nonsense to talk of twoness
added to twoness. Thus, here too it might be said we require
a class of intermediate arithmetical objects, resembling sensible
things in being many, but resembling the Forms in being
eternal and unchanging, and as such belonging to the intelligible
world. We can thus see that within the framework of the
theory of Forms there is a case for a sub-division of intelligible
objects into the Forms themselves on the one hand, each unique,
and on the other hand into a class of intermediate mathematical
objects which, like the Forms, would be eternal and unchanging
and perfect, but unlike the Forms would in each case be many:
i.e. there would be a plurality of mathematical triangles,
mathematical units, and so on. In this way appropriate objects
would be provided for mathematical thinking. Moreover,
apart from this general argument for an intermediate class of
objects, there are two further considerations which might be
regarded as pointing in the same direction. First there is the
evidence of Aristotle. He tells us in the *Metaphysics* (987b
14 ff.) that "further, besides sensible things and Forms he [i.e.
Plato] says there are the objects of mathematics, which occupy

an intermediate position, differing from sensible things in being eternal and unchangeable, from Forms in that there are many alike, while the Form itself is in each case unique" (Ross's translation). Secondly, we have seen in Book V (477c ff.) that Plato holds that powers or faculties are distinguished by their objects, i.e. that each power has its own distinct type of object (what Mr. Hardie in *A Study in Plato*, p. 32, has called Plato's 'objectivist bias'). Thus, granted that thinking is a distinct power or state of mind, one would expect it to have its own distinct type of object, namely "intermediates" as distinct from Forms. When we turn now to the text of the *Republic* itself, some commentators claim that Plato intends us there to understand that the objects of the third section of the Line are these "mathematicals" or "intermediates" — Mr. Hardie, for example (*op. cit.*, p. 52), writes "it seems to me clear that it is the explicit doctrine of the *Republic* that, just as understanding is 'between belief and reason' (511d), so its objects are between sensible objects and forms". There are, however, considerations which suggest a different conclusion, of which the most important is this. Apart from a passing reference at 74c of the *Phaedo* to "the equals themselves", which could be understood of mathematical equals, there is no reference in the dialogues earlier than the *Republic* to the doctrine of mathematical intermediates. If then the doctrine does appear in the *Republic*, it is something new, and one would expect Plato to introduce it as such, explain it, and express it in unambiguous language. In fact, however, this is not done. At 510d, when he tells us that the geometrician is not thinking about the sensible diagram but about "the square itself" and "the diagonal itself", the Greek here is one of the regular Greek phrases Plato uses when he is referring to Forms. It is quite true that the phrases could also stand for perfect particulars as well, i.e. for "the mathematical square", "the mathematical diagonal"; but it would be, to say the least, odd if Plato, without any further indication, expected us to take them in this latter way, when in fact they are his regular expressions for referring to Forms. In this connection the passage at 524 ff., where Plato is discussing arithmetic as a higher study, is less conclusive. At 524e the mind is represented as being compelled to ask what "the one itself is", where again the Greek phrase is one of the regular phrases for referring to Forms, i.e. in this case to the Form Unity; and so again at 525d the same expression is used (though this time in the plural) where the mind is described as reasoning about "the numbers themselves", i.e. as we would naturally understand the Greek, in this case the Forms of numbers. On the other hand, this is immediately followed by a discussion of "the one itself" where the mathematician is represented as resisting all attempts to divide it up, and as insisting that "every one is exactly equal to every other one and contains no parts". Here "the one" under discussion seems to be the unit, i.e. the mathematical unit, as distinct both from sensible "ones" and from the Form Unity; and it will be noted that a plurality of these units is recognised exactly equal to one another. Again, however, even in this passage, Plato makes no comment calling attention to a distinction between the Forms and mathematicals. The evidence of the actual text then (and particularly the Divided Line passage at 510d) points to the conclusion that in the *Republic* there is not an explicit doctrine of intermediates, and that consequently, since the objects of the third section of the Line must be intelligibles of some sort, its objects are Forms. If this is so, however, the question arises whether this can be fitted in with Plato's view that different powers have different objects, his 'objectivist bias' noted above; for he clearly regards "thinking" and "intelligence" as different powers, and if, as seems clear, Forms are the objects of the latter, the conclusion we have just reached would mean that Forms were also the objects of "thinking", and thus we would have failed to preserve the principle of different powers, different objects. It is true that Plato's main interest in the whole upper half of the Line is in the contrast between the methods of the mathematician and the philosopher, and he is silent about the difference between the objects they study by these differing methods; but presumably he would have held, in conformity with the principle just mentioned, that there is a corresponding difference of objects. In fact, however, to anticipate part of what is said later, this difference of objects can still be preserved, and a distinction made between Forms as they appear in the third section of the Line and as they appear in the fourth, such as to maintain the principle. In the third section of the Line the Forms are still seen as separate and unconnected and our understanding of them is in this way incomplete and fragmentary. On the other hand, in the fourth section they are seen in their inter-connection with the supreme Form, the Form of the Good. They are now connected in a coherent system dependent on the Good, and our knowledge of them is complete in that we understand them in the light of the whole system to which they are seen to belong. It is not implausible to say that seen in their isolation and fragmentariness the Forms are different objects from what they are when seen in their connectedness and their dependence on the Form of the Good. Thus in our diagram on p. 230 we have opted for the view that the objects of "thinking" are Forms, but Forms not yet seen in their connection with the Form of the Good.

(ii) Secondly, let us consider briefly in a general way the role Plato assigns in mathematics to the sensible diagram. Whether the objects which the mathematician is thinking about are Forms or intermediates, at any rate it is clear that on Plato's view they fall within the upper main section of the Line and thus are intelligible objects and not sensible objects. The latter are only aids to the study of the former — as he puts it at 510d, the mathematicians "use as aids the visible figures and discourse about them, though they are not thinking about these, but about the originals [i.e. Forms or alternatively intermediates] which they resemble" (510d). Plato then, in considering the mathematics of his time, would reject the sort of view of mathematics which we find later in the nineteenth-century philosopher J. S. Mill. Mill was an empiricist, i.e. the sort of philosopher who makes sense experience fundamental in all our knowledge. Thus when he came to deal with mathematics, here too he tried to account for mathematical thinking in terms of sense experience. For him the objects with which the geometrician, for example, is concerned are the objects we see and touch, in fact the sensible diagrams or models which Plato says the mathematician uses as an aid in thinking about the non-sensible. Thus, in discussing geometry in his *System of Logic*, Volume I, Book II, Chapter v, § 1, Mill says "We are thinking, all the time, of precisely such objects as we have seen and touched, and with all the properties which naturally belong to them; but for scientific convenience, we feign them to be divested of all properties, except those which are material to our purpose, and in regard to which we design to consider them". As we have seen, Plato denies that the geometrician is "thinking all the time of precisely such objects as we have seen and touched". On the other hand, he does regard the use of sensible diagrams as a characteristic feature of geometry (and indeed, as 510c, with its reference to "those engaged in geometry and calculation [arithmetic] and such things" indicates, of mathematics generally). It is true that he does not, as he does with the second feature of mathematics which he singles out, namely its use of assumptions, say explicitly that these sensible aids are a necessity for the mathematician; but this is pretty clearly implied. His view then would be that though the objects about which the geometrician is thinking are intelligible objects and not the sensible diagrams he uses, he still cannot deduce the properties of these objects without constructions in space, i.e. without drawing sensible figures and apprehending their implications. Thus, while Plato would have rejected Mill's view that it is the sensible diagrams that are the objects of the geometrician's thinking, he would equally have rejected another later view of mathematics which seeks to reduce mathematics to pure logic. With this logicist position the names of Frege, the German nineteenth-century mathematical philosopher (although he confined the view to arithmetic), and in England Bertrand Russell are especially connected. Russell maintains that geometry is a deductive system proceeding by reasoning alone from a set of postulates and definitions, and that no intuition of space or spatial constructions is necessary. Against any view of such a kind Plato appears to be maintaining that space as we experience it in sense perception cannot be dispensed with in geometry — that geometry, though it is concerned with the intelligible world, is nevertheless rooted in the space that we experience. In this respect it is worth comparing the position Plato takes about mathematics as he knew it with that of Kant. Kant, writing in the eighteenth century, and with Euclid's geometry, handed down from the Greeks, still the only geometry known, held too that geometry was concerned with the space we experience and could not dispense with spatial intuition. The propositions of geometry were necessary propositions. They were not empirical contingent statements about the objects of sense perception. Nevertheless they still described the space that we experience — they were descriptive of the pure *a priori* intuition we have of space and of the constructions we make in it. Unlike the later logicists, then, Kant held that the pure intuition of space was necessary to geometry, that geometry could not be reduced to logic, and that the geometrician could not dispense with his spatial constructions. In this tying of geometry to space one can see an affinity between Kant and Plato when the latter singles out as one of the marks of geometry its use of sensible diagrams. In modern philosophy of mathematics Kant's influence is still recognisable in the formalist and intuitionist movements, both of which are opposed to the logicist programme of reducing mathematics to logic. It is hardly necessary to add that the references we have been making to these later views are summary and incomplete and designed simply to stimulate interest. Mill's views and Kant's views must be studied in their own right; and modern developments within mathematics, which have produced the differing positions of the logicists on the one hand, and the formalists and intuitionists on the other, in themselves constitute a whole field of study.

(iii) Lastly, to return directly to our text, it is the use of sensible aids by the mathematician and their abandonment by the philosopher that Plato makes one of the distinguishing marks between mathematics and philosophy. The latter, he holds, is concerned entirely with the intelligible world, and he puts this strongly at 511c where the philosopher is described as "never using anything sensible, but only Forms, moving through Forms from one to another and ending with Forms". For Plato the mathematician is half-free from the changing, imperfect world of sensible particulars; but only half-free, in that he still has to use sensible diagrams while thinking of the non-sensible. It is for this reason that Plato regards mathematics as a bridge-study leading the student from the sensible to the intelligible, and why it is the various branches of mathe-

matics that provide the initial training for the philosopher in
Book VII of the *Republic*. They are still, however, only an
initial training, in that the philosopher proper dispenses entirely
with sensible particulars and studies the Forms in and by themselves. But how in fact he is to do this is a point that requires
thinking about. It is quite clear that he does not use diagrams
or models in the way in which, if Plato is right, the geometer,
for example, does; if a philosopher is interested in, say, justice
or in knowledge, no diagrams or models are likely to help him.
On the other hand, to say that what he is concerned with is
simply the pure Form or concept of justice, or the pure Form
of knowledge, and that he uses "only Forms, moving through
Forms from one to another and ending with Forms", leaves
the actual procedure the philosopher is to follow obscure. Suppose the philosopher is interested in the notion of justice and
its relation, say, to the notion of goodness, and we ask ourselves how he is to set about studying this problem. It seems
as though his first and obvious move is to consider some actual
cases, or, one might prefer to say, the way people actually use
the words 'just' and 'good' in particular circumstances. He
will, in this case, to use Platonic language, be studying the
Form in the particular instances. In so far, however, as particular instances, sensible particulars, in a wide sense of the
phrase, are still involved in this procedure, Plato clearly will
not be satisfied. The philosopher by his training will somehow
be able to apprehend the Forms in question and the relations
between them independently of their sensible manifestations.
He will move all the time in the intelligible world, the world
of universals, and will have no need to have recourse to the
embodiment of these universals in particular instances. He
will be able to map out the relationships between the Forms
entirely within the intelligible world. One is inclined, however,
to say that it is difficult to see how this can be done. Agreed
that the philosopher does not use sensible diagrams or aids as
the mathematician does, and agreed too, to put it in a modern
way, that the philosopher is concerned with concepts and the
relations between concepts, it would seem that the latter concern is served by the study of actual situations or the language
people use in actual situations, that it is by this sort of study

R

that concepts and their logical geography are clarified, and that this clarification is intimately bound up with the world in which we live and act. (It is of interest to compare John Locke's discussion of the possibility of turning morals into a deductive system — *An Essay concerning Human Understanding*, Book IV, Chapter 3, §§ 18-20.)

The second mark by which Plato distinguishes the mathematician from the philosopher is their differing attitude to what he calls their ὑποθέσεις (*hypotheseis*) ; and in the present context what Plato means by a *hypothesis* is what we would call an assumption. In 510c-511d he explains the difference. The mathematician makes certain assumptions and then, taking them for granted as though they were self-evident and known to be true, he proceeds from them, using them as first principles, to derive the conclusions in which he is interested. The philosopher, on the other hand, recognises the initial assumptions for what they really are, namely unexamined assumptions whose truth has still to be established. Instead, then, of using them as first principles and proceeding downwards from them to a conclusion, he seeks to give an account of the initial assumptions themselves. Thus he proceeds, as it were, in an upward direction, seeking to derive the initial assumptions from more general assumptions, and pursuing this process until he comes (511b) to something that is non-hypothetical, i.e. no longer assumed but now known to be true, namely the first principle of everything (and by this Plato almost certainly means the Form of the Good). When he has reached this unhypothetical first principle he can now proceed in the reverse direction, retracing his steps through the various assumptions he has used in the upward path, establishing each of them as true by demonstrating how it is derived from the first principle which is known to be true, until he finally reaches a true conclusion. To put the distinction generally, Plato is saying that while the mathematician constructs a consistent system given his initial premisses, he does nothing to establish the truth of these premisses — they are left as unexamined assumptions. Consequently while the whole system he constructs may be consistent, and while the conclusions may follow logically from the premisses, since the latter have not been shown to be true, neither the system itself nor the conclusions reached by it have been shown to be true. As Plato himself says at 533c, "if your beginning is something you do not know and your conclusion and the intermediate steps are constructed out of what you do not know, your reasoning may be consistent in itself, but how can it ever amount to knowledge?" It is the philosopher's task, by contrast, not to leave any assumptions unexamined but to reach a genuine first principle known to be true. When it is reached, then the propositions deriving from it will not only be logically consistent with one another, but, since they follow from a premiss known to be true, will themselves be true. Thus the philosopher will have knowledge (or "intelligence"), whereas the state of mind of the mathematician is (511d) something between belief and "intelligence", namely "thinking" (*dianoia*).

There are a number of points here that require comment. (i) First there is a point discussed in the last chapter (Chapter 9, pp. 218-220), which relates to the general interpretation of the Line simile. It will be remembered that in the ratios of the Line the whole upper part of the Line (CB) is to the whole lower part of the Line (AC) as the fourth (topmost) segment (EB) is to the second segment (DC), and also as the third segment of the Line (CE), i.e. "thinking", with which we are especially concerned at the moment, is to the lowest segment of the Line (AD), i.e. the state of mind which we have called "illusion". These relationships are explicitly drawn by Plato at 534a, and they indicate a parallelism between CE ("thinking") and AD ("illusion"). Now we have just seen that Plato singles out two features of "thinking" which are distinctive of it, namely the use it makes of sensible diagrams or models, and secondly the feature under discussion, its attitude to its assumptions. The question then arises in respect to which of these two features Plato intends us to see a parallelism with the lowest segment of the Line. On the view that understands the state of mind symbolised by the lowest segment of the Line, for which, it will be recalled, Plato uses the Greek word *eikasia*, as a state that seeks to apprehend originals through their images, the parallelism will lie in the first feature of "thinking", i.e. its use of sensible diagrams. That is, as the mathematician

uses his sensible aids as a means of apprehending the intelligible
objects with which he is concerned, so the man in a state of
eikasia tries to guess at originals through their shadows or reflections.   On this view then, *eikasia* will appropriately be
translated 'conjecture' — conjecturing about originals through
their shadows or reflections.   Now it will be recalled that in
the previous chapter reasons were given for preferring a different view about *eikasia*, namely the view that a man in the state
of *eikasia* takes what is in fact a copy or image for the original
without realising that it is a copy.   His state then is one of unquestioning acceptance and here the translation suggested for
eikasia was 'illusion'.   On this view the parallelism with "thinking" will lie in the second distinctive feature of the latter,
namely its attitude to its "hypotheses" or assumptions.   These
are accepted without question, taken for granted; and it will
be recalled that reference was made in this connection in the
previous chapter to the metaphor of dreaming which Plato
uses of the mathematicians in 533b-c, when he describes them
as "dreaming about being . . . so long as they leave the assumptions they employ unquestioned and can give no account of
them".

(ii) An interesting question arises whether Plato thought
there was any necessary connection between the two features
of mathematics, its use of sensible diagrams and its use of
assumptions.   Various suggestions have been made about this.
The most convincing is that of Mr. Robinson and will be found
on pp. 155-156 of his book, *Plato's Earlier Dialectic*.   Plato
criticises the mathematicians on the ground that they treat
their starting-points, their initial assumptions, as certainties,
whereas in fact they are only assumptions, are really only,
using the word in a general sense, hypotheses that require to
be themselves established.   The suggestion is that the mathematicians adopt this confident and dogmatic attitude to their
assumptions because they seem to be directly given in sense
experience, i.e. in the diagrams or models they use.   Thus the
assumptions are, in the words Plato uses at 510d, 'plain to all',
(*panti phanera*) in the sense of being there to be seen embodied
in the sensible diagrams or models the mathematician uses.
"In geometry", Robinson says, "the appeal to spatial intuition

and the claim that one's postulates are certainties go together."
The point would be that the mathematician fails to see the need
to question and give an account of his assumptions because the
sensible diagrams, which are there to be seen, appear to bear
out the assumptions. Thus no further proof of the assumptions
seems necessary beyond the appeal to the sensible diagram.
One must remember that Plato is criticising the mathematician
not for using assumptions, but for his failure to recognise that
they are assumptions, i.e. for his failure to recognise that they
should be regarded as hypothetical, as simply assumed and as
such themselves in need of examination and proof. One might
say that the mathematician is criticised not for using a hypothetical method, but for his failure to use a hypothetical method.
It is the philosopher who recognises the assumptions for what
they are, i.e. that they should be treated not as certainties but
as genuine assumptions, i.e. as hypotheses which themselves
require to be established. In this connection too we must
remember that we are dealing with Greek mathematics, with
the sort of geometry systematised a little later in Euclid's
Elements. L. M. Blumenthal writes (*A Modern View of Geometry*,
p. 16), "as late as the second decade of the nineteenth century
geometry was thought of as an idealised description of the spatial
relations of the world in which we live. In writing his *Elements*,
Euclid chose for his postulates statements that had their roots
in common experience. He thought of them as being true,
self-evident, . . . and factual. Euclid's task was to proceed
from those simple facts and establish more complicated ones
which, like the postulates, would be regarded as idealisations
of the way in which the physical world behaved." Greek
geometry then was rooted in the space we experience in our
everyday life, and its assumptions or postulates seemed to be
guaranteed by our spatial intuition. In terms of what we have
just said above, the geometer of Plato's day would not think of
questioning his assumptions, because the figures he drew embodied them. The development of geometry in the last hundred
years has altered the position radically. It has been found
that, given different postulates from those Euclid adopted, new
geometries can be developed that are consistent in themselves.
This has led to the abandonment of the view of geometry as a

description of actual space, and to the recognition of the fundamental part played by postulational procedure. Thus any simple appeal to the drawn figure in actual space to guarantee one's postulates or assumptions no longer operates, and complicated questions arise about the role of spatial intuition in geometry, and about the notion of truth itself in mathematics. Euclid thought of geometrical statements as either true descriptions (the world is like that) or false descriptions (the world is not like that). The modern mathematician would say that this sort of view is mistaken : it turns geometry into a branch of physics, whereas in fact geometry is a branch of mathematics and mathematics is not concerned to describe the actual world. Clearly, however, we cannot pursue questions of this kind here, and the interested reader must follow them up for himself. Before, however, we finally abandon the topic, it is interesting to ask oneself, in the light of what he says in the *Republic*, what Plato might have thought of these modern developments. He himself sees it as a defect in the mathematician that he is tied to his sensible diagrams, and in this respect one might imagine that he would approve of the modern abandonment of the view of geometry as a description of actual space. On the other hand, and this is a point that will occur again, he would not have been happy with the avowedly postulational procedure of modern geometry. His second complaint against the mathematicians of his own time was that they failed to establish their assumptions or postulates, that they failed to recognise that they were hypothetical in character and should not be left as such but should somehow be shown to derive from what was non-hypothetical. Presumably then, so far as modern geometry is deliberately postulational in its method, so far Plato would still be dissatisfied with it.

(iii) We must next try to find out a little more about the assumptions (or we may now call them hypotheses to bring out Plato's point discussed above that that is what they really are) of the mathematician, and about the philosopher's treatment of them. In this connection two passages in the text are particularly relevant. The first is 510c where Plato gives some examples of mathematical hypotheses, "odd and even numbers and the various figures and three kinds of angles and other kindred data". Presumably Plato mentions these as typical of the assumptions that the mathematicians of his time made, and we might suppose, as Mr. Robinson suggests (*Plato's Earlier Dialectic*, p. 103), that the assumptions are that every number is either odd or even, that three or more straight lines will enclose a plane figure, and that every plane angle is either a right angle or an acute angle or an obtuse angle. The second passage is at 533c where Plato, again contrasting mathematics with philosophy or dialectic, says "the method of dialectic alone proceeds in this way, destroying the hypotheses, to the beginning itself, to secure confirmation". The phrase translated "destroying the hypotheses" (*anairousa tas hypotheseis*) has caused a good deal of discussion. It seems at first sight to mean that dialectic "destroys" hypotheses in the sense of refuting them, showing them to be false. Taking this as the meaning, A. E. Taylor in *Mind*, Volume XLIII (1934), pp. 81-84, took a different view of the examples at 510c. He suggested that Plato in fact knew or suspected that these hypotheses were false. We need not follow Taylor in detail in his discussion of the hypotheses, but a little about them will indicate his general line. The first we have understood as the assumption that every number is odd or even. Taylor suggests that what this hypothesis really amounts to is that all numbers are integers, that is, that whatever is a number must be either odd or even, and that this would exclude irrational numbers which are neither. But, the argument runs, Plato knew about irrationals, and therefore this hypothesis is an example of the false assumptions made by the mathematicians which dialectic "destroys". Similarly, Taylor holds that the other two examples Plato gives are again intended as examples of false hypotheses — the second about "the figures" leads to difficulties arising from the fact that there are only five regular solids that can be constructed in a circle, and the third, which he understands as the assumption that there are angles formed by straight lines, angles formed by a straight line and a curve, and angles formed by two curves, to difficulties about the angle formed by a circle and its tangent. Historically, this view is improbable. It is true that in the *Theaetetus* (147d ff.), which was probably written later than the *Republic*, there is a reference

to a problem about irrationals, but there is no evidence that
when Plato wrote the *Republic* he was specially interested in
the problem; and Taylor's account of the other two hypotheses is even more difficult. There is nothing in Euclid's
Elements, which reflects the geometry of Plato's time, that at all
answers to Taylor's suggestions about the last two hypotheses.
Thus, Taylor's interpretation is on historical grounds implausible. Apart from this — and we have to remember
throughout this discussion that Plato is presumably, as we said
above, quoting typical examples of mathematical hypotheses
— if by 'destroying the hypotheses' Plato meant showing
them to be false, he would be implying in the phrase, and
implying without any further explanation or justification, that
the mathematics of his time was radically mistaken, that its
typical assumptions were false; and this again is hard to believe.
It seems, then, that we must find some other meaning for the
phrase 'destroying the hypotheses'. It should be understood
not as destroying hypotheses in the sense of refuting them, but
in the sense of destroying their hypothetical nature. That is,
dialectic, the method of the philosopher, seeks to derive the
hypotheses with which it begins from more general hypotheses
and finally from a non-hypothetical first principle. As it does
this the hypotheses lose their hypothetical character, are destroyed as hypotheses. This does not mean, however, that
they are destroyed in the sense of being proved false. Some
may be, but presumably many will survive, only now in the
form not of hypotheses, but of propositions known to be true.
The mathematician simply assumes certain propositions without knowing whether they are true or false, and proceeds to
make deductions from them; the philosopher cannot rest content with this. Pursuing his dialectical method he establishes
the truth, or it may be in some cases the falsity, of the propositions concerned. Thus, the state of mind of the mathematician
is one of assuming or hypothesising, while the state of mind of
the philosopher is one of knowledge. The mathematician may,
within his assumptions, have constructed a system that is consistent, but whether it is also true he does not know. On the
other hand, for the philosopher consistency is not enough;
with whatever hypotheses he is working he cannot leave them

as hypotheses, but must show them to be true propositions or, it may be, in some cases, reject them as false. Hence the point of Plato's remark at 533c, already quoted on p. 243, in which he denies knowledge to the mathematician, and hence, too, the metaphor of 533b-c, in which he describes the mathematicians as "dreaming about being" so long as they leave their hypotheses unexamined and can give no account of them.

(iv) Finally, in this discussion of the differing attitudes of the mathematician and the philosopher to their hypotheses, it is desirable, if we can, to obtain a clear view of the procedure which it is envisaged the philosopher will follow. Mathematics, Plato tells us at 511a-b, cannot ascend from assumptions to a first principle, whereas dialectic proceeds upwards from hypotheses to "something that is not hypothetical, the first principle of all", and only then proceeds on a downward path to its conclusion. In fact, however, Plato tells us little in detail in the *Republic* of the upward and downward path, and the matter has been much discussed. There seems a good deal to be said for the view that a passage in the earlier dialogue the *Phaedo*, which discusses hypothetical method, throws light, in part anyhow, on what is said in the *Republic*. In the *Phaedo* discussion we can distinguish three stages. (1) At 100a the procedure described is to accept whatever hypothesis seems to be best founded, and then to accept as true whatever follows from it. 101d-e explains what is to be done if the hypothesis itself is challenged. First (stage (ii)) it has to be checked by drawing the consequences and seeing whether any of them are inconsistent with one another. If they are, the hypothesis will have to be abandoned. If they are not, i.e. if no contradictory consequences follow, and if nevertheless the hypothesis itself is still questioned, then (stage (iii)) a similar process must be gone through, i.e. another hypothesis "the best of those above" must be assumed from which the hypothesis under question is shown to follow, and this process is continued until "something adequate" (or "sufficient for the purpose" — the Greek phrase is τι ἱκανόν (*ti hikanon*)) is reached. (For a non-propositional view of this passage in the *Phaedo*, see R. S. Bluck, *Plato's Phaedo*, Appendix VI, p. 160 ff.) A point arises in this

Phaedo passage which we should attempt to dispose of at the
outset. The reader may be perplexed by the notion in it that
a hypothesis could in itself entail consequences that contradict
each other; for, he would say, any propositions that follow
from a given proposition are necessarily consistent with each
other. Thus, so far from this passage helping us with the
Republic, it is logically absurd in itself. There are, however,
two ways in which the apparent absurdity can be accounted
for. First, if the initial proposition is in fact latently a complex
proposition, then it may give rise to a consequence that contradicts another of its consequences; or, secondly, the contradictory consequences may arise because it is not the immediate
hypothesis alone that is being used, but the hypothesis along
with one or more of our standing assumptions, which are being
employed tacitly, and which we fail to recognise as explicit
premisses within our system. It is worth observing that in
much of our everyday reasoning our conclusions often involve,
along with the premisses we explicitly recognise, other premisses
drawn from our standing beliefs which are tacitly employed.
No doubt in either case the reasoning is lacking in full logical
rigour, but we can at least understand how Plato could have
supposed that a single hypothesis might produce contradictory
consequences, and we can follow what he is saying in the
Phaedo without dismissing it out of hand as involving a logical
impossibility. Granted this, we can see a considerable resem-
blance between the method described in the *Phaedo* passage and
the upward path of the *Republic*, and it is not unreasonable to
suppose that Plato intends stages (ii) and (iii) of the *Phaedo*
procedure to be followed by the dialectician in the *Republic*. It
will be noted, too, that the *Phaedo* path is also an "upward"
path — the hypothesis under examination is to be derived
from "the best of those above". The *Phaedo* does not explain
the significance of the notion of "above" in this context, and
this is unfortunate because of the reappearance in the *Republic*,
in a similar context and again without a clear explanation,
of the concept of "above". It is clear that the "lower" hypothesis follows from the "higher" hypothesis, and thus 'higher'
must at any rate in part mean that from which the original
hypothesis follows. One feels, however, that more than this

must be involved, that in some sense or other the "higher" hypothesis is more general than the "lower" (this is why, for example, on p. 248 we spoke of dialectic as deriving its hypotheses from "more general" hypotheses). Mr. Robinson also suggests, in discussing the *Phaedo* passage (*Plato's Earlier Dialectic*, p. 137), that Plato "may also be thinking that the higher, as nearer to the source of entailment, is grander and more important", and it may be suggested that this is even more applicable in the case of the *Republic*, since the source there from which everything follows is the non-hypothetical first principle of everything, the Form of the Good. This mention of the Form of the Good brings us to our last point in this discussion of philosophical procedure in the *Republic*. There is one very important respect in which the account in the *Phaedo* differs from that in the *Republic*. In the *Phaedo* the process of deriving a hypothesis from a higher hypothesis is continued until something "adequate" or "sufficient" is reached; and the context shows that 'adequate' means agreed by all parties in the discussion. What happens there is that the search for a higher hypothesis arises because one of the parties to the discussion takes objection to the original hypothesis — he says in effect, "granted your conclusion follows from the hypothesis you have put forward, I am not happy about the hypothesis itself", and this difficulty is met by showing the hypothesis itself to be a valid conclusion from a higher hypothesis (let us call it hypothesis (2)). But the objector may still be unhappy about our hypothesis (2), and if so the process is repeated, i.e. hypothesis (2) is in turn derived from hypothesis (3), and so on until an adequate hypothesis is reached, i.e. one which all parties to the discussion are ready to accept. The important point about this is that the process ends when general agreement is reached, and the method of reaching general agreement is to continue pushing back hypotheses until all parties are satisfied. That is, agreement is reached, the "something adequate" is attained, within the hypothetical method. In the *Republic* the position is different in an important way. There, the hypothetical method is to be pursued, not until something agreed by all parties is reached, that is, a hypothesis which all parties are prepared to accept, but until, as described at 511b, we

arrive at "the non-hypothetical, the first principle of everything", by which Plato presumably means the Form of the
Good. The goal, then, in the *Republic* is knowledge of the Form
of the Good, and when we attain to this there is no element
of hypothesising left. It is no longer a question simply of all
parties agreeing to a proposition, but a matter of knowledge
and certainty. This indeed is a fundamental point in the
Republic. Those, like the mathematicians, who are content
with assumptions or hypotheses are still only dreaming about
being. The philosopher alone attains to knowledge and certainty; and indeed it is because he alone has knowledge that
he alone is entitled to rule. Granted, however, that the goal
in the *Republic* is knowledge, and granted that we are right in
supposing that the method envisaged for the philosopher is
the hypothetical method of the *Phaedo*, an obvious difficulty
arises. In the *Republic* Plato seems to think that in some way
or other a point comes in the hypothetical method when we
step right out of the realm of hypotheses and attain to what is
certain and true and known once for all. The hypothetical
method as described in the *Phaedo* is tentative and provisional
and approximative — as you ascend to higher and still higher
hypotheses you are presumably approaching closer and closer
to truth and knowledge; but even at the best the final hypothesis is still provisional, still open to possible challenge, adequate or sufficient but no more. To reach the unchallengeable
you would have somehow at some point to step outside the
hypothetical method; and this is what in the *Republic* Plato
seems to envisage. At the same time, if we are correct in what
we have been saying, the method provided is still the hypothetical method of the *Phaedo*, which will not in itself lead to
the absolute certainty, the knowledge, that Plato requires in
the *Republic*. This is why earlier we said that the *Phaedo* throws
light only in part on what is said in the *Republic*; the part that
remains obscure is the final step beyond hypotheses to the non-
hypothetical first principle, and unfortunately Plato does not
help us about this. Presumably the hypothetical method has
to be supplemented in the end by intuition. That is, after
deriving hypotheses from higher hypotheses, the philosopher
may eventually reach a hypothesis such that, after this long

training in hypothetical method, and after much thought and discussion, it suddenly dawns on him that this is the truth at last, that at last he has reached a proposition which he knows, which is certainly true. It has frequently been pointed out that Plato constantly uses the metaphors of sight and touch when he is discussing knowledge — 510b itself provides an example when dialectic is described as 'grasping' the first principle. This feature in Plato's thought can be exaggerated, but it seems true that in the *Republic* the hypothetical method has to be supplemented at its final stage by some sort of immediate awareness, an immediate grasping or seeing of the non-hypothetical first principle; or to use the metaphor we used a moment ago, at some point it must dawn on one that this is now the truth. That such an element is not foreign to Plato's thought can be seen in various parts of his work. The *Seventh Letter*, usually accepted now as written by Plato, is a good illustration, where Plato at 341c says of philosophic truth, "it cannot be expressed like other learning, but from much discussion of the matter itself by men leading a common life, it suddenly appears in the soul like light kindled from a leaping fire, and thereafter sustains itself"; and again at 344b there is this metaphor of the 'flash' of truth. Thus the view that the method recommended in the *Republic* is the hypothetical method of the *Phaedo* has to be supplemented by importing this notion of the final flash of intuition. The hypothetical method, in which the notions of provisionality and approximation are predominant, and intuition, with its notion of once-for-all certainty, are not easy bed-fellows, and this is why Mr. Robinson in Plato's *Earlier Dialectic*, p. 146, rightly speaks of a conflict between Plato's epistemology in the *Republic* (his view that absolute incorrigible knowledge is attainable) and his methodology (his recommendation of the method of hypotheses). At the same time, the difficulty which arises from this conflict must not lead us to underestimate the importance of this part of the *Republic*. It contains many ideas that have been fruitful in later thought, and not least the idea of pushing back one's original hypotheses as far as they will go. What Plato has to say about hypothetical method contains the seed of the notion of axiomatisation, which has become fundamental in later mathematics, and this is why one German commentator regarded the Line simile as "unambiguously the proposal to axiomatise". With it, too, we may compare a quotation from Russell's *Introduction to Mathematical Philosophy* borrowed from G. C. Field's book *The Philosophy of Plato*, p. 40: "Instead of asking what can be defined or deduced from what is assumed to begin with, we ask instead what more general ideas and principles can be found, in terms of which what was our starting-point can be defined or deduced". One must recognise that in modern mathematics axiomatisation is pursued for its own sake; whereas for Plato its importance lies in its connection with the unhypothetical first principle, which is itself not postulated but known. For Plato, once we reach the first principle we can retrace our steps on the downward path, but now, while the validity of each step is guaranteed by our axiomatic system, at the same time, since each step follows ultimately from the first principle, known to be true, so each step in turn will no longer be a postulate but a truth known as such, since it derives from the supreme truth, the Form of the Good. With this *caveat*, however, we may agree with Field's comment on the Russell passage that it "appears to express Plato's demand exactly, and in language not so very different from that which he might have used himself".

Mathematics then differs from and is inferior to philosophy in respect to the two features we have discussed above, its use of sensible aids and its attitude to its hypotheses. But though these are defects, Plato nevertheless regards a training in mathematics as an essential preliminary to philosophy or dialectic. It is to form part of the higher education of the philosopher, and he explains why and outlines his scheme of mathematical education in 521-531. He begins by asking what form of study will draw the soul from the world of change to reality (521d), and it is this objective that is central throughout the recommendations that follow. It is this that is the test for any study's inclusion in the higher education — its power to lead the mind away from the changing unstable world of sense experience to a world of stable, unchanging objects grasped by the intelligence. 521c-524d, to which we have already referred in connection with Book V (Chapter 7, p. 154 ff.), discusses the power

of relational attributes to stimulate thought, and then in 525 it
is agreed that arithmetic has a similar power, granted (525c)
it is pursued not for commercial ends, but "to help in the conversion of the soul itself from the world of becoming to that of
truth and reality". Arithmetic then, pursued in this way, is
the first of the higher studies, and it is followed in order by
Geometry (526c-527c), Solid Geometry (527d-528e), Astronomy (528e-530c) and Harmonics (530c-531c). In every case,
as we have said above, the ground for the inclusion of each
discipline is its ability to turn the mind away from the changing
sensible world to the unchanging intelligible world. Plato is
interested in all these studies in so far as they are concerned
with *a priori* necessary truths, i.e. truths that are independent
of sense experience, that no experience could refute, that must
hold always. This explains his attitude to astronomy and
harmonics which he includes in his list. They are there not
as observational disciplines concerned primarily in the one
case with the visible heavens and in the other case with the
sounds we hear. They are there rather for the problems in
pure mathematics which they throw up, i.e. as with all the
other disciplines, for the power they have to stimulate thought
and lead us away from the sensible world. Hence the well-
known remark at 530b in the discussion of astronomy, "we
shall proceed as we do in geometry, by means of problems, and
leave the starry heavens alone". This is why, too, it is misleading, as some commentators, e.g. Nettleship, have done in the
past, to speak of this part of the higher education in the *Republic*
as an education in "the sciences". Plato is not interested here
in what we mean nowadays by 'science', in the sense of the
natural sciences. The latter are concerned, in however refined
a way, with the sensible world, with observation and experi-
ment, with describing nature. Plato is not interested in science
in this sense as part of his higher education, but only, if we want
to use the word at all in this connection, with the pure sciences,
i.e. in summary, with pure mathematics. He wants for his
higher education disciplines which take us right away from the
natural world. If the question could have been raised with
him to which section of the Line he would have allocated what
we call science, it seems as though the answer would have been

that, in the main, as a description of the natural world, it
belongs to the lower section of the Line, to the world of belief;
and in this connection it is to be noted that he himself describes
the account he gives of the physical world in the *Timaeus* as
no more than a "likely story", since the physical world is only
a likeness of unchanging reality. Plato's aim then in his higher
education is to turn the mind from the sensible to the intelligible, and it is mathematics that he regards as the best
instrument to achieve this. 532b-c recalls the simile of the
Cave in stating this — it is "the whole course of study in the
arts we have reviewed" (i.e. the mathematical disciplines,
arithmetic, geometry, etc.) that "has the corresponding effect
of leading up the noblest faculty of the soul towards the contemplation of the highest of all realities". In this passage
mathematics is described as operative throughout a man's
release from his chains, from the time he turns from the shadows
in the Cave to the objects which cast the shadows and then
from these to the divine reflections and shadows in the sunlit
world outside the Cave. This latter stage clearly symbolises
"thinking", and in this corresponds to the third sub-section of
the Line. It has been objected, however, that the four-stage
view of the Cave, which takes the prisoner's progress within
the Cave not simply as illustrative, would require that mathematics should come down into the Cave, and mathematics
has no place in the world of belief. The answer to this is that
it is not pure mathematics that comes down into the Cave, but
mathematics as simple applied calculation — the sort of thing
Plato has in mind at 522c as used by all the arts. This simple
sort of calculation, as he says at 523a, is one of the studies he
is looking for as naturally awakening the power of thought,
though no one makes a right use of its tendency to lead the
mind to reality. When properly developed it will eventually
turn the mind from "collections of material things which can
be seen and touched" (525d) to the intelligible world, and from
"belief" to "thinking". It is interesting to compare here the
discussion of arithmetic in the *Philebus* 55-57, and particularly
the distinction at 56d between "popular" and "philosophical"
arithmetic; though the *Philebus* is a later dialogue, and must
therefore be used with caution in relation to the *Republic*.

This training in mathematics (on which ten years are to be spent — see the educational programme at 535a ff.) is, however, only a "prelude" (531d) to dialectic, which is the "coping stone" (534e) of all these studies, and dialectic itself is discussed from 531c-535a, discussed somewhat briefly, since, as with the Form of the Good earlier, despite Glaucon's request at 532d for a full discussion, Socrates draws back on the ground that Glaucon will not be able to follow further. Most of what is said here is familiar from what we have been already told in Book VI about the difference between mathematical method and dialectic, the method of the philosopher, and parts of the present section have already been discussed in detail. There are, however, one or two points to which attention should be called. (1) It should be clear from earlier discussion that dialectic, as Plato uses the notion in the *Republic*, should not be confused with the later Hegelian or Marxian 'dialectic'. Nor, though this is more disputable, should it be identified with the method of dialectic as it appears in some of Plato's own dialogues subsequent to the *Republic*. In these dialogues — the *Politicus* (285) and the *Philebus* (16-18) are examples — dialectic appears as a method of collection and division, the latter phase of "dividing by kinds (or species)" being particularly important. Whatever hints there may be of this later dialectic in the *Republic*, it would be a mistake to interpret (as some have done) the "upward" and "downward" path of dialectic in the *Republic* in terms of this later method. (2) The "synoptic" nature of dialectic is stressed — the dialectician is the man who "sees things together" (537c); the philosopher's training must be continued "to the point at which reflection can take a comprehensive view of the mutual relations and affinities which bind all these studies [the mathematical studies] together" (531c); and the final aim is to see how everything eventually stems from the first principle of everything, the Form of the Good. (3) The recapitulation of the Cave simile in 532 should be noted, with the equation at 532a of dialectic with the prisoners looking at the living creatures outside the Cave, then at the stars, and finally at the Sun itself; and also the recapitulation of the ratios of the Line at 533e-534a.

This chapter has been primarily concerned with what

Plato conceives to be the task of the philosopher, and how it
differs from that of the mathematician. To conclude it, however, let us look now in a more general way at the Sun, Line and
Cave similes to see what we can gather from them about Plato's
general philosophical position as represented in his theory of
Forms. We must be very tentative in any inferences we draw,
since, as will be clear from the last chapter, the interpretation
itself of the similes is so much disputed. In particular, as we
saw, it has been denied that the sensible world figures at all
in the similes in a philosophically significant way, or that the
Line and Cave are parallel; and though we have rejected
these views, it must nevertheless be recognised that this part of
the *Republic* does not provide sound enough ground for any
sweeping inferences about Plato's general metaphysical views.
Granted this proviso, it will be remembered that, when we
were discussing the theory of Forms in Chapter 8, p. 195,
one of the things that puzzled us was the relationship between
Forms and sensible particulars. Do the similes throw any
light on this? There is a good deal in the similes which
emphasises the poorness of the sensible world in contrast to
the intelligible world — in the Sun simile, for example, the
sunlit world of the Forms "irradiated by truth and reality" is
contrasted sharply with the "twilight world of things that
come into existence and pass away" (508d); in the Line
simile, the shadow-or-reflection-or-image as opposed to original
metaphor would again suggest that the sensible world is but a
shadow of the intelligible; and again in the Cave simile the
dimly lit Cave, symbolising the world of sense, is sharply contrasted with the sunlit world outside. All this might suggest
the distinctness and the separation of the world of Forms from
the sensible world. On the other hand, in the Line simile
Plato does not represent the sensible world by one line and the
intelligible world by another. Instead he uses a single line,
the whole lower part of it representing the sensible and the
whole upper part the intelligible; and this suggests a continuity
between the sensible and the intelligible. In this connection,
too, we must remember the important passage at the end of
Book VI (511e) where we are bidden to assign to each of the
states of mind symbolised by the four parts of the Line "a

degree of clearness and certainty corresponding to the measure
in which their objects possess truth and reality"; and this
suggests a continuing scale of increasing clearness in states of
mind, and of increasing reality in the objects, with no sharp
and absolute break between sensible objects and intelligible
objects. Similarly in the Cave there is a progress from the
lowest state of contemplating the shadows on the wall of the
Cave to the final vision of the sun in the world outside. It is
not an easy progress (see for example the description at 515c-d
of the bewilderment of the prisoners at the first stage of the
rescue, and again, in reverse, at 517d, of the plight of the rescued
prisoner who has to return to the darkness of the Cave and dispute about the shadows of justice). Still, it is a progress, though,
to use a phrase Mr. Hardie uses also of the Line, "a progress
punctuated by crises of conversion". Indeed, even the image-
original metaphor as Plato uses it in the Line suggests this:
it will be remembered that the everyday objects of the second
part of the Line, which are the originals of the images in the
first part of the Line, are themselves images in turn relatively
to the intelligible objects of the third part of the Line, a point
which has led W. D. Ross to remark that this is "the clearest
evidence . . . that there is a continuity between all four sub-
sections of what is symbolised" (*Plato's Theory of Ideas*, p. 47).
Thus one might say that there are a number of indications in
the *Republic* that Plato wishes to avoid a two-world view, i.e.
the notion of a world of Forms entirely cut off from sensible
particulars; though whether this part of the *Republic* helps us
to understand with any more precision how they are related
is perhaps a moot point. The general picture that emerges is
that in each of the first three stages in the Cave (symbolised
also by the first three sections of the Line, which we agreed
was the map of the country through which the prisoner had to
travel) what we apprehend is fragmentary and disconnected,
second-hand and provisional, as shadows or images are. At
the same time we are content with it; we do not realise that it
is only a world of shadows. The change from one stage to the
next above, i.e. from shadows or images to their originals, is
an abrupt one and it takes time before we come to recognise
that our new world is more real than the old. Nevertheless,

there is not at any point a complete break — the new world of
the higher stage is more real, but the old world we have left is
not completely unreal. It is only an image, but still an image,
and perhaps in the image-original metaphor Plato thought he
had a way of conveying at the same time the continuity and
the difference between the sensible world as a whole and the
world of Forms.

As we remarked above, in general it is rash to make too
much of the Sun, Line and Cave similes in connection with
general issues concerning the theory of Forms. All commentators are agreed, however, that the similes do clearly add one
new element to the theory of Forms as we discussed it in Chapter
8. This new element is the special position Plato assigns in
all three similes to the Form of the Good. In the *Republic* it
appears as the supreme principle. In the words of the Sun
simile, 509b, the objects of knowledge (i.e. the Forms) "derive
from the Good not only their power of being known, but their
very being and reality ; and Goodness is not the same thing as
being, but even beyond being, surpassing it in dignity and
power" ; and in all the similes clearly the vision of the Good
is the ultimate goal of philosophy. At the same time, this is
the only dialogue in which the Good appears in this way as the
supreme principle, and neither the dialogues earlier than the
Republic nor the later dialogues are of help in understanding
what Plato says about it in the *Republic*. Unfortunately too,
from what he does say, it is very difficult indeed to form any
clear idea of what was in Plato's mind, and he himself, it will
be remembered, at 506e leaves the question of what the Good
is in itself and offers only 'the offspring' of the Good, in the
analogy of the Sun. Hence a critic like Popper speaks of "the
emptiness of the Platonic Idea or Form of the Good". As we
have seen from our earlier discussion, one of the few things
Plato does indicate clearly is that the principles of the mathematical disciplines are to be derived from the Form of the Good,
and this itself is puzzling. It is less difficult to understand what
Plato would mean in holding that moral principles must be
seen in their connection with the Form of the Good — he himself refers explicitly to this at 504d-505a, and possibly also at
534b-c. But what would it mean to say, as Plato seems to be

saying, that the division of numbers into odd and even (one of his own examples at 510c) can only be shown to be necessary because it is "good"? Is 'good' here being used in the same sense as when we talk of a "good" man or of justice being "good"? Discussion of this would take us far afield; and the immediate point is that there is nothing in this part of the *Republic* to help us. The situation is much the same in the difficult passage in the Sun simile at 508e-509b, part of which we quoted above. There are puzzling hints about the position of the Form of the Good in the world of Forms; for example, it is the source of being of the other Forms, but itself is not the same as being, but beyond being in dignity and power. Here again, though all sorts of suggestions have been made, and the passage has had a powerful influence, for example on Plotinus and the neo-Platonic philosophers, Plato does not say enough to enable us to state at all clearly and discuss what he means. In short, what Plato has to say about the Form of the Good here is one of the most celebrated passages in his writings, and has been the stimulus to much thought and conjecture; but what he does say is so brief and so obscure that most comment tends to become speculation, and to take us too far from the text of the *Republic*, which is our immediate interest.

Chapter 11

COMPARISON OF JUST AND UNJUST LIVES

In Books VIII-IX Plato takes up the topic which he had begun at the end of Book IV, but had put on one side to deal with the epistemological and metaphysical problems raised by the need to answer the question whether the city was possible, and to find the right educational programme for future Guardians. At 543 he recapitulates what he has said at 445c-e, that in contrast with the one good form both of city and of individual man (which he calls aristocracy, using the word literally, to mean 'government by the best'), there is an unlimited number of bad forms, four in particular deserving mention. He then proceeds to give a vivid and impressionistic sketch of these four kinds of state, and of the corresponding four kinds of individual in the order: timocracy and the timocratic man (544c-550c), oligarchy and the oligarchic man (550c-555b), democracy and the democratic man (555b-562a), and tyranny and the tyrannical man (562a-576b).

While Plato prefaces this long passage with a warning that even the best state can go to the bad (545-546), and while he represents each type of state as one that comes into being through some corruption of the better elements in the state before it, so that he talks of aristocracy turning into timocracy, timocracy into oligarchy and so on, it is surely a mistake to interpret him as speaking historically. On that interpretation, he would be saying that constitutional history proceeds in a single sequence, from its start in aristocracy to its end in despotism — a view of history for which Plato must have known that it would be impossible to produce evidence. This attempt to interpret Plato's account of the various kinds of political degeneracy as a continuous historical decline is as implausible and unnecessary as the corresponding interpretation of the sequence of cities in Books II-IV : primitive, sophisticated and ideal. In both cases he is observing an order, but not a chronological order. At the beginning of the *Republic* he starts with the minimal necessary condition of a city's existence, that it should be economically self-supporting, and then he proceeds to add what he regards as those further necessary conditions which will jointly constitute a sufficient condition of a satis- factory state. At the end of the *Republic*, having argued that justice is a kind of harmony, he wishes to exhibit the different degrees of discord which injustice can manifest. The obvious sequence to follow is to list them as they are further and further removed from the political embodiment of justice ; and to present them as one changing into another is a very natural and graphic way of doing that. They correspond, too, to the different levels of the soul. As aristocracy has been shown to be government by reason, so timocracy is government by the spirited element, oligarchy government by the money-making appetite, democracy government by all the appetites in un- bridled competition, and tyranny is the enslavement of all else by a single overriding appetite of the kind that, in normal man, appears only in sleep, when control by the rational conscious self is totally withdrawn. Furthermore, it enables Plato to round off the *Republic* in a satisfying manner (for, important although Book X is, it must be regarded as an appendix). By contrasting the tyrannical kind of individual with the aristo- cratic kind of individual, i.e. the extreme of injustice with the extreme of justice, he is enabled to give his firm reply to the question which he had deliberately left inconclusively answered at the end of Book I — whether the just or the unjust man has the better life, i.e. which of them is to be regarded as being the better off.

The perfectly just man, as we have seen, is the man the elements of whose soul are kept in their proper balance by the chief element, reason. He has the appetitive desires and spirit in the right degree to manifest the virtues of self-restraint and courage, and he has the virtue of wisdom to direct them both aright, true wisdom, as it eventually turns out, being attainable only through philosophical knowledge. The perfectly unjust man, on the other hand, is the tyrannical man, as far removed

from rationality as he can be, "friends with nobody, master
to some men and slave to others, never tasting real freedom or
friendship" (576a).

The question which of these two men has the happier life
is so heavily loaded by the description given of each as to have
become pointless. The perfectly just man being the completely
integrated man, and the perfectly unjust man being an advanced
psychopath, the answer to the question can be neither in doubt
nor interesting. But the three arguments which Plato uses
are interesting, because they (precisely, the second and third)
confirm the point mentioned earlier, viz. Plato's identification
of the just man with the philosopher. The first is scarcely an
argument at all but consists of a more detailed statement of the
unenviable predicament of the man of tyrannical character,
especially the extreme case of such a man, when not only is
he of such a character but also he has the misfortune to be
an actual political dictator (576-580). While Plato produces
nothing here which could count as philosophical argument, his
account merits attention as a remarkably graphic and pene-
trating picture of morbid psychology; the dictator who, as
time goes on and fortunes grow worse, more and more shrinks
from public appearances is not only a twentieth-century phe-
nomenon.

The next argument (580d-583a) refers back to the tripartite
soul, each part having its own desires and pleasures, those of
appetite, of personal ambition, and of the pursuit of knowledge
respectively. Some men's characters are governed by one of
these elements, some by another, so that we have three basic
types of men : the appetitive or acquisitive, the ambitious or
honour-seeking, and the philosophical or lovers of truth (581c).
If we ask each of these men which of these lives is the most
pleasant — and Plato insists that that is the question to be
considered, not which is the better or more noble (581e) —
each will choose his own. But as the basis of a decision between
them must be threefold — actual experience, sound judgment,
and reason (582a) — as the philosopher alone of the three has
experience of all three kinds of pleasures, and as he alone has
the required powers of judgment and reason, he is the only
one competent to make a comparison; he must therefore be

right in saying that the philosopher's life is most pleasant.

If we are to pay Plato the doubtful compliment of taking that argument seriously, then two points need noticing. First, there is the abruptness of the switch from talk of the just man to talk of the philosopher. In the first argument the contrast had been between the most just and the most unjust man (580c); in the course of the present argument neither of these words occurs even once, although its conclusion is stated to be that "the just man has now defeated the unjust twice running" (583b). Next, as Plato is explicitly considering which of the three lives is the most pleasant, he may be criticised for treating pleasantness as though it were a property which an experience or a way of life would have, regardless of the tastes or preferences of the individual whose experience or life it was. J. S. Mill later used a somewhat similar argument when, having insisted, as against the earlier utilitarians, that some kinds of pleasure are superior in quality to others, he suggested that the only people competent to judge between the rival claims of two pleasures to be the "better" (as it might be, classical music versus swing, or bridge versus poker) were those who had had the necessary experience of both. Now Mill, whatever his difficulties of detail, has this strong point to his argument that values, including aesthetic values, have some objectivity about them, and that anybody who maintains that the experience of enjoying *Puss-in-Boots* on ice is qualitatively as high as the experience of enjoying either Shakespeare's or Verdi's *Macbeth* is just wrong, and wrong through ignorance. But Mill carefully refrains from arguing that higher-grade pleasures are more pleasant, that the man who enjoys Shakespeare enjoys him more than the man who enjoys pantomime on ice enjoys that. But Plato, while refusing here to compare the life of philosophy with those of position-seeking and money-making in terms of "quality" (that is deferred until the third argument), does take the unwarranted step of concluding that because the philosopher enjoys philosophy more than he enjoys either of the other lives, and because neither of the other two men knows anything of the pleasures of philosophy and is therefore not competent to judge, the life of philosophy is more enjoyable. To which the answer is that while it may be more enjoyable

to the philosopher, it does not follow either that it is more
enjoyable to him than the pursuit of power and wealth are to
the other men, or that there is any sense in which one can speak
of a way of life as being pleasant or enjoyable without reference
to the man, or kind of man, who is going to lead it. If one
insists, as Plato does, on keeping "quality" out of the argument,
then questions of what is more pleasant or enjoyable than something else are questions of preferences; and there are no
preferences without people. The philosopher may think it
odd that the business-man should want to buy wealth with an
ulcerated stomach, but if the business-man says he enjoys his
life, and appears to enjoy it, the philosopher has no right to say
that it is less pleasant than his own — except in the sense that
he would not choose to live it. The question "which is the
most pleasant life?", unless it means "which would *you* prefer?"
is not a properly formed question at all. Plato's argument
presupposes that it is a properly formed question, and that
there could be such a thing as an absolutely most pleasant life,
irrespective of individuals with their likes and dislikes.

The third and final argument (583b-587a) for the proposition that the just man's life is more pleasant than the unjust
man's is extremely complicated; and it is difficult to be confident that one has sorted out all the threads of it. It depends
basically on a contrast between "the real" (sometimes "the
more real") and "the less real", which is familiar from the
metaphysics of Books V-VII; and on a corresponding contrast
between "real pleasures" (or "more real pleasures") and "less
real pleasures", the latter being referred to (586b) as *images*
and *shadows* of the former — a reintroduction of the language
used in the Line and the Cave. The Greek words (sometimes
alethes, sometimes the present participle of *einai*) which we translate as 'real' have to be understood as, in some degree at least,
terms of value, as the English word 'real' (and close relatives
like 'genuine') often is. (Cf. "This is the *real* thing", "this
really *is* whisky", "What a genuine person she is", etc., v.
p. 185.) In saying of some pleasures that they are not real
Plato is not saying that the people experiencing them are not
really pleased, but he is saying that what pleases them has
something spurious or second-rate about it. He offers two

different criteria of a pleasure's being real; and in that he may perhaps be open to the criticism of overstating his case. First, a pleasure (or a pain) is real only if it is not just relief from its opposite (583-584): if, say, a man is in physical pain, relief from it will be welcome and pleasant, but it would be wrong to think of such relief as real pleasure, however pleasant it may be. The pleasure of relief from pain has to be contrasted with the pure pleasures, notably those of smell, which do not arise from a painful condition nor leave one behind when they end (584b). Plato is clearly thinking of physical desires as principally being "pains" which are relieved by achieving the object desired, e.g. the pleasure of a good meal when hungry is relief from the "pain" of the hunger. And with this he contrasts the pure physical pleasure, such as the suddenly caught smell of a rose, which is a real pleasure because it comes unsought and not in answer to a need. Plato's model is of a three-level structure, the top level being Up, the bottom Down, and the middle Neutral. Real pleasure is a movement from Neutral to Up, and real pain a movement from Neutral to Down; movement from Down to Neutral is an improvement and is pleasant, but is not real pleasure, for it is only negative removal from pain.

His other criterion is quite different: pleasure is real (or more real) if it characterises an activity concerned with real objects. More specifically, he uses the metaphor of filling, and asserts that the pleasure of being filled with what is more (rather than less) real is itself a more (rather than less) real pleasure. The application of this is obvious: the food and drink which fill the body are less real than the knowledge and understanding which fill the mind, therefore mental pleasures are more real than bodily pleasures. Plato claims to have reached this conclusion, that the pleasures of the mind are more real than those of the body, separately by each criterion. But in fact neither succeeds. His use of the second criterion would lead to the desired conclusion only if supplemented by the further condition that pleasure is so inextricably bound up with the activity of filling as to derive its (degree of) reality from that of the activity. Plato does not argue for this condition, but Aristotle (*Nicomachean Ethics*, X, 4-5) more interestingly does.

The use of the first criterion would provide the conclusion that mental pleasures are more real than bodily pleasures only given the further proposition that bodily pleasures are relief from pain, and that mental pleasures are not. But Plato himself only says that *most* bodily pleasures are of the relief-from-pain kind, and admits that some are not, giving smell as an example. That is to say, not all bodily pleasures are the fulfilment of a previously felt need or desire. And he does not consider at all that many mental pleasures are, or arise from, the fulfilment of desire, e.g. the desire to find out or to know. Consequently, his two accounts of real pleasure do not converge quite as neatly as might appear. The use of the first criterion excludes from the category of "real pleasure" that satisfaction of bodily appetites which he wishes to exclude, but it excludes also some mental pleasures. The use of the second criterion lets in all mental pleasures, but keeps out the few bodily pleasures which he thought of as being something better than regrettable necessities.

So far justice has not appeared in the discussion at all; and we may wonder how he hopes to show by it that the just man has the happier life. But by a simple twist of the argument he works it in. The man who, in pursuit of the pleasures either of appetite or of ambition, follows the guidance of knowledge and reason will achieve the most real pleasures of which he is capable (586d). Therefore, a man will achieve the best and most real pleasures that he can, provided that his whole soul obeys the rational element, the other two elements performing each its proper function. And this is exactly the description of the real or inner justice given in Book IV, the harmony of the three elements of the soul maintained by the rational element. It is not at all clear how having one's appetitive or ambitious desires controlled by reason makes the pleasures which are their fulfilment any more *real* than if they were not so controlled; for the pleasures are still those of appetite or ambition rather than of reason, and they are pleasures from achieved desires. Plato seems to think that the fact that the pleasures peculiar to reason, in the pursuit of knowledge, are the most real, and the fact that the just man is he whose soul is controlled by reason, confer some higher degree of reality than they would

otherwise have had on his pleasures of appetite or ambition ;
but he suggests no reason why we should think so.   Having
given an account of justice such that strictly only the philosopher can be just, and having used as arguments for the greater
attractiveness of justice than injustice two arguments which
are concerned with the philosopher as philosopher, not as just
man, Plato then at the end blurs the distinction, so as to suggest
that what he has established is that the just man, in the less
strict sense, enjoys more real pleasures than the unjust man.
The conclusion, that the man who is not a prey to his appetites
nor to the drive of self-assertiveness is likely to be happier than
the man who is, is, no doubt, quite acceptable ; but it is another
question whether Plato's final argument provides any reason
why we should accept it.

With a playful arithmetical demonstration that the aristo-
cratic (or just) man lives 729 times more pleasantly than the
tyrannical (or unjust) man, and with a short summary of their
conclusions about the nature of man, to give the answer to the
claim, made seriously by Thrasymachus and eristically by
Glaucon, that injustice (with a reputation for justice) is more
profitable than justice, Plato brings the main discussion of the
Republic to a close.

Chapter 12

ART

In the first part of Book X Plato discusses art (in particular poetry). He begins the discussion by congratulating himself at 595a on having (in Book III) excluded from his ideal state all imitative poetry (in Cornford's translation "the poetry of dramatic representation"), and goes on to explain in the next sentence that the rightness of this move is all the clearer now that the parts of the soul have been distinguished (in Book IV and also in Books VIII and IX); and, as we shall see, he also makes use of the metaphysical doctrines of Books V-VII.

Before we consider the present discussion in Book X, it will be useful to recall what was said in Book III, and here the relevant section for our present purposes runs from 392c-398b. In the immediately preceding section (376e-392c) Socrates has laid down certain principles of censorship for the content of literature, and now at 392c he turns to the question of the form in which this content should be presented. The storyteller or poet, he explains at 392d, tells his story either in simple narrative, or by means of imitation (*mimesis*), or he may employ a mixture of both; and he illustrates this from the beginning of the *Iliad* where Homer, speaking in his own person, describes how Chryses begged Agamemnon to release his daughter (this is simple narrative), but later, speaking in the character of Chryses, does his best to make us think it is the latter and not Homer himself who is speaking (this is imitation, *mimesis*). The *Iliad* and *Odyssey*, Plato points out, are a blend of these two forms of presentation, namely simple narrative and imitation. Thus (394b) poetry can take three forms. It may proceed wholly by imitation, as in tragedy and comedy; it may proceed wholly by narrative, the poet speaking in his own person throughout, as in the dithyramb; or it may employ both

methods as in epic poetry, of which the *Iliad* and *Odyssey* are
examples. The question to be decided is which form or forms
from among these three are to be allowed in the ideal state.

Before we come to Plato's answer, this is a convenient point
to call attention to a difficulty in the translation of the Greek
word μίμησις (*mimesis*), which is a key word both here and in
Book X. The verb *mimeisthai* means 'to mimic', 'imitate', 'represent', and similarly the noun *mimesis* means, generally,
'imitation'. It is these words Plato uses when, for example,
in the illustration from Homer in the preceding paragraph,
he speaks of Homer as no longer talking in his own person but
in the character of Chryses, the old priest, and so 'imitating'
the latter. Similarly, when at 595a he talks of the poetry he
has excluded in Book III, he describes it as 'imitative' poetry,
using the adjective *mimetike*. Now, in fact, in English we would
not normally say that Homer 'imitates' Chryses, but rather that
he represents him saying such and such, or again of an actor
(and again it is the word *mimesis* that Plato uses here), we
would not say that he 'imitates' a character but rather that he
represents him, plays the part of so and so. As Cornford says
(p. 78 of his translation), "the actor does not 'imitate' Othello,
whom he has never seen; he represents or embodies or repro-
duces the character created by Shakespeare". Again, of the
play or the poetry, we would not say that it is 'imitative', but,
though it is not easy to find a single word in English to convey
this, that it is representative or dramatic. Indeed if in English
we said of a play or a poem or a work of art generally that it
was imitative, we would normally mean something quite different. We would mean that it copied other works of art, that it
lacked originality. Hence Cornford's translation of the passage
at 595a as "the poetry of dramatic representation" and Lee's
translation "dramatic representation". Nevertheless, despite
these difficulties, in the discussion that follows where Plato is
using the word *mimesis* (or the corresponding verb or adjective
forms) we shall use the English words, 'imitation', 'to imitate',
'imitative', since in fact there are shifts in Plato's meaning
such that while in one context the most appropriate English
rendering might be 'representation', even perhaps 'impersonation', in another these renderings would be inappropriate.

Such a shift can be seen within the present section of Book III — in 395 (Cornford's translation) the Guardians are not to "enact the part of a woman, old or young", they are not to "impersonate men working at some trade", they are not to "imitate horses neighing and bulls bellowing, or the noise of rivers and sea and thunder" — where the same word *mimeisthai*, 'to imitate', is used throughout. For the understanding of the discussion, both in Book III and in Book X, it is important that the reader should be aware when Plato is using the same word *mimesis*, and the purpose of adhering to the translation 'imitation' in what follows is to bring this out.

To return now to Book III, it seems at 394 that the choice of the poetry suitable for the Guardians has to be made from the three classes, imitation only, narrative only, or a mixture of both. In fact, however, as the argument develops, the position is not so simple as this. Plato, taking the view that the audience identifies itself with the characters in the play or poem, and in this way imitates or acts the parts of these characters, appeals at 394e to the principle of one man one job, used in constructing the ideal state. The Guardians have the job of ruling the state, they are "the artificers of their country's freedom". This is their sole task and they should play no other role nor should they imitate. Plato, however, then goes on to say that if as audience or spectators they do imitate, they should from childhood upward imitate only the types of character appropriate to their own task as Guardians, that is, men who are brave, religious and so on ; and he adds that imitation, if carried on from youth, leaves its mark on a man's character and nature. Thus, the Guardians are banned from imitating women, bad and cowardly characters, men working at a trade, and so on. At the end of 396 (in a passage omitted from Cornford's translation) it is explained that the virtuous man (in Lee's translation 'the decent man') will be prepared to imitate the speech or action of a good character in a play or poem, but will not imitate characters inferior to himself "except perhaps for the purpose of amusement". His style, then, will be like that of Homer's epics as described earlier, that is, it will be a combination of imitation and simple narrative, but the proportion of imitation will be small. At the other extreme will

be the more-or-less completely imitative style, which men will
be the readier to adopt the worse they themselves are. Such
men, Plato says at the beginning of 397, will think nothing
beneath them and be prepared to imitate anything and everything. We thus have these two styles, the style of the good man,
primarily narrative but allowing imitation of a good character,
the other, one of unrestricted imitation. We now come back
to the question whether we are to admit to the ideal state both
of these styles, or one of them, or a combination of both, and
Adeimantus replies that his vote goes to "the unmixed imitator
of the good man". Socrates points out that the mixed style
has its attractions, while the opposite style to that which
Adeimantus has chosen is much the most acceptable to the
general public. Both are, however, to be rejected, and at 398
the writer who is clever at imitating anything and everything is
banned from the ideal state. "For our own good", Plato says,
"we shall employ the more austere and less attractive poets and
story-tellers who will imitate the style of the good man".

It will be seen then that while at 394 it seems that the
choice of the poetry suitable for the ideal state has to be made
from narrative poetry, imitative poetry, or poetry that is a
mixture of narration and imitation, the position changes as the
argument develops. What we have at the end is a choice
between poetry that is mainly narrative, but allows imitation
of good men and good actions, poetry that is unrestrictedly
imitative, and poetry that is a mixture of both, and it is the
first that is chosen for the ideal state. In it the imitator is himself good and will only imitate characters who are good like
himself. Such being the position in Book III, a difficulty
appears to arise over the opening words of Book X, where
Plato refers to the earlier exclusion of all imitative poetry,
since in Book III, as we have just seen, some imitative poetry
in some sense of the word 'imitative' is apparently retained.
We shall return to this apparent discrepancy after we have
considered what is said in Book X.

The discussion in Book X falls into two parts. In the first
part (595a-602b) imitation and its products are discussed in
the light of metaphysical and epistemological distinctions with
which Books V-VII have made the reader familiar, and in the

second part (602c-608b) the conclusions reached in the first part are related to the psychological doctrines of Book IV. Plato begins (at 595c) by asking what in general imitation is, and proceeds to give an answer in terms of the theory of Forms. There are various points in his exposition here to which we shall have to return, but to put the argument in summary form, it runs thus. Take any class of particular things in our ordinary, everyday world — for example the class of things each of which we call a bed. Now, as we know from the theory of Forms, the particular beds are all beds in virtue of the Form of Bed. Thus there is first of all the Form of Bed, which is unique (597c-d), which exists in the nature of things, and which we might say was made by God. Secondly, there are all the particular beds, and these are made by the craftsman (in this case the carpenter) looking to the Form (596b). As we also know from the theory of Forms, the Form of Bed alone is completely real, while the bed the craftsman makes is not completely real — it is a somewhat shadowy thing as compared with reality (597a). In addition, however, to the divine craftsman (God) who makes the Form, and the ordinary craftsman who makes the particular bed, there is another sort of craftsman who can make anything — indeed we could do this ourselves by taking a mirror and turning it round in all directions (596d), though, of course, we would only be producing appearances and not actual things. The painter, Socrates says, is a craftsman of this kind. He too in a sense produces a bed, but not an actual bed, only the appearance of a bed. We can now use this to clarify the nature of imitation. God makes the Form, the craftsman makes the particular bed, but we cannot describe the artist as making a bed. What he does is to imitate what the others have made (597e). Moreover it is in fact the products of the craftsman that he imitates, and he imitates these not as they are but as they appear (598a). Imitation, then, is concerned with appearances, the artist is an imitator, and his work is at the third remove from reality. Similarly the tragic poet, who is an imitator, and all other imitators are "as it were third from the throne of truth" (597e).

This view is now developed (598d-601b), particularly in relation to the tragic poets, amongst whom Homer is now

included as their leader. It is sometimes thought that they
have a knowledge of all forms of skill and know all about
morality and religion. This, Plato argues, is quite false —
rather, as he puts it at 600e, "all the poets from Homer on-
wards are imitators of images of virtue and of everything else
about which they write and have no grasp of the reality".
They know nothing except how to imitate.

By way of clinching his point about the artist's ignorance
of his subject-matter, Plato adds a final brief argument (601b-
602b). We can distinguish three arts concerned with any
object, the art of using it, the art of making it, and the art of
imitating it. It is the man who uses the object who has knowledge about it. He can, from his knowledge, instruct the
maker, who thus comes to possess correct belief about it. The
imitator, on the other hand, has neither the knowledge that
derives from use nor the correct belief which comes from being
instructed by the user. He will thus have neither knowledge
nor correct belief about the goodness or badness of the things he
imitates, but will aim only at pleasing the taste of the ignorant
multitude. The conclusion then is that the imitator knows
little or nothing about what he imitates, that imitation is a
form of play and not to be taken seriously, and that all those
who write tragic poetry, whether in dramatic or epic form,
are in the highest degree imitators.

Imitation then, whether in painting or poetry, is concerned
with what is at the third remove from truth, and Plato now
turns in the second part of the present discussion (602c-608b)
to its psychological effects. He begins with painting. Objects
seen at a distance appear smaller than when close at hand, a
straight stick appears bent in water, and so on. The confusion
caused by these perspectival variations can be dispelled by
measuring, counting and weighing, and this is done by the
reasoning element in the soul. When the latter has done its
measuring it may be contradicted by appearances. But (and
here, at 602e, Plato refers to the principle he used in Book IV
at 436b) it is impossible for the same part of us to hold contrary
opinions simultaneously about the same objects. Thus the
part of us that agrees with the measurements must be different
from the part that disagrees, and the part that agrees with

measurement and calculation is the highest part of the soul, while the part that goes against them must be inferior. But painting is concerned with appearances, is far removed from reality, and thus appeals to the inferior part of our soul that is far removed from wisdom. A similar argument is applied to imitative poetry (603c). A man of high character, as had already been said in Book III (387d ff.), will not indulge the lower irrational element in his soul and give way to excessive grief. Rather he will listen to the best part of his soul, the law-abiding part, which bids him resist his grief. It is, however, the lower element of the soul, with its excessive lamentations, that gives scope to the imitative poet. It is the imitation of this element that will win the imitative poet success with the motley audience in a theatre, who would find the imitation of the rational and controlled element hard to understand, since it is alien to their own habit of mind. Thus the imitative poet is the counterpart of the painter. His works are poor things in relation to truth and reality, and his appeal is to an inferior element in the mind. Further, the gravest charge still remains. The imitative poet has great power to move even the best of us, so that we surrender ourselves to the performance and share in the feelings of the characters, and the more he is able to do this, the more we praise him. But in all this, the poet is gratifying the lower part of our nature, and the control by the best element in us is relaxed. Yet in fact to enter into another's feelings must have an effect on our own (606b — compare Book III, 395c-d). We identify ourselves with, and thus imitate, characters whom we would ordinarily condemn. When then Homer is praised as the educator of Hellas and as a guide in all the affairs of life, it may readily be agreed that Homer is the first and greatest of the tragic poets; but only hymns to the gods and praises of good men are to be allowed in the ideal state (607a). Finally Plato refers at 607c to the "long-standing quarrel between poetry and philosophy" but nevertheless makes it clear that if "poetry for pleasure's sake and imitation" (Cornford 'the dramatic poetry whose end is to give pleasure') can show reason why it ought to exist in a well-ordered state, then he would welcome it back. Unless, however, it can be shown to be not only a source of pleasure but of benefit to human society and human life, it must be renounced, for what is at stake is the choice of becoming a good man or a bad.

Such is Plato's attack in Book X. The question is what is he attacking? Many writers have regarded what he is saying here as an attack on art as such and have supposed that the artist is banished from the ideal state. On this R. G. Collingwood in *The Principles of Art* (p. 46) says, "This Platonic 'attack on art' is a myth whose vitality throws a lurid light on the scholarship of those who have invented and perpetuated it". We must then take a closer look at what Plato is doing.

He begins Book X by congratulating himself on having in Book III excluded "all imitative poetry" — if we translate the Greek word for word, the actual phrase is "of it (poetry) such as is imitative"; he then raises the question of the general nature of imitation; and it is by and large true that in the subsequent discussion whenever he mentions poetry or literature, the qualification 'imitative' is explicitly, or clearly implicitly, present. Thus it would seem that the short answer to our question is that the object of Plato's attack in Book X is imitative poetry. He excluded it in Book III and he is now further justifying that exclusion. It would also seem as a consequence that there is some other non-imitative type of poetry which is immune from this attack. This, however, is too short an answer. We can see this if we ask ourselves what this other non-imitative poetry is which Plato would allow. What he does allow in Book III is, as we have seen above, poetry which imitates the good man, and in Book X, hymns to the gods and praises of good men. Clearly the first of these is imitative poetry in some sense or other, and this brings us back to the difficulty about the relation between Book III and Book X already referred to (p. 273). Collingwood (*Principles of Art*, pp. 46-48) takes the view that Plato's attitude changes between Book III and Book X and that while some imitative poetry (Collingwood uses the translation 'representative') is retained in Book III, all imitative poetry is banished in Book X, because it is imitative; and he consequently holds that what is left in Book X, namely the hymns to the gods, etc., is regarded by Plato as not imitative. This view, however, is not convincing.

T 2

For one thing, Plato deliberately refers to the Book III discussion at the beginning of Book X, and represents himself as having in Book III excluded all imitative poetry. Collingwood's view leaves this reference unexplained — presumably all one could say would be that Plato was either misrepresenting or mis-remembering what he had actually said in Book III. Again it seems unlikely that Plato did regard the hymns to the gods, etc., which are left in Book X, as not imitative. It is true that when he originally introduced the notion of 'imitation' in Book III, it appeared at first to have a purely stylistic reference — a poet could use pure narrative or again he could imitate, i.e. he could employ direct speech and follow a dramatic style; and in this purely stylistic use of 'imitation', the hymns to the gods and praises of good men of Book X would not be imitative — i.e. they would not be dramatic in form. In the subsequent discussion, however, and particularly in Book X, 'imitation' is no longer being used with this narrowly stylistic reference, and in this wider sense non-dramatic poetry too, such as the hymns to the gods, etc., could be imitative or representative — they would imitate or represent the actions of gods and so on. In the *Laws*, where at 801 the same sort of poetry is allowed as we have here in Book X, Plato has earlier said (at 668) that all 'musical' compositions (this of course includes poetry) are imitative and representative. There is no reason to suppose that he had a different view about the hymns, etc. of Book X.

Collingwood's view then is unconvincing. A much more convincing line of explanation is suggested by Professor Tate (*Classical Quarterly*, Vol. XXII, 1928, and Vol. XXVI, 1932). He argues that Plato was using 'imitation' in two senses, a good sense and a bad sense. In the good sense not only is the model imitated good, but the poet himself must be a good man and understand the principles of goodness. Granted this, though he will use mainly the narrative form, there will be no objection to his adopting direct speech in some passages, where he is speaking in the character of a good man like himself. The point of this type of poetry will be its restriction of the dramatic element. This is the type of poetry allowed in Book III. We could call it restricted imitation. From the point of view of the audience, in this case the young Guardians, the imitation involved in listening to such poetry will be an imitation of their own ideal character — thus, as Tate puts it, such imitation will lead to "not the suppression but the development of the personality", and the one-man-one-job principle will be preserved. Adeimantus, as we noted above, describes such a poet as "the unmixed imitator of the good man", and Plato contrasts this style of poetry with imitative poetry, i.e. in this context he is regarding imitative poetry in the good sense as non-imitative. Imitative poetry in the bad sense then will be the poetry that involves what we could call unrestricted imitation — in this case, to use the language of Book III, the worse the poet is himself the readier he will be to imitate anything and everything. Thus when at the beginning of Book X Plato refers to the earlier exclusion of "all imitative poetry", this is consistent with Book III if we understand that Plato is using 'imitative' in the bad sense. Thus, the ban in Book III and the justification for it in Book X are concerned only with imitative art in the bad sense of imitation. In this case the poet or artist himself is ignorant of that which he is imitating. He can copy only the external appearances and his work is thrice removed from the truth.

This explanation has much to commend it. It makes sense of the relation between Book III and the opening words of Book X, it accounts for the implication that there is some art other than imitative art (in the bad sense) that is allowable, and it accounts for the retention of the poetry that is in fact retained — the latter is, in the required sense, non-imitative. It is clear too that what is primarily worrying Plato throughout the whole discussion is imitation in the bad sense, i.e. unrestricted imitation. In this case it is not merely that the model may be bad, but that the poet or artist himself has no understanding of what he is imitating and yet is professing to have. In the words of 598d, he sets out to be "a person who is a master of every trade and knows more about the subject than any specialist", and Plato will have none of him. His work is all impersonation — "is at the third remove from reality, nothing more than semblances, easy to produce with no knowledge of the truth". It is this sort of work which we suggested

earlier (Chapter 9, p. 223) belonged to the lowest division
of the Divided Line. We may then agree with Tate, in answer
to our own question earlier, that what Plato is primarily
attacking throughout is imitative art in the bad sense of imitation, i.e. unrestricted imitation. At the same time, the reader
who consults Professor Tate's articles will see that a good deal
is said there about imitation in the good sense and the place
Plato assigned to imitative art of this latter sort. Tate's view,
put very briefly, is that the kind of poetry or painting that is
imitative in the good sense is that which imitates the ideal
world — "What it produces is not merely a copy of this or that
concrete object as perceived by the deceptive faculties of sense,
imagination and opinion, but a copy of the ideal realities
which the object 'imitates' or 'partakes in' . . . And this
kind of artist must be a man who enjoys the vision of the ideas
of justice, beauty, etc., so that he may embody them in his
work. He must be a true philosopher, a man of wisdom and
(therefore) of virtue . . ." (*C.Q.*, XXVI, 1932, pp. 161-162).
It is not possible to discuss in detail here the evidence on
which Tate ascribes this positive view of imitation in the good
sense to Plato. For instance, he refers a good deal to the passage at 500e ff., the simile of the painter-legislator which we
already noted in Chapter 7, p. 136. The legislator is there
likened to a painter who copies the Forms directly and the
passage thus may be taken as suggesting a higher status for
the artist than that of Book X. As however we said at the
time, too much cannot be made of these fairly incidental
references ; and in general it is arguable — though the reader
who is interested must examine the matter for himself — that
the evidence Tate adduces scarcely supports the positive view
of good imitative art which he ascribes to Plato. If, however,
Plato did have such a view, a number of interesting questions
would arise. For example, one might ask whether then the
poet would have the same education in mathematics and dialectic as the philosopher. Presumably the answer to this
would have to be yes, since the good poet is to have knowledge
of the Forms, i.e. of Justice itself, Goodness itself, and so on.
Again one might ask, granted this, what then would be contributed by the specifically poetical element in his work — his

use of metre, simile, metaphor, poetic language, and so on. This latter does not seem at all an easy question to answer within Plato's general philosophical position — rather for him, as he makes Socrates say in the *Phaedo* (61a) "philosophy is the noblest music" (compare also the suggestion in the *Laws* (811c) that the discussion recorded there is "very like a sort of poem"). In this, however, we are moving further and further away from the *Republic* itself. In the latter it is easier to see what Plato is against than what he is for. He is against unrestricted imitation where the poet is ready to imitate any character or action, good or bad, having himself no understanding of what he is imitating, and thus dealing in mere appearances. This is the sort of art that is banned from the ideal state. About the nature and status of the art that is to be left, the position is more obscure.

To return now to Collingwood's remark quoted on p. 277 that the "Platonic 'attack on art' (in the *Republic*) is a myth", from what has been said it should be clear that there is substance in this. All art is not excluded from the ideal city; and some art of some sort is intended to survive the attack in Book X, whatever its precise nature and status may be. On the other hand, it is equally clear that the works of Homer and the dramatists come under Plato's ban, that they are the sort of art that Book X attacks as bad imitation, third removed from the truth. This being so, it might be argued that when we are thinking about art it is exactly to the *Iliad* or the *Prometheus Vinctus* or the *Antigone* that we would refer as typical examples of great art — that these provide, so to speak, an ostensive definition of what we mean by a work of art. So, it might be said, if Plato is attacking these, he is in effect, after all, attacking art, in any important sense we can give to that term; and further, to suppose as he does that such works are third removed from the truth is to stray very far from the mark. Indeed it does seem that Plato's position here is quite unacceptable. When, however, we are criticising him, as we should, there are several points to be borne in mind. First, there is a certain similarity between Plato's position here and his position in political matters. We remarked in Chapter 9, p. 199 that if we disapproved of Plato's anti-democratic views in politics, they were nevertheless based on arguments which Plato believed to be sound and interlocked with his philosophical views in such a way that the latter must be shown to be wrong or defective before his anti-democratic proposals can be dismissed. Somewhat similarly in the present case, in Books V-VII he has argued that the Forms alone are truly real and are the sole objects of knowledge ; that the philosopher alone can attain to this knowledge ; and that he only attains to it after a long and arduous training in mathematics and dialectic. If then claims are made against Plato of the sort that the poets he condemns have in fact an insight into the nature of things, that their works so far from being an imitation of an imitation reveal reality to us, it is necessary to show what is wrong or defective in the philosophical arguments by which Plato has reached his own position. Moreover, it is not enough simply to say the poets are inspired. Plato was well aware of that claim and did not rate it highly. The *Ion* is witness to this, or again the *Apology*, where at 21c-d Socrates says, "then I knew that it was not by wisdom that the poets produced their works, but by a sort of natural gift and by inspiration, like the prophets and soothsayers ; for they too say many fine things, but know nothing about that of which they speak". Secondly, the context in which the present discussion of art arises has got to be remembered. Plato is not writing a treatise on aesthetic theory, but a treatise on politics. The question of art first arises in connection with the education of the young Guardians, and then more widely in connection with the sort of people the members of his ideal state are to be. Plato then throughout is thinking primarily in terms of the educational and social function of art. It is true that the fact that he will only admit such art into his state as satisfies his educational and social demands does imply that he thought art had no other over-riding claims to admittance — but that he did think it had some other claims to consideration can be seen from stray remarks in the *Republic* itself. There is, for instance, the somewhat curious passage at 396e where the good man will not imitate bad characters "save for the purpose of amusement", which implies that the pleasure which art gives, and which Plato readily admits, cannot be entirely bad (otherwise the good man

will not indulge it); or again the suggestion in the passage at
387b where a ban is put on terrifying language that "this may
be all right by reference to another standard". Moreover we
must remember that the champions of Homer and the trage-
dians were prepared to defend them on educational and social
grounds similar to those which lay behind Plato's attack. This
can be very clearly seen in the passage at 598d ff., and again
at 606e ff. It is claimed for the poets that they know all about
human conduct, good and bad, that Homer has been the
educator of Hellas, that we should model our lives by him.
Indeed we can see from Book I how in fact men like Cephalus
and Polemarchus carried this out in practice. Thus it was the
common Greek view that the poets had an educational and
social role, that they had a knowledge which other men did
not possess, and that by this knowledge they were fitted to
guide and educate the rest of Greece. It is these claims against
which Plato is protesting. Lastly, and closely connected with
what has just been said, the view Plato took of the attitude of
the audience to a work of art must be borne in mind. He
believed that the audience identified themselves with the characters on the stage, in this sense imitated them, and that this
imitation had an effect on their own character and actions.
Thus, given this view of the effect of art on practice, Plato aimed
at ensuring that the art allowed in his state would be such that
its effects on practice could only be good. The pity and fear
aroused by a tragedy might be pleasurable, but for Plato these
emotions inhibited the manly actions he expected of his
Guardians. Hence his demand at 607d that before the poetry
he has banished can be restored it must be shown to be "not
merely pleasant but also beneficial to society and to human
life". Collingwood in *The Principles of Art* (especially Chapters
III, IV and V) makes an interesting distinction between what
he calls 'amusement art' and 'magical art', the latter being
designed to cause emotions in order to discharge them into
practical life, and argues (p. 49) that "what Plato wanted to
do . . . was to put the clock back and revert from the amusement art of the Greek decadence to the magic art of the archaic
period and the fifth century". He also points out (p. 50 ff.)
that Aristotle in the *Poetics* takes up Plato's demand at 607d

and seeks by his doctrine of purging (*katharsis*) to show that the emotions aroused by watching the performance of a tragedy do not inhibit subsequent action, but rather are discharged in the experience of watching the tragedy, so that after it is over the audience are released from these emotions rather than burdened by them. The effect then, as Collingwood adds, would be the opposite of what Plato had supposed.

So far we have been considering the first part of Book X in its bearing on Plato's views about art. Before we leave it finally, however, we ought to note certain particular points in it that have a special interest for the theory of Forms. They are scattered through the discussion and the simplest way to deal with them is to list them with brief comments. Before we do this, there is one general observation that is worth making. Commentators have often remarked that the first part of Book X has the air of a digression or an appendix. It is as though Plato were still worried by what he had said in Book III and, whether because what he had said there had become known (though there is no actual evidence for this) and had provoked criticism, or whether because he wanted to fortify himself further against the attractions of poetry and provide a fully satisfactory antidote (595b), felt he must say more in support of his stand in Book III. However that may be, one gets the impression that he now musters every argument he can think of in justification of what he had said earlier, and that in so doing he is in places less strict in the statement of an argument than he would be elsewhere, and in places less heedful than one might expect of whether the arguments he uses fit in with one another. We shall see instances of this in certain of the points which we now proceed to list. (i) 596a. Imitation is under discussion, and it is proposed that "the accustomed method" should be followed, and this, on a straightforward translation of the passage, consists in "positing a single Form for every set of things to which we apply the same name". This is a passage to which we have already referred in Chapter 8, p. 181, in discussing Forms as universals. On this argument for the Forms, the range of the Forms would be unrestricted — for all the individual acts we call just there will be a Form Justice, for all the individual things we call trees, a Form

Treeness, for all the individual things we call tables, a Form
Tableness, and so on. Three points arise about this. (a) The
reader should compare *Parmenides* 130a-e where Socrates
appears to hesitate about forms of lowly objects, such as hair,
or mud, or dirt, and where on the principle of the present passage, such hesitation would be unwarranted. (b) Plato himself in the *Politicus* 262d points out that the division of mankind
into Greeks and barbarians is wrong — though there is one
name for the latter they do not form a genuine class. For a
genuine class we must "divide . . . at the joints established
by nature" (*Phaedrus* 265e). (c) These latter quotations are
connected with the question whether Plato allowed Forms of
manufactured objects. Aristotle says (*Met.* 1070a18) that
"Plato recognises Forms just as many as the things that exist
by nature", the implication being that Plato did not recognise
forms of manufactured objects. There would then be a difficulty about the Forms of Bed and Table which appear specifically in this part of the *Republic*. Ross's explanation of the
apparent difficulty (*Plato's Theory of Ideas*, pp. 174-175) seems
correct. Plato's point was not, as Aristotle understood it, to
contrast natural objects and artificial objects in this connection,
but to insist, as the *Politicus* and *Phaedrus* quotations indicate,
that there are only Forms answering to natural divisions in
things. Thus, as Ross says, "there is no real evidence that
Plato ever denied the existence of Ideas answering to the
objects of the useful arts". (ii) 596b. Here the craftsman is
said, in making a bed or table, to have before his mind the
appropriate Form. According to the doctrine of Books V-VII,
this could not be so — only the philosopher, after long training,
is able to grasp the Forms. There is a passage in the *Cratylus*
(389b) where the craftsman is similarly said to "look to the
Form", but it is doubtful whether in that dialogue Plato is
using the notion of a Form in the way in which it occurs in the
central books of the *Republic*. On the other hand, in our present
passage it does seem to be being so used — compare the
reference at 597b to the first bed, the Form of Bed, which
"exists in the nature of things". But if it is a Form in this
sense, then this is a place where Plato is less strict in his argument than he ought to be. (iii) 597b. Plato describes the

Form of Bed as "made by a god". This is quite contrary to his usual view that the Forms are eternally existing, completely independent entities. In the *Timaeus* the divine craftsman does not make the Forms — he fashions the visible world on the model of the Forms. Adam in his edition of the *Republic* seeks to identify the god here with the Form of the Good, but to say as he does that "Plato is merely saying in theological language what he formerly said in philosophical" (Adam is referring to what was said about the Form of the Good in Book VI) is unconvincing. Rather it is the exigencies of the argument and the desire to produce a symmetrical scheme — Form of Bed made by God, ordinary bed made by carpenter, etc. — that seem to underlie the present passage, and the same general comment is applicable to it as to (ii). (iv) 597c. This is an interesting passage, particularly in relation to the discussion of the theory of Forms in the first part of the *Parmenides* (130-135) to which we referred at the end of Chapter 8 (p. 195). One of the arguments used there by Parmenides (it is to be found at *Parmenides*, 131e-132b) against the theory of Forms is what came to be known as the Third Man argument (or at least one form of the Third Man argument) and is as follows. According to the theory of Forms, all individual men are men in virtue of the Form, Man. Let us call this Form Man_1. But the individual man and the Form Man_1 have then the characteristic of being a man in common. But to account for this characteristic common both to individual men and the Form Man_1, we require another Form, Man_2, in virtue of which individual men and the Form Man_1 possess the common characteristic of being a man, and so on in an infinite regress. Now the interest of the present *Republic* passage is this. Plato argues here that there must only be one Form of Bed — if there were say two Forms of Bed, then there would have to be a third Form of Bed "whose character these two would share", and it would be this Form of Bed that would be, so to speak, the real Form. It is said then that he recognises here that given entities of the same order (whatever order it may be) which have a characteristic in common, a Form is required to account for the common characteristic; and the inference is that in the case of, for example, particular men and the Form

Man he sees no difficulty, since particular men and the Form
Man are for him not entities of the same order, and thus the
difficulty about a further Form (Man$_2$) does not arise. This is
not convincing. The real point is whether given what Plato
says about Forms, and given what he says about the relation
of Form to particulars, he can avoid the Third Man regress.
There is a great deal more to be said on this topic which unfortunately cannot be said here, and the reader must be referred to the *Parmenides* discussion and the literature on it,
notably perhaps to the article by G. Vlastos in the *Philosophical
Review*, Volume LXIII (1954). (v) Lastly, at 601c-602b we
have the argument that the user has knowledge, the maker
right belief, and the imitator neither. (In the *Cratylus* 390b-c
it is similarly the user who has knowledge and instructs the
maker.) This seems to be an additional argument which has
no direct connection with the theory of Forms. If we are
thinking of the central books of the *Republic*, it is not the user
who has knowledge, in the distinctions drawn there, but the
philosopher. And again, it is not easy to reconcile the statement here that the maker of an object has only right belief
with what is said of the craftsman in the passage referred to at
(ii) above, where he is described as looking to the Form. To
repeat what was said earlier, at certain points in Book X, of
which this again is one, one feels that Plato is mustering all the
arguments he can think of, sometimes at the expense of accuracy
and consistency, to demonstrate that the art he is attacking is
an imitation of an imitation.

In the remaining pages of Book X Plato returns to the just
man and proposes now (612b) to restore to him the honours
and rewards, the consequences of his justice, which had been
excluded as a result of the representations of Glaucon and
Adeimantus at the beginning of Book II (see Chapter 3, p.
66). He begins (608c-611a) with a proof of the immortality
of the soul. Each thing is only destroyed by its own peculiar
evil; wickedness is the peculiar evil of the soul; but wickedness
does not destroy the soul; therefore the soul must be immortal.
The argument is open to various objections; for a discussion
of this and other proofs of immortality in Plato (there is a
reference to "the other proofs" at 611b), see R. S. Bluck,

Plato's Phaedo, pp. 18-33, especially pp. 28-29. Glaucon is, however, satisfied with it, and Plato adds (611a-612a) a comment on the nature of the soul. In Book IV the soul had been regarded as a composite, made up of three parts (there is probably a reference to this in the words in 611b "as we recently supposed the soul to be"). Now, Plato suggests that such a composite could hardly be eternal, and that to understand the soul in its truest nature we must see it in its pure form, freed from its association with the body and from earthly evils, as loving wisdom and akin to the divine. Only then will we be able to see its true nature, whatever that may be, whether composite or incomposite.

After these preliminaries the honours and rewards that are in fact the consequences of justice are restored. At 612e the just man is beloved by the gods, at 613b he is honoured and rewarded by his fellow men, at 614a still greater recompense awaits him after death, while in each case the unjust man suffers the opposite; and the *Republic* ends with the Myth of Er, which describes what happens in the after-life. In the Myth itself it is worth noting first that, however prominent a part necessity may subsequently play in a man's destiny, at the critical moment when the life he is to lead has to be chosen, the choice is in his own hands. If anything goes wrong with the choice "the blame lies with the chooser; god is blameless" (617e). Secondly, we see here again the fundamental importance Plato attaches to the philosophic life, as opposed to any other sort of life. Thus in the Myth (619b-c) in the making of the supreme choice it is *philosophia*, the pursuit of wisdom, that is all-important. The first to make the choice is a man who "had come down from heaven, having lived his previous life in a well-governed state, and become virtuous from custom without pursuing wisdom". He makes a dreadful mistake and chooses the greatest tyranny, with all its attendant evils. Thus at the moment of greatest danger, right belief is not enough; it is philosophy, with the knowledge that it brings, that alone can save a man.

BIBLIOGRAPHY

The list of books and articles given below is not intended to be exhaustive, but contains suggestions for further reading. Books marked with an asterisk are those considered likely, for one reason or another, to be most useful to the less advanced student.

1. GENERAL

Adam, J. (ed.), *The Republic of Plato* (2nd ed.) with an introduction by D. A. Rees (Cambridge, Cambridge University Press, 1963).

Burnet, J., *Greek Philosophy — Thales to Plato* (London, Macmillan, 1914; paperback, 1961).

Crombie, I. M., *An Examination of Plato's Doctrines* (London, Routledge, 1963. Two volumes).

*Field, G. C., *Plato and his Contemporaries* (3rd ed.) (London, Methuen, 1967; paperback, 1967).

*Field, G. C., *The Philosophy of Plato* (2nd ed.) with an appendix by R. C. Cross (London, Oxford University Press, Oxford Paperbacks University Series, 40, 1969).

Grube, G. M. A., *Plato's Thought* (London, Methuen, 1935).

Murphy, N. R., *The Interpretation of Plato's Republic* (Oxford, Clarendon Press, 1951).

*Nettleship, R. L., *Lectures on the Republic of Plato* (2nd ed.) (London, Macmillan, 1901; paperback, 1963).

Popper, K. R., *The Open Society and Its Enemies* (4th ed.) (London, Routledge, 1962; paperback, 1962).

Schuhl, P.-M., *L'Œuvre de Platon* (Paris, Hachette, 1954).

*Taylor, A. E., *Plato: The Man and his Work* (7th ed.) (London, Methuen, 1960; paperback, 1960).

2. MORALS AND POLITICS

(a) *Books*

Adkins, A. W. H., *Merit and Responsibility* (Oxford, Clarendon Press, 1959).

Crossman, R. H. S., *Plato Today* (2nd ed.) (London, Allen and Unwin, 1959; paperback, 1963).

*Foster, M. B., *The Political Philosophies of Plato and Hegel* (Oxford, Clarendon Press, 1935).

Gould, J., *The Development of Plato's Ethics* (Cambridge, Cambridge University Press, 1955).

*Joseph, H. W. B., *Essays in Ancient and Modern Philosophy* (Oxford, Clarendon Press, 1935 (Chs. I-V).

Prichard, H. A., *Moral Obligation* (Oxford, Clarendon Press, 1949) (Ch. V).

Weldon, T. D., *States and Morals* (London, Murray, 1946; paperback, 1962).

(b) *Articles*

Foster, M. B., "Mr. Joseph and the *Republic*" (*Mind*, N.S., Vol. XLV, 1936).

Joseph, H. W. B., "A Reply to Mr. Foster" (*Mind*, N.S., Vol. XLV, 1936).

Foster, M. B., "A Mistake of Plato's in the *Republic*" (*Mind*, N.S., Vol. XLVI, 1937).

Mabbott, J. D., "Is Plato's *Republic* Utilitarian?" (*Mind*, N.S., Vol. XLVI, 1937).

Foster, M. B., "A Rejoinder to Mr. Mabbott" (*Mind*, N.S., Vol. XLVII, 1938).

Kerferd, G. B., "The Doctrine of Thrasymachus in Plato's *Republic*" (*Durham University Journal*, 1947-8).

Gallop, D., "True and False Pleasures" (*Philosophical Quarterly*, Vol. 10, 1960).

Sachs, D., "A Fallacy in Plato's *Republic*" (*Philosophical Review*, Vol. LXXII, 1963).

Vlastos, G., "The Argument in the *Republic* that 'Justice Pays'" (*Journal of Philosophy*, Vol. LXV, 1968).

Vlastos, G., "Justice and Psychic Harmony in the *Republic*" (*Journal of Philosophy*, Vol. LXVI, 1969).

3. EPISTEMOLOGY AND METAPHYSICS

(a) *Books*

Bluck, R. S., *Plato's Phaedo* (London, Routledge, 1955).

Blumenthal, L. M., *A Modern View of Geometry* (San Francisco and London, W. H. Freeman, 1961).

Collingwood, R. G., *The Principles of Art* (Oxford, Clarendon Press, 1938; paperback, 1963).

Hardie, W. F. R., *A Study in Plato* (Oxford, Clarendon Press, 1936).

Joseph, H. W. B., *Knowledge and the Good in Plato's Republic* (Oxford Classical and Philosophical Monographs, Oxford, Clarendon Press, 1948).

Körner, S., *The Philosophy of Mathematics* (London, Hutchinson University Library, 1960).

Robinson, R., *Plato's Earlier Dialectic* (2nd ed.) (Oxford, Clarendon Press, 1953) (espec. Chaps. IX-XI).

*Ross, W. D., *Plato's Theory of Ideas* (Oxford, Clarendon Press, 1951) (espec. Chaps. III-IV).

Ross, W. D. (ed.), Aristotle's *Metaphysics*, 2 vols. (Oxford, Clarendon Press, 1924).

*Russell, B., *The Problems of Philosophy* (London, Oxford University Press, Home University Library, 1912).

*Woozley, A. D., *Theory of Knowledge, An Introduction* (London, Hutchinson University Library, 1949).

(b) *Articles*

Allen, R. E., "The Argument from Opposites in *Republic* V" (*The Review of Metaphysics*, Vol. XV, No. 2, 1961).

Cherniss, H., "The Philosophical Economy of the Theory of Ideas" (*American Journal of Philology*, LVII, 1936).

Cross, R. C., "Logos and Form in Plato" (*Mind*, N.S., Vol. LXIII, 1954).

Ferguson, A. S., "Plato's Simile of Light, Part I" (*The Classical Quarterly*, Vol. XV, 1921).

Ferguson, A. S., "Plato's Simile of Light, Part II" (*The Classical Quarterly*, Vol. XVI, 1922).

Ferguson, A. S., "Plato's Simile of Light Again" (*The Classical Quarterly*, Vol. XXVIII, 1934).

Hamlyn, D. W., "*Eikasia* in Plato's *Republic*" (*The Philosophical Quarterly*, Vol. 8, 1958).

Murphy, N. R., "The 'Simile of Light' in Plato's *Republic*" (*The Classical Quarterly*, Vol. XXVI, 1932).

Murphy, N. R., "Back to the Cave" (*The Classical Quarterly*, Vol. XXVIII, 1934).

Paton, H. J., "Plato's Theory of *Eikasia*" (*Proceedings of the Aristotelian Society*, Vol. XXII (1921–2)).

Raven, J. E., "Sun, Divided Line, and Cave" (*The Classical Quarterly*, N.S., Vol. III, 1953).

Tate, J., "'Imitation' in Plato's *Republic*" (*The Classical Quarterly*, Vol. XXII, 1928).

Tate, J., "Plato and 'Imitation'" (*The Classical Quarterly*, Vol. XXVI, 1932).

Taylor, A. E., "Note on Plato's *Republic*, VI, 510c 2-5" (*Mind*, N.S., Vol. XLIII, 1934).

Vlastos, G., "The Third Man Argument in the Parmenides" (*The Philosophical Review*, Vol. LXIII, 1954). (See also Strang, C., and Rees, D. A., "Plato and the Third Man", *Proceedings of the Aristotelian Society*, Suppl. Vol. XXXVII, 1963.)

(Some of the articles mentioned above are reprinted in Allen, R. E. (ed.), *Studies in Plato's Metaphysics* (New York, Humanities Press; London, Routledge, 1965)).

INDEX

Figures in bold type give references to chapters

145; distinguished from 'is' as copula, 162-164

Faculty (*dynamis*), criteria for distinguishing, 146-151
Falsehood, 196-197
Ferguson, A. S., 208; interpretation of Line and Cave, 209-216; 291
Field, G. C., xiii, xiv, 254, 289
Forms, theory of, 140-144; **8,** 178-195; 258-260, 284-287
Foster, M. B., 289, 290
Foundation myth, 103
Freedom, and Economic Class, 107-109
Frege, G., 239
Function, argument from, 57-60

Gallop, D., 290
Good, Form of the, 260-261
Goods, three kinds of, 65-66
Gorgias, xii, 221
Gould, J., 290
Grube, G. M. A., 289
Guardians: introduction of the term, 95; distinguished from Auxiliaries, 96; whether administrators or legislators, 101-103; wisdom their virtue, 105; correspondence to rational element in soul, 119; as philosophers, 199-201

Hamlyn, D. W., 291
Happiness: and *eudaimonia*, 56-57; of just man, **11**
Hardie, W. F. R., 236, 259, 290
Heracleitus, 153
Hippias Minor, 14
History: economic interpretation of, 83; constitutional, 262-263
Hobbes, 71-72
Hume, 85; contrasted with Plato on Desire and Reason, 117-119; 122
Hypotheseis (assumptions), *see* Mathematics

Idea, translation of, 178-179
Ignorance, 145-146
Images, 204-205, 212, 218-224, 226, 259-260
Imitation (*see Mimesis*), **12,** 270-284
Injustice: not more profitable than justice, 51-56; life of not better than that of justice, 56-60; life of compared with that of justice, **11,** 263-269; 288

Inspiration, of poets, 282
Intermediates, *see* Mathematics
Ion, xii, 282

Joseph, H. W. B., 4, 290
Justice: as truth-telling and repaying debts, 2-3; as rendering to each man his due, **1,** 3-22; not a skill, 15-19; as the interest of the stronger, **2,** 24-60; in the city, 109-111; in the soul, **6,** 124-127
Just man, identified with philosopher, **9,** 264-269

Kant, I.: holy will and good will, 106; 138; on mathematics, 239-240
Kerferd, G. B., 290
Kinds of city and men, 262-263
Knowledge: virtue as knowledge, 53-55; and belief, **7,** 138-165, **8,** 166-178; as dispositional, 149-150; by acquaintance and by description, 171, 177
Körner, S., 290

Laches, xii, 1
Laws, xii, 223, 278, 281
Lee, H. D. P., vii, 25
Letters, large and small, 76
Letter, Seventh, 253
Liking, distinguished from approving, 19
Line, simile of, **9,** 203-206, 230
Locke, J., 71-72, 242

Mabbott, J. D., 290
Mathematics and philosophy, **10,** 232-258
Mathematics: objects of, 233-238; role of sensible diagrams in, 238-240, 244-246; assumptions (*hypotheseis*) in, 242-249
Melian dialogue, 27-28
Meno, xii, 169, 181
Mill, J. S., 238-239, 265-266
Mimesis (see Imitation); translation of, 271-272
Moral, standards, xiii; reformer distinguished from philosopher, xiv-xv
Murphy, N. R., 144, 158, 215; interpretation of Line and Cave, 216-217; 289, 291

Natural community, contrasted with artificial, 99-100